Yugoslav Communism and the Macedonian Question

Stephen E. Palmer, Jr.
Robert R. King

ARCHON BOOKS
1971

© 1971, The Shoe String Press, Inc.,
Hamden, Connecticut
ISBN: 0-208-00821-7
Library of Congress Catalog Card Number: 79-116904
All rights reserved

To our wives, Nancy and Kay

The views expressed in this book are entirely
those of the authors and do not necessarily reflect
those of the Department of State or the Foreign
Service of the United States. No official U.S.
Government Sources were used.

CONTENTS

LIST OF ILLUSTRATIONS

ABBREVIATIONS

ASNOM	Anti-Fascist Council of National Liberation of Macedonia
AVNOJ	Anti-Fascist Council of National Liberation of Yugoslavia
CC	Central Committee
CP	Communist Party
CPA	Communist Party of Albania
CPB	Communist Party of Bulgaria
CPM	Communist Party of Macedonia
CPY	Communist Party of Yugoslavia
EAM	National Liberation Front of Greece
ELAS	Greek People's Liberation Army
FNRJ	Federal People's Republic of Yugoslavia
IMRO	Internal Macedonian Revolutionary Organization
KKE	Greek Communist Party
LCM	League of Communists of Macedonia
LCY	League of Communists of Yugoslavia
MANAPO	Macedonian People's Movement
MPR	Macedonian People's Republic
NOF	National Liberation Front
SFRJ	Socialist Federal Republic of Yugoslavia
SKOJ	Union of Communist Youth of Yugoslavia
SNOF	Slavo-Macedonian National Liberation Front
SRM	Socialist Republic of Macedonia

PREFACE

This book is the result of research that began some sixteen years ago and has continued intermittently since that time. Consequently, the two of us are indebted to numerous people and institutions widely separated in time and space. The project was begun at Indiana University where Dr. James F. Clarke and Joseph Strmecki provided valuable advice and assistance. Miss Lenore Schwartz assisted in typing the manuscript at this stage of the project.

The manuscript was finished in Cambridge, Massachusetts. Professor William E. Griffith generously made available his materials at the M.I.T. Center for International Studies. The staffs of the Russian Research Center and of the Widener Library, both at Harvard University, were most co-operative in granting access to their extensive collections. Professor Uri Ra'anan read and offered helpful criticism on portions of the manuscript.

We are grateful to Harry Stritman of the Library of Congress for calling an earlier version of the manuscript to the attention of the publisher. Finally, we must particularly thank Peter Krogh, currently Dean of the Foreign Service Institute of Georgetown University, for being the essential link in bringing the two authors together.

We express our deep appreciation to those who have assisted us in this work. For errors in judgment and fact, we alone are responsible.

Robert R. King
Radio Free Europe

Stephen E. Palmer, Jr.
Madras, India

YUGOSLAV COMMUNISM AND THE MACEDONIAN QUESTION

The Macedonian Question presents, on the one hand, such a medley of jarring races, long standing animosities, and ever-recurring atrocities, and, on the other hand, such a jumble of ethnographical uncertainties, unreliable statistics, assertions and counter-assertions flatly contradictory on every point, that one almost despairs of an idea as to how it ought to be settled, or of the hope of ever seeing it settled at all.

C.H. Haskins and R. H. Lord in
Some Problems of the Peace Conference

INTRODUCTION

Any treatment of things "Macedonian" conjures controversy. A century of Serb, Greek, Bulgarian and occasionally Albanian struggle for the territory and its people has produced a tangle of conflicting claims and counter-claims. When entering the maze of primary and secondary material on Macedonia, one is struck by the obvious bias of the great mass of it. Reasonable arguments and farfetched fancies have been employed by the contestants for Macedonia and their backers to prove the Macedonians belonged to one or another of the "older" Balkan nationalities. The standards of "scientific" proof were opportunistically varied: history, language, religious affiliation, cultural affinity, anthropology, and folklore were prostituted in the service of political ambitions. A major weapon in this battle has been the use of ethnographic maps. Although the peripheral parts of Macedonia were clearly enough Bulgarian, Albanian, Greek, and perhaps Serbian—even this fact was and is disputed by some of the respective claimants—the core of the region was claimed by all of the contending nationalities. In disputes over this core scores of maps were drawn, a great many of them highly imaginative. Whereas a Serbian map of 1848 did not recognize the existence of any Serbs in Macedonia, one in 1889 showed Christian and "Muslim" Serbs dominating almost the whole of Macedonia including the environs of Salonika. Some Greek maps showed as "Greek" territory almost up to Belgrade. "Disinterested" ethnographers and cartographers joined the fun. After 1915, the British "discovered" that elements of the Macedonian population which were previously regarded as Albanian, Bulgarian, Greek, Rumanian, or Turkish were really Serbian after all. It was all a matter of one's point of view and the shifting political scene; the standards were adjusted accordingly. The population statistics on which most Macedonian maps were based were almost worthless, for the lists of definitions which could be made for Macedonian Slavs, Bulgarians, Serbs, Albanians, Turks, and Vlahs rendered possible an almost infinite variety of concurrent ethnographic conclusions about the region.[1]

The ascertainable history of Macedonia is less significant to a study of the region's present than are the conflicting legends which have evolved from historical data. While chauvinistic manipulation of political and ethnic mythology is not unusual, the Macedonian issue has been beclouded by an extraordinarily copious mixture of deliberate misrepresentation and popular misinterpretation. Macedonia was hardly more than a loose geographical expression for at least 2,300 years. But even as a geographical entity Macedonia has been in dispute. It is now generally accepted that, in terms of current boundaries, Macedonia consists of the southernmost part of Yugoslavia presently called the Socialist Republic of Macedonia, with its northern limits along the watershed of the Šar and Crna mountains; the southwestern corner of Bulgaria, south from Blagoevgrad (Gorna Dzhumaya) and west from the Mesta River; and that segment of central northern Greece from the Aliakmon River in the west to the Nestos (Mesta) River in the east. The Yugoslav communists use the terms Pirin and Aegean Macedonia for the Bulgarian and Greek parts, respectively, and the Yugoslav section is frequently called Vardar Macedonia. The region is a zone of transition between and overlapping the Dinaro-Pindus range and the Rhodope massif, with a jumbled topographical pattern of basin, gorge, and mountain. Macedonia has provided its inhabitants with a precarious livelihood from subsistence farming and herding. The fact that Macedonia is bisected by the strategic north-south Morava-Vardar passage from Serbia to Salonika has contributed much to making it a traditional zone of conflict.

Slav migrations into the Balkan Peninsula in the sixth and seventh centuries A.D. and seventh century invasions of the Finno-Ugrian Bulgars surrounded, but did not eliminate from Macedonia, the Illyrian and Dacian population from which Albanians and Vlahs derive their origin.[2] Although Slavic tribes penetrated the entire Greek Peninsula, it was only in the north that large and compact Slav settlement persisted. In the ninth century, Cyril and Methodius, missionaries from Salonika, were instrumental in developing the first written Slavic language, now known as Old Church Slavonic or Old Bulgarian, and in spreading Orthodox Christianity throughout Slavdom. As differentiations among the South Slavs deepened, those living in Macedonia remained an ill-defined group, transitional between the Serbs and the Bulgarians, with closer affinity to the latter. The Byzantine Empire, two "Bulgarian" empires, and a "Serbian" empire were in turn masters of Macedonia.

Turkish domination of Macedonia was secured by 1371. For nearly five centuries the Slavs suffered varying forms and degrees of exploitation, largely ignored by the European powers. Taxes were crushing, violence frequent, degradation general. In the Macedonian vilayets of Kosovo, Monastir (Bitolj) and Salonika, the Turks allowed relative freedom of religion but all the Orthodox Slavs were put under the ecclesiastical direction of the Roum Millet of the Greek Phanariot Church. There followed a process of cultural Hellenization which had some success among the urban Slavs and the Vlahs.

But the Slavic peasantry came to associate the Greek church, especially its heirarchy, with the oppressive Turkish regime. The dynamics of the nineteenth century Bulgarian cultural revival and political evolution stirred Macedonian hopes for liberation. The fear of Russian expansion through a client regime in Bulgaria made Macedonia a major European issue. The conflicting power drives of the neighboring states, fired by militant nationalism, had much to do with Macedonia's becoming the cause of wars and of continuing Balkan instability.

The national orthodox churches were the chief bearers of the awakening Greek, Serbian, and Bulgarian national ideals. Macedonia become an ecclesiastical battleground. The Greek Patriarch had seen to it that the Bulgarian Patriarchate in Ohrid was abolished in 1767. The Serbian Patriarchate at Peč had been abolished the previous year. The Greeks and Serbs, on the periphery of European Turkey, had attained political independence and were already inclined towards expansion in Macedonia by the time the Bulgarians gained some freedom of action. Bulgaria's liberation struggle, initially directed against the Greek church in Bulgaria and Macedonia, was not welcomed by Serbia. So in the last quarter of the nineteenth century a three-cornered struggle developed for the souls of the Macedonians. It was conducted by priests, by teachers and later by armed bands.

Two closely related occurrences in the 1870's served further to precipitate and frame the Macedonian question. The first was the successful outcome of the campaign by the Bulgarian Church to secure autonomy. The Turkish Porte granted the Bulgarian Exarchate in 1870. This step was denounced by the Serbs, who had received their church independence forty years earlier, but were declared schismatic by the Greek Patriarch. Bulgarian Exarchist churches and schools in Macedonia became centers of activity against the Turks, the rival Greeks and Serbs, and even the Vlahs and Albanians. The Turks could hardly have devised a better way of pitting Balkan Christians against one another than the principle of local majority rule as the basis for Exarchist jurisdiction in Macedonia. The second major factor was the abortive Treaty of San Stefano in 1878. This treaty utilized the diocesan boundaries of the Exarchate, which included most of Macedonia, to outline the borders of a Greater Bulgaria. Although Macedonia was restored to the Turks upon the intervention of the Western European powers at the Berlin Conference later the same year, San Stefano remained the blueprint for Bulgaria's thwarted national ambitions.

Balkan national appetites, whetted by these two developments, thwarted normal cultural development in Macedonia. In the earlier part of the nineteenth century there had been a few distinctly Macedonian cultural manifestations which in other circumstances might have burgeoned into forms of

MAP 1

THE BULGARIAN EXARCHATE AND SAN STEFANO BULGARIA

BOUNDARIES OF BULGARIA IN THE TREATY OF ──────
    SAN STEFANO

BOUNDARIES OF DIOCESES IN WHICH THE ·········
EXARCHATE POSSESSED THE BISHOPRICS

BOUNDARIES OF DIOCESES IN WHICH THE ─ ─ ─ ─
EXARCHATE POSSESSED NO BISHOPRICS
BUT WAS OFFICIALLY REPRESENTED

more pronounced regionalism or nationalism. But for the most part Macedonian literary iniative was swept along in the main current of the Bulgarian literary and cultural revival, and after the issue was joined, evidences of Macedonian particularism were proscribed.[3] In 1894 Exarchist Bishop Theodosi of Skopje organized a group called the *Lozari* (Grapevine) in an attempt to obtain approval for an independent Macedonian Orthodox Church. He favored the use of the local dialects and was against annexation by Serbia or Bulgaria. The political significance of such a program ran counter to Bulgarian aspirations and the Bishop was promptly transferred to Sofia.

The existence of medieval empires encompassing Macedonia provided Balkan nationalists with opportunities to incite passions on the basis of slanted historiography. In the ninth and tenth centuries there was the First Bulgarian Empire, with its last capital at Ohrid, and in the twelfth and thirteenth centuries the Second Bulgarian Empire existed. For several decades in the fourteenth century there was a Serbian Empire of Stefan Dušan, with its capital at Skopje. These realms were really multi-ethnic entities in which nationalism in the modern sense was utterly lacking. Dušan called himself "Emperor of the Roumelians [Eastern Romans, i.e., Greeks], Serbians, Bulgarians, and Albanians." Yet several nineteenth and twentieth century generations of Serbian and Bulgarian school children were inculcated with "national" histories in which the attributes of modern nation states were transferred to these medieval supranational despotisms. Thus, Macedonia was and is imagined to be the very cradle of both Serbian and Bulgarian nationalism.[4]

By the turn of the century the Macedonian problem had been inexorably swept forward, often as a result of external power politics rather than of local issues, to the point where it was inevitable that the competing armed bands and cultural agents be supplemented by national armies. The Serbo-Bulgarian War of 1885 achieved nothing except to worsen relations between those countries and render Macedonia even more of a tinderbox. Macedonia became the all-absorbing interest of the Bulgarians, who plotted for its annexation. In 1893, when Bulgarian, Greek, and Serbian irregulars were roaming over Macedonia, the Internal Macedonian Revolutionary Organization was founded at Resen. Damian Gruev, Goce Delčev, Petar Tošev, and Hristo Matov were among the early leaders of the Organization, which aimed at taking direct indigenous action against the Turks. But the IMRO needed outside help, and the Bulgarians were eager to assist. There developed a basic split over the ultimate disposition of Macedonia when the Turkish yoke should be lifted—autonomy or annexation by Bulgaria. In Sofia the annexationists, Bulgarians and Macedonians, formed the Supreme Macedonian Adrianopolitan [Thracian] Committee in 1895.

On the festival day of Saint Ilia, August 2, 1903, the IMRO ordered an uprising. Perhaps as many as 25,000 Macedonian Slavs gave vent to pent-up hatreds and frustrations in one-sided skirmishes against the stronger Turkish troops. Some socialistically inclined insurgents organized a short-lived "Kruševo Republic," which, though a minor development in the uprising, has become a celebrated event for the Macedonian communists. Within three months the Macedonian insurrection was suppressed. Yet the Ilinden Uprising drew the attention of the outside world to the plight of the Macedonians. Under foreign pressure, ineffectual reforms were promised by the Turkish Porte and subsequently forgotten.

The European crisis of 1908 gave Serbian territorial ambitions a geopolitical push away from the Adriatic and towards the Aegean. It was at this time that the renowned Serbian ethnographer Professor Jovan Cvijić discovered the existence of the Macedo-Slavs who, he claimed, were neither Serbs nor Bulgarians. In his latter works, Cvijić varied the distribution of the three Slav groups in Macedonia to suit Serbia's strategic requirements. The Young Turk Revolution and reforms of the same year spurred efforts on all sides to obtain control of Macedonia while the new Turkish Government was preoccupied with domestic problems. Exploiting the Italo-Turkish War of 1911, Bulgaria, Greece, Montenegro and Serbia hastily formed an uneasy alliance against Turkey. Bulgaria and Serbia ceased feuding long enough to negotiate a secret agreement for the division of Macedonia which included a provision that the Russian Tsar would arbitrate a large contested area between them. In the First Balkan War of 1912-1913 they liberated Macedonia and much of the rest of Turkey's holdings in Europe. However, disagreement among the victors over division of the Turkish spoils provoked the Second Balkan War in the summer of 1913. Greece, Montenegro, Serbia and later Rumania allied themselves against Bulgaria, and the latter lost considerable territory it had won from Turkey. The treaty of Bucharest (1913) ending the Second Balkan War created the basis for the contemporary phase of the Macedonian question by establishing the international division of Macedonia which is essentially still in effect. Bulgaria received about ten percent, Greece about half and Serbia the remainder of Macedonia. [5]

The Serbian government began a religious, educational and political campaign in Vardar Macedonia to reorient the pro-Bulgarian Macedonians, but this was cut short in less than a year by World War I. Bulgaria sided with the Central Powers and temporarily controlled a large portion of Macedonia, but the prewar boundaries, adjusted slightly in favor of Serbia, were restored by the peace treaties. Although the outcome of World War I failed materially to alter the Macedonian situation, it radically changed the position of

after Crimea turk revenge mix & move people so slavs born in greek v-v.

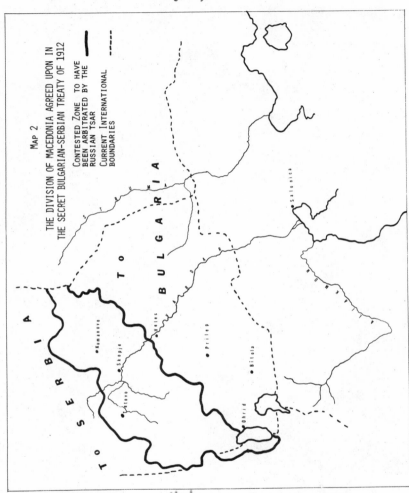

Map 2

THE DIVISION OF MACEDONIA AGREED UPON IN
THE SECRET BULGARIAN-SERBIAN TREATY OF 1912

CONTESTED ZONE TO HAVE
BEEN ARBITRATED BY THE
RUSSIAN TSAR

CURRENT INTERNATIONAL
BOUNDARIES

1939 was called Vardarska

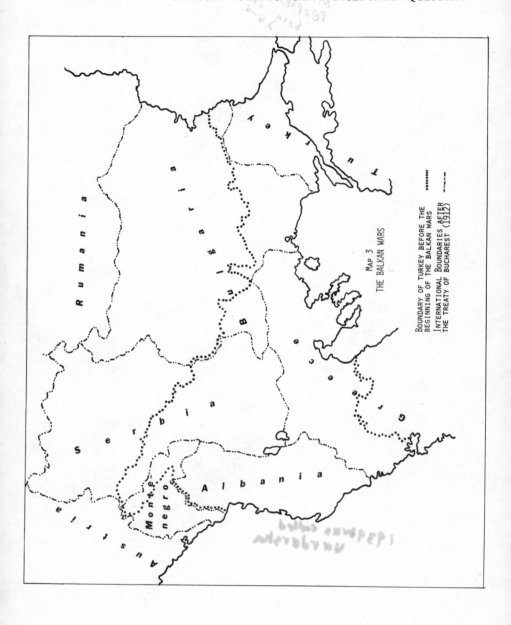

MAP 3
THE BALKAN WARS

BOUNDARY OF TURKEY BEFORE THE
BEGINNING OF THE BALKAN WARS
INTERNATIONAL BOUNDARIES AFTER
THE TREATY OF BUCHAREST (1913)

Serbia, with the creation of the Kingdom of Serbs, Croats, and Slovenes. In spite of the long tradition of the Yugoslav ideal, the first opportunity to forge bonds of real unity among most of the South Slavs instead brought to the surface basic differences in background and aspirations. The hard-bitten, Orthodox Serbs had acquired statehood by great sacrifices in blood. Their strong national feeling was reinforced by dreams of past glory and of new fields yet to conquer. Most of the western-oriented, Roman Catholic Croatians, having struggled for and attained a degree of autonomy in Austro-Hungary, had in mind some sort of a cooperative federation. The conception of "unity" varied from the most extreme Serbian view that the new state was to be an extension of Serbia, to the most extreme Croatian position favoring a separate Croatian state or one with only a shadow of guidance from Belgrade. That the non-Serb Yugoslav groups obtained no precise preconditions as to the organization of the state can be attributed at least in part to the fact that the Serbian Army was in control of Croatia and Macedonia. The negotiating position of the non-Serbs was weak but there was increasing agitation for nationality rights as the new kingdom took form.

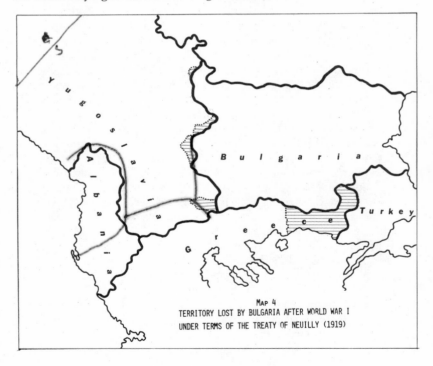

MAP 4
TERRITORY LOST BY BULGARIA AFTER WORLD WAR I
UNDER TERMS OF THE TREATY OF NEUILLY (1919)

Macedonia, called "Southern Serbia" by the Serbs, entered the kingdom with no reasonable hope for any kind of autonomy. The Bulgarian occupation during World War I had been well received, some of the IMRO leaders had held responsible positions. The Macedonians naturally desired a fair share of governmental participation, but the Serbs persecuted those who had actively cooperated with the Bulgarians and discriminated against the rest of the Macedonian Slav population which had at least passively cooperated. This provoked bitter resistance and led IMRO leaders to flee with many of their followers to Bulgaria, whence in subsequent years they conducted guerrilla operations against the Serbian authorities in Vardar Macedonia. Bulgaria was a willing accomplice of the Macedonian revolutionaries. Aroused by the restoration of the 1913 division of Macedonia at the Versailles Conference, Bulgaria commenced two decades of determined maneuvering for another chance to recover its irredenta. The Macedonian issue poisoned inter-war Yugoslav-Bulgarian relations and made it possible for extremists to dominate the Sofia government from 1924 to 1934. [6]

The process of forced Serbization was carried on with vigor. Bulgarian speech was forbidden. Serb-colonizers poured in. It was unfortunate that often the least able types of Serbian military and civil officers were sent to adminster Macedonia. Because of the hostility of the populace and the region's backwardness, an assignment to Macedonia was usually received as a form of punishment. The primary basis of the ensuing trouble, however, was the self-righteous spirit of rampant nationalism with which the dominant Serbian elite of Yugoslavia was infected. This kind of ethnocentric psychosis, in which the group's absolute faith in its superiority is reinforced by self-interest, was not peculiar to the Serbs, but it was to play a major role in the unfolding of the Macedonian drama in the inter-war period.

From the end of World War I through World War II, the Macedonian Slavs were exposed to four conflicting forces. First, Serb-dominated Yugoslavia, holding that portion of Macedonia in which most Macedonian Slavs lived, attempted to bring about the integration of the Macedonians with the Serb national group. This attempt, in which considerable coercion was used, met with almost total failure. There were among the Yugoslav Macedonians very few "Serbomans" who supported the Belgrade regime. Some Macedonians, never organized, identified themselves with the original federal "Yugoslav" ideal, which could not be realized because of the nationality outlook of the inter-war elite in Yugoslavia.

Second, Bulgaria laid claim to Yugoslav Macedonia. There was some variation in the avowed aims of various Bulgarian parties; Stamboliski's Agrarian Party was far less irredentist than the usually dominant cliques of conservative nationalists and bourgeois parties. However, until the period of Bulgarian occupation in World War II, many if not most Yugoslav Macedonians were in favor of this Bulgarian solution. This is admitted even by the Yugoslav communists. The severe Serbian persecutions of those evincing Bulgarian proclivities bore witness to the extent of Bulgarophilism in Yugoslav Macedonia during the inter-war period.

Third, there was the influence of the Internal Macedonian Revolutionary Organization, concentrated in and led from Bulgaria. Most of the leaders and activists of the IMRO were refugees from Yugoslav Macedonia. Divergent tendencies were apparent in the Organization. During the 1920's the faction which supported a vaguely defined autonomy under Bulgaria and the faction which favored Macedonian independence were at odds, very sanguinarily so. While the Organization had many members and supporters in Yugoslav Macedonia, it is difficult to ascertain which of the two basic programs was more acceptable to the rank and file, and to the "pacified" majority of people in Macedonia. The latter had no chance to express themselves freely. Certainly, an overwhelming majority of Yugoslav Macedonians was prepared to experiment with almost any solution, in preference to living in a virtual Serbian colony. With the assumption of IMRO leadership by Ivan (Vančo) Mihailov in 1924, and the increasing realization that the Organization was a band of ruthless terrorists closely allied with Great Bulgarians in Sofia and with Fascists in Italy and Hungary, the group lost some of its power to evoke sacrificial responses from the Yugoslav Macedonians.

Fourth, there were numerous Communist initiatives vis-a-vis the Macedonian problem. They varied according to time, place, and tactical opportunity. While the main Communist aim was to exploit the revolutionary potentialities of the disruptive Macedonian situation, the Yugoslav, Bulgarian, and Greek Communist parties usually qualified their respective interpretations and implementations of Moscow's flexible Macedonian line in consonance with the probable effect of that line on their own domestic positions. The Greek Party was unwilling to support the highly unpopular proposal that Greece should cede Aegean Macedonia. The Bulgarian party held that all Macedonia was properly in its domain. The Yugoslav party, after much stumbling over the touchy Macedonian issue, finally came up with the policy that Macedonians were a distinctive national group and that Macedonia must be regarded as an integral part of the Yugoslav federation.

The decision to recognize a Macedonian nationality is the key event in our examination of Yugoslav Communist treatment of the Macedonian question. The CPY policy on Macedonia, which is closely linked with its line on the Yugoslav nationality question, was fashioned by internal disputes, Comintern intervention, and expediency. In Macedonia the CPY was at an almost complete loss during most of the twenties and thirties. Yet when the opportunity came during World War II to exploit the party's decision to recognize a Macedonian nationality, party operatives efficiently and successfully carried out the party's program under the greatest adversities. In postwar Yugoslavia, policy has been implemented and the Macedonians have been granted the political and cultural forms permitted the other major Yugoslav nationalities. However, enough of the old tensions remain and enough new ones have arisen to render Macedonia a challenge to Belgrade and a continuing source of international contention. The Macedonian question has not been eliminated by the Yugoslav decision to acknowledge a Macedonian nationality, but it has been profoundly altered.

Despite the recognition of the Macedonian nationality and its equality within the Yugoslav federation, there is still disagreement about whether a Macedonian nationality really exists. "Nationality" implies a conscious feeling of distinctiveness which one group has in relation to all other groups; an ascertainable degree of realized homogeneity which leads one segment of the human race to draw a meaningful line between "we" and "they." National consciousness adds a name, a selective history and a set of related symbols to a people. The Macedonians, by the end of the last century, had evolved from a relatively undifferentiated segment of the South Slavs to a group largely conscious of Bulgarian nationalism. During the ninety years or so since Macedonia became a major Balkan problem evoking much international concern, the issue of whether there has been a further evolvement of Macedonian nationalism has occasioned masses of conflicting evidence. These contradictory views about the nature of Macedonians and their political aspirations are still very much alive, not only in scholarly circles but among political strategists and hopeful emigre groups.

It is reasonable to hold that, prior to World War II, the Slavs of Yugoslav Macedonia considered themselves Bulgarians, but they developed reservations during Bulgarian occupation in World War II. They could have developed into thoroughly nationalistic separatists, but they did not resolutely struggle when they had a fair chance for perogatives of independence. Whether the Macedonians would eventually have evolved into a separate nationality is an open question. The Yugoslav communist policy has encouraged the national consciousness of the Macedonian Slavs. However, since it is still dangerous today for a Yugoslav Macedonian to admit that he considers himself a Bulgarian, there is no accurate way to determine the real national feeling of the Macedonian Slavs. They have passively, if not positively, accepted their status. We will seek to explain which factors led to the failure of the traditional disputants and the success of the Yugoslav communists. In examining this question, it is well to bear in mind the continuing international significance of the region—the facts that some Yugoslavs and Bulgarians still entertain claims to now-trisected Macedonia as a whole, that Albanians and Greeks would like to have additional parts of it, and that there exists support for Macedonia's unification and its independence of all of these claimants.

Although often overlooked in propaganda tracts treating the area, the ethnographic make-up of greater Macedonia has been greatly altered in the last forty years. Greek Macedonia, following the expulsions of Bulgarians in the early 1920's and in 1944, and the Greek-Turkish population exchange in the early 1920's, became more solidly Greek. The Slavic element was further diminished by the attritions of World War II and the Greek Civil War. However, pockets of Slavs, perhaps a minimum of 80,000 (the Macedonian Political Organization estimates upwards of 200,000) remain in the northwestern part. A Bulgarian census was conducted in 1946 in which the inhabitants of the Pirin region were urged to declare themselves Macedonians, but the results of this census were never made public. According to CPY figures in 1950, there were 226,700 Macedonians in the Pirin district, about 6,000 Turks and 2,300 of other nationalities. The 1956 Bulgarian census listed a Macedonian population of 187,789 of which 178,862 (or 95.3 percent) lived in Pirin Macedonia where they made up 63.8 percent of the population.[7]

Yugoslav Macedonia, like the rest of Yugoslavia, is ethnically heterogenous. The Slavo-Macedonian inhabitants of the Macedonian republic make up about 70 percent of its population and their number increased from 789,648 in 1948 to just over one million in 1961. About 200,000 Albanians live in west and north-west Yugoslav Macedonia and make up about 15 percent of the population of the republic. Over 130,000 Turks are also scattered about, mainly in the Vardar River Valley. The Serbian population, though remaining relatively small, has grown to more than 42,000. Vlahs, now largely assimilated by the dominant nationality, are dispersed through all three parts of Macedonia.

If one adds the Slavs in Yugoslav Macedonia who are classified as Macedonian by Belgrade to the Slavs living in Bulgarian and Greek Macedonia, the grand total of Macedonians or potential Macedonians approaches one and a half million. Given the strategic position which this bloc of Slavs occupies and until recently their lack of a markedly discrete national consciousness, it is not surprising that for almost a century they have been the subject of rather constant advances by whichever of their neighbors happened to be most powerful and audacious.

PART I

THE INTER-WAR PERIOD

CHAPTER 1
FIRST CPY APPROACHES
TO THE MACEDONIAN PROBLEM
(1919 — 1923)

The nationalist dissatisfactions which debilitated inter-war Yugoslavia and which led directly to its downfall, were apparent as soon as the Kingdom's administration was constituted along lines rendering Serb dominance probable. In Croatia and Macedonia there were fundamental misgivings about Serb insistence on a high degree of centralization. The situation was ripe for Communist exploitation, but the Communists failed to capitalize on this opportunity. They limited themselves to parliamentary opposition. In the Constitutional Assembly of 1921 the fifty-eight Communist delegates voted against the centralistic constitution finally enacted by the combined strength of all the Serbian parties. (The Croation Peasant Party boycotted the Assembly.) Yet the Communist Party had virtually no nationality program of its own during the formative years of the new state. The Party was in confusion on many vital questions. When direction did come it was from the predominant Serbian wing. So, although the CPY publicly stood for forms of regional and local autonomy, it could not, either constitutionally or by means of revolutionary agitation, fully exploit the nationality issue at first.

However, while the traditional Serbian parties exacerbated the issue by endeavouring to bypass or suppress national yearnings, the CPY made an effort to analyze the problem and to find a solution. This effort took a full four years. There was much wavering. Often domestic pressures for an effective nationality line were supplemented by blunt advice from Moscow. But the direction was towards the crystallization of a policy which the CPY labeled the "Communist solution of nationality problems." The prenatal development of this policy bears close examination, for the tendencies which delayed its evolvement until 1923 were not fully eradicated with subsequent drastic overhauls of Party leadership, and are of concern to the Government today.

The root of early CPY hesitation on the Macedonian and Croatian problems lay in the composition and prevailing nationality outlook of the Serbian Social Democratic Party which spawned the Communist organization. In the chaotic situation in Yugoslavia immediately following World War I, the Social Democrats, organized in sections according to provincial boundaries, engaged primarily in social agitation. In principle they supported the new state and the need for national "unity." The Social Democrats had active organizations in all Yugoslav provinces, but their following was limited. According to Tito, the Serbian SD Party, by far the strongest left-wing political group in the prewar kingdom at the time, received 30,000 votes in the Parliamentary elections of 1912. Its rural membership consisted of only 2,300 in 1914. [1]

The Bolshevik Revolution in Russia occasioned the same sort of ideological division among the Yugoslav Social Democrats that occurred elsewhere. There was a cleavage between the partisans of a reformist, Marxist policy and those moved by Lenin's more radical, active approach. In the Serbian SD Party the radical group prevailed. It was they who took the initiative in uniting the Yugoslav leftist parties in a national Communist Party. Immediately after the institution of the state, the dominant left wing of the Serbian Social Democrats, led by Sima Marković, created an Initiative Committee which sent agitators to the provinces.

A Congress of Unification was held in Belgrade, April 20-23, 1919, with Social Democrats from all provinces except Slovenia participating. From Macedonia, over which the Serbian SD Party had jurisdiction, came 20 delegates from local socialist organizations. [2] The basis for unification had been worked out by Marković according to Lenin's model. The new organization was named the Independent Workers Party of Yugoslavia (Communist). This Congress criticized the Second International and joined the Third International, which had been founded only six weeks previously. Thus, the Yugoslav Communists enjoy the distinction of having been the first outside party to join the Comintern, as well as the first to leave the Cominform.

The pervading note of the founding Congress, as far as the nationality question was concerned, was that voiced by the Marković group. In the spirit of a Serbian SD Party proclamation made the previous November, it held that Serbs, Croations, and Slovenes were one nation, for they had one language and their other ethnic characteristics were the same. The Congress decided that the Party should support the idea of national unification and struggle against some working class opinion that the Serbs, Croations, and Slovenes were different peoples. The newly elected Central Party Council, in a logical corollary, took the position that Macedonians, Montenegrins, and Bosnians were Serbs, and that any attempt to oppose this proposition must be characterized as chauvinistic nationalism. Despite this stern warning, a number of delegates attacked this super-Serbian line and were duly criticized.

The nationality controversy was particularly timely, for the Congress had to take a stand on the Green Cadre movement which was then very active in striving for an independent Croatia. A number of Croatian Communists who had recently returned from the Soviet Union were playing important roles in the Green Cadre's revolutionary activities. Marković held the movement to be chauvinistic and bourgeois inspired. He dispatched a member of the Central Council, Djuro Cvijić, to Zagreb to order Communist disassociation from the Green Cadre. Marković was later severely criticized by Moscow for not having exploited the revolutionary potentialities of this Croatian group.[3]

Besides the Slovene Social Democrats, a large number (including the leadership) of the Croatian-Slavonian SD Party's members had absented themselves from the Congress of Unification, although Tito claims that a "huge majority" of the membership attended.[4] The Congress' decisions caused such dissension that many delegates left the new party then and there, having recognized that their views on the nationality question and on plans for revolutionary activity were too basically at variance with those of the dominant group to render collaboration attractive.

Despite its own ideological confusion, the Communist Party tried to capitalize on the inability of the Pašić Government to mellow its xenophobic view of non-Serb Yugoslavs. Social, economic, and national dissatisfactions were exploited, with agitators gingerly endeavoring to straddle all sides of the prickly nationality issue. The Party began to set up local organizations. On January 7, 1920, a Provincial Committee was created for Macedonia and Old Serbia. On that date a resolution was passed with regard to the Party's role in the forthcoming county (opčinski) elections. Attention was called, in very general terms, to the "almost unbearable conditions" in Macedonia. A section of the resolution read: "The newly-founded bourgeois parties in Macedonia are using this condition purely for their own class aims, putting above all else nationalistic, chauvinistic dispositions and actions which only deceive and stupefy the masses of working people."[5] There was no command for specific Communist exploitation of the Macedonian nationality problem, but it was made clear that pro-Bulgarian agitation would not be countenanced. Thus, while the Macedonian Communists clearly recognized the national problem as an important political factor, the Party line was such that they could not aptly manipulate it to their ends. However, Party activities met with significant success in some Macedonian districts;

at least Koliševski claims there were 1,000 members in Skopje alone at the beginning of 1920. [6]

Nation-wide Communist agitation was rendered fruitful by conditions of general unrest, largely promoted by dissatisfaction with the government's policy on the structure of the state. When the Second National Party Congress was held in Vukovar, Croatia,[7] 374 delegates assembled. They claimed to speak for about 60,000 Party members. The Party also exercised control over many of the 300,000 trade union members in the Kingdom.

As the Communist leaders were preparing for the Vukovar Congress, basic differences on fundamental issues continued to be debated. The important factions coalesced, in traditional Party fashion, into three groups — left, center, and right. The overriding divisive factor was the question of the proper approach to the Party's seizure of state power. The right wing, supported by most of the centrists (these two groups were composed mainly of former syndicalist leaders) opposed any "premature" armed struggle against the bourgeois government. The left wing, led by Marković, favored a thoroughly revolutionary approach.

The Vukovar Congress opened in an atmosphere of great tension. Party statutes, strategy, and tactics were hotly discussed before being decided upon. The main points of the announced program were: the struggle for a Soviet Republic of Yugoslavia, the creation of a Red Army, the expropriation and socialization of industry and trade, and the separation of church and state. Apparently there was no resolution specifically addressed to the national problem which was rocking the nation. However, the participants were seemingly united in their acceptance of the correctness of a centralistic state. Tito, while admitting that the Congress marked the "end of the process of unification" and the purification of the Party by purges of the "most opportunistic leaders of the social-democratic movement," took a dim view of its handling of the nationality question.[8] In quoting the Congress' view that the "CPY will further stand on the defense of national unity," he stated that it had a "complete misunderstanding of the national question."

The Vukovar Program represented a victory for the Marković line — for the sharpening of the revolutionary class struggle. The resulting intensity of Communist agitation evoked strong reaction on the part of the Government. But Belgrade's subsequent characterization of all opposition to state centralization as "Communist" was short-sighted, for it stiffened the anti-regime tendencies of non-Serb democratic elements. The decisions at Vukovar offered no hope to the Macedonian Communists who were eager to utilize "officially" the most agitating issue in the province — the strong reaction against the processes of Serbization.

Although the Macedonian Communists were deprived of their most potent campaign issue by the Serb-oriented CPY, they were able to rally considerable popular support. They were justifiably regarded as being in general opposition to Belgrade, and this alone sufficed to win votes. The Party scored important victories in elections for county officials and for delegates to the Constituent Assembly. In local elections, Communists won majorities in Kumanovo, Veles and Kavadarci, and took over local administrative organs in a number of villages.[9] The Party was forced to prepare for the November 1920 general elections for the Constituent Assembly under conditions of police repression. The Communists and their sympathizers, as well as non-Communist Macedonian nationalists and pro-Bulgarian elements, were all disparagingly labeled "Bugaraši."[10] Government-subsidized bands of armed Serb irregulars, the Četas, roamed the countryside searching for those known to be antipathetic to the regime. The Communists were indirectly helped, however, by the Government's refusal to allow any party except the essentially nationalist Serbian Radicals and Serbian Democrats, the Communists, and the regime-sponsored Moslem Džemiet group to contest the general elections. According to CPY accounts, the three non-Communist parties cooperated in limiting the influence of the Communists, even to the point of using slogans about an autonomous Macedonia.

At a meeting held in Veles on October 17, 1920, 3,000 Macedonian Communists adopted resolutions which gave further evidence that they were enjoined not to exploit anti-Serbism beyond a very limited extent. Among the resolutions were the following:

> Call on the Macedonian people to frustrate, insofar as they can, every *comitadji*[11] action, to express its solidarity with the Yugoslav peoples in their struggle for the freedom of the working masses from the capitalistic rulers, marching under the banner of the CPY.
>
> Make known to all the manipulators of Bulgarian chauvinistic propaganda, that the Macedonian people have come to their senses and no longer will allow themselves to be playthings in the hands of reactionary exploiting men. The Macedonian people are against fratricidal slaughter. They are for the struggle which the proletariat of the entire world is carrying out for its liberation.
>
> Demand that the Yugoslav rulers prohibit the Serbian Četnik groups, which, on the assumption that the Macedonian people are aiding the Bulgarian *comitadjis,* are carrying out the most awful terroristic activities and thus forcing the Macedonian people, willingly or not, to take the woods.[12]

It will be noted that the resolutions were within the bounds of the Marković nationality line. In the Constitutional elections the CPY did come out for certain forms of administrative autonomy, but not based upon nationality considerations. The Communists favored a degree of decentralization in general, on any sort of regional or local basis. Unofficially, some Macedonian Communists played this proposal for all it was worth. A former resident of Bitolj recalls that the IMRO adherents there supported Communists in order to increase the anti-Belgrade vote. One successful Communist candidate promised to denounce Serb chauvinism on the floor of the Assembly and to declare that Macedonians were Bulgarians. He failed to do so. Upon his return to Bitolj to mend political fences, he was promptly pushed into the Draga River by a boisterous group of students.[13]

Most of the IMRO adherents boycotted the elections. This factor, combined with police measures to discourage anti-Serbs from voting, resulted in the exercise of the franchise by only 55% of the registered Macedonian electorate. The Communists received 38% of the votes cast, thus becoming the strongest single party in Macedonia and electing 15 of the region's 45 deputies. It appears probable that, of the 198,736 votes obtained by the CP in the Kingdom as a whole, about 25% were garnered in Macedonia, whose population was but 6% of the Yugoslav total. The Moslem Party received about 30,000 votes in Macedonia. It is a reasonable estimate that almost one-half of Macedonia's non-Moslem vote went to the Communists.

The striking Communist success in Macedonia has been interpreted by all non-Communist observers as a protest vote against Belgrade centralism and Great Serbism. No Macedonian party having been permitted, the Communists were considered by the voters as the most anti-Government legal group. Thus, one cannot attribute the Party's victories in Macedonia to pro-Communist sentiment. The 45% of the registered voters who boycotted the election were patently anti-Government. It follows that almost three-fourths of the Macedonian electorate, in their first (and only) opportunity to express themselves on Yugoslavia as conceived by the Pašić group, were openly anti-regime.[14]

Meanwhile, factional struggles over the principle of armed revolution continued to occupy the top CPY leadership. The Centrist group, in a manifesto of opposition to the key decisions of the Vukovar Congress, demanded a referendum of party members on that issue. Marković led a delegation to Moscow in December 1920 to discuss the matter with Third International and Bolshevik Party officials. It was "confirmed" that conditions in Yugoslavia were ripe for an armed revolt and the CPY was directed to prepare for an uprising. However, the Government's security organs were alerted to the plot by the creation of a Communist Workers' Defense Organization and by individual acts of terrorism. The CPY was severely compromised by police capture of some highly incriminating revolutionary plans, which may have been planted by government agents.

The CPY leaders, having "resolved" the question of armed revolution only to forewarn the authorities by their preparations, therefore, found it more and more difficult to keep the lid on the boiling intra-party disagreements about nationality policy. General agitation, including non-Communist, was still giving evidence of widespread popular concern about the nationality issues rather than economic and social factors. In Croatia, anti-Belgrade emotionalism was canalized into the Croation Peasant Party of Stjepan Radić. In Macedonia, support of the IMRO increased in direct proportion to the growing stringency of Serbian rule. The Communists, with their locally unpopular nationality line, were becoming less attractive as an outlet for Macedonian frustrations. It became obvious that the Party was losing large numbers of potential supporters to the Bulgarophiles and to the few, poorly organized groups favoring complete autonomy. Therefore, the Macedonian Communist leaders requested of the Central Committee a drastic revision of the Party's nationality position.

By that time, however, the Yugoslav Party leadership was faced with a situation the seriousness of which greatly overshadowed that of the internal Party crisis. Police agents were reporting details of Communist revolutionary plots to the Ministry of the Interior with regularity. The general public was reacting negatively to individual acts of Communist violence. Belgrade capitalized on the public's mood by intensifying efforts to label all expression of centrifugal nationalism as "Communist," a device which it used for the next fifteen years. Finally, the Provisional Government decreed the dissolution of the Party's organizations and suspended its press. In retaliation, the Party assassinated the author of the decree. An unsuccessful attempt by a Party youth named Stejić to assassinate Prince Regent Aleksandar brought the full wrath of the regime upon the Communists. In August 1921 Parliament passed an anti-extremist law, the *Obznana* (Notification), by a vote of 190 to 54. This sweeping measure, which had been presented by Minister of the Interior Milorad Drašković, forbade all Communist, anarchist and terrorist propaganda and all agitation to change the form of government. It denied to the Communists the right to hold public office. The administration was authorized to deport to other parts of the Kingdom the relatives, and even innocent co-villagers, of fugitives who refused to surrender.[15]

The *Obznana* was effectively employed to drive the CPY underground, and it was fervently applied against the non-Communist Macedonian revolutionaries and Croation nationalists. Thus, after a strong start, the Party lost its Parliamentary representation of fifty-eight and was faced with the greatest difficulties in staying alive at all. For awhile only sporadic terroristic acts were undertaken, the most notable of which was the assassination by Alija Alijagić of Drašković, author of the *Obznana*.

The CPY was clearly unprepared to cope with its new illegal status, especially as Government administrative authority was by then firmly established and the police had honeycomed the Party's organizations with spies. But the factor which contributed most to the Party's subsequent weakness was the deeply divisive nationality issue. Communist activities in Macedonia fizzled out, while the IMRO increasingly became the symbol of resistance. In Croatia the Party's chances to counteract the popularity of the Peasant Party of Radić were minimized by the Communists' Serbian nationality line. While the Party leadership was indecisively debating whether to be content with strictly illegal activities or to establish a legal front organization, the Comintern instructed the CPY to recommence legal political activity under another name. To lay concrete plans, a Party Conference was held in Vienna on July 14, 1922, and the "Independent Workers Party of Yugoslavia" was set into motion. This front organization was formally launched in Belgrade on January 14, 1923.

At the time when the Croatian and Macedonian Communists were rebelling most vehemently against the rigidity of the nationality line imposed by Marković, Moscow was beginning to play with the revolutionary potentialities of the Macedonian problem. All loyal Balkan Communists were expected to engage in this game in accordance with changing rules set by the Comintern. The Comintern's Macedonian line fluctuated widely, and the Balkan CPs were hard put to reconcile it with domestic political needs. The abstract merits of the Macedonian case, even as determined by the later stated Stalinist nationality policy, were sometimes overridden by the Comintern. The Soviet Union saw in Macedonia an explosive situation worth using in its plots against the bourgeois Balkan regimes.

The Comintern's first approaches were muddled, but Zinoviev, President of its Executive Committee, referred specifically to "Macedonian Bulgarians" in Yugoslavia. In a message to the CPs of "Bulgaria, Rumania, *Serbia,* and Turkey," he wrote:

> New national divisions, which were created after the defeat of Austria-Hungary and the dismemberment of Bulgaria and Turkey, have intensified the national problem so that it is now more serious than before the war. Many segments of foreign nationalities have come under rule of the victors. A more powerful desire for freedom is encouraged by the policy of national oppression and of insatiable militarism. . . . *Macedonian Bulgarians,* Albanians, Montenegrins, Croats and Bosnians are rising against the rule of the Serbian bureaucratic landowning oligarchy . . . .

> A new era of bitter national agitation, national hate, and national-bourgeois wars threatens the Balkan and Danube peoples. . . . Only triumph of a proletarian dictatorship will unite all the masses of the peoples in a Federation of Socialist Balkan (or Balkan and Danube) Soviet Republics, and preserve them . . . from colonial enslavement and national conflict. The Communist Party is called by the current situation to undertake an even greater role in the Balkan Peninsula than in capitalist countries which have no nationality problems. [16]

Yet, three months later a Communist from Skopje, Dušan Čekić, was one of the signatories of a CC CPY manifesto which averred that the outside world was exaggerating Yugoslav nationality differences. [17]

The Balkan Communist Federation was founded on Bulgarian initiative and continued under Bulgarian domination. It was, therefore, inclined towards a Bulgarian solution of the Macedonian issue, an attitude vigorously opposed by the Serbian and Greek Communists. As early as 1922 the question of Macedonian autonomy was raised at a Federation Conference by the Bulgarian Vasil Kolarov, but discussion was postponed at the request of the Greek representative.

Thus, the first attempts of the Comintern and the Bulgarian CP to capitalize on the Balkan nationalities problem were rebuffed by those Parties which had the most to lose by Communist agitation for a change in Macedonia's status. Opposition to the current Comintern line on Macedonia was invariably excused by the offenders, and sometimes even by the Kremlin, on the ground that adherence to the line would severely undercut Communist support among dominant national groups. This excuse was frequently advanced by the CPY and by the Greek Communists, who held that exploitation of the Macedonian problem was not worth the consequent reaction of the Serbs and the Greeks.

Now Stalin himself subjected the Balkan situation to close analysis, paying special attention to the peasantry. This interest directed his attention to Croatia. Radić, whose Peasant Party was still refusing to participate in the Belgrade Parliament, visited Moscow to investigate the possibility of Soviet assistance to his struggle for a Croatian Peasant Republic. [18] The Kremlin perceived the impossibility of CPY progress in Croatia as long as the Marković nationality line prevailed. Accordingly, the Comintern's Executive Committee summoned the Yugoslav Communist leaders to Vienna for serious consultation.

The Vienna meeting between the representatives of the Comintern and the CPY brought a showdown on the nationality line. The gathering, in May 1923, was officially called the Second Conference of the CPY. Prior to the Conference, the former factional nomenclature of the Party had become meaningful in terms of a member's position on the nationality question rather than on the necessity for an armed revolution. Those such as Marković who continued to favor the acceptance of the "unity of Yugoslavia" were now termed "rightists," albeit they might support armed revolt. To be a "leftist" now meant that one stood for the exploitation of national issues in Croatia and Macedonia. Referring to the Second Conference, Tito stated that the CPY leadership "for the first time gave a little serious attention to the national question, but it did not at that time definitely take a stand on it, even though the Party leadership then went 'left.'"[19] In dismissing with this judgement the Conference's focus on the nationality issue, Tito glossed over an interesting development.

When the Conference convened, the right-wing (essentially pro-Serb) faction had a majority of the delegates. The Comintern was by this time thoroughly disenchanted with the pro-Serb element. Its representatives saw to it that the CPY delegation was so reconstituted that the leftists had the majority. Marković was not present at the Conference, being in prison at the time. The Conference concluded that the left-wing stand on the nationality question was indeed the correct one; that each Yugoslav "nation" should have the right to self-determination. Marković, who proved to be ideologically supple, was retained in the top Party position. Nonetheless, for the next several years during which he remained as Secretary General, he continued to be the spokesman for the rightists. The basic controversy was not yet resolved.

About this time, in early 1923, the entire CPY leadership was called to Moscow for a seven-day conference with the Executive Committee of the Comintern. This pilgrimage is not mentioned in the Party's public chronicles. Whether the trip was made before, during, or after the Second Conference is immaterial. The Moscow sessions were important in that the Comintern made obvious to Marković and the other rightists its agreement with the left-wing's nationality stand. The Yugoslav representatives were informed that the principal cause of CPY failures lay in its incorrect position on the national question and its disregard of the possibilities in exploiting peasant unrest. The "Great Serbian" orientation of the Party was specifically attacked. The Comintern advised that the slogan of the "unity of Yugoslavia" be abandoned and that, *for propaganda effects,* the CPY adopt a program for the organization of the state along federalistic lines. The right of independence, not only of the Croatian and Slovenian people but also of the Macedonians, should be supported. For the next three years the Marković group bowed gracefully but continued to argue that the national question was primarily a "constitutional" one, that the Croatian and Macedonian national movements were bourgeois-inspired, and that all priority should be given to the accomplishment of a proletarian revolution.

In this period, when the CPY's professed nationality position was being superficially renovated, there occurred two incidents which gave evidence of the extremes to which party factionalism went. Croatian Party leaders carried on an exceedingly acrimonious correspondence with the CC as a result of the latter's prohibition of Communist participation in Croatian Peasant Party demonstrations. At the height of the Croatian quarrel, some of the Macedonian comrades lost their lives as a result of having organized a nationalist demonstration. On August 2, 1923, Serbian gendarmes had fired into an assembly held to commemorate the Ilinden Uprising. Ten persons were killed. On the following day the Skopje Party Committee organized a demonstration against "Great Serb hegemony and Belgrade terror." The CC CPY expelled eight Skopje ringleaders from the Party, characterizing them as chauvinists and enemies of the working class. To insure that the culprits had learned their lesson the Party published their names in a leaflet. The eight were arrested and allegedly passed away in Belgrade's Glavnjača Prison.

It was not surprising that by late 1923 the Macedonian Communists had lost almost all of the public support they had been able to muster in 1920. Koliševski's historical review coupled the "mistaken and unclear stand on the national question" with the effects of the *Obznana* as the basic reasons for the Party's loss of its "great influence on the Macedonian masses."[20] He admitted that some of the lost sheep went over to the "Great Serbian and bourgeois" Democratic Party, then in opposition to the Radical Government. He also acknowledged that the activities and influence of Ivan Mihailov's IMRO were rendered more potent by the CPY's mistakes. The CPY's nationality line was not, until after the Third Party Conference in December 1923, at all helpful in providing ammunition for Macedonian Communist attacks on, for instance, the Government's unpopular Serb colonization program. Contemporary Macedonian Communists record many instances of the rigorous and short-sighted measures undertaken in Belgrade's application of the Serbization policy. It must have been extremely frustrating to their forerunners to have been kept off the only popular bandwagon, anti-Serb resentment, by their own Central Committee. But any claims made by the Yugoslav Communists, and such claims are sometimes implied, that the Party was consistently at the forefront in the struggle for Macedonian rights, or that the Party during the first years of the 1920's took any real initiative with regard to Macedonia, must be dismissed as wishful afterthinking.

However, the faint beginnings of a new nationality line were evolving by 1923. As we have seen, the Comintern, as well as the CPY's own "nationalists," had perceived the futility of a nationality approach which differed little in essence from that of the traditional Great Serb elements ruling the Kingdom. Many raids by the IMRO were being made into Yugoslav Macedonia from the sanctuary of the Pirin region and Todor Aleksandrov, the fiery leader of the revolutionists, had caught the imagination of many Macedonians. The Bulgarian CP, through the Communist Balkan Federation, had shown its intention to play upon the extensive anti-Serbism in Yugoslav Macedonia. With the Party's plight in Croatia just as serious as in Macedonia and its country-wide position in a shambles, a radical revision of its tenets was clearly indicated.

CHAPTER 2
THE CPY ADOPTS
A NEW NATIONALITY POLICY
(1923 — 1928)

When the Third International found it necessary to "suggest" a third CPY conference, the nationalities problem had come into focus as by far the most difficult challenge to the Belgrade regime. General prosperity and a moderate land reform program had eased peasant dissatisfaction, whereas the nationality problem had become a seemingly hopeless tangle of reprisal and counter-reprisal. No doubt there were many Serbian politicians and administrators who sincerely believed that a stern hand over the troublesome Macedonians and Croatians was essential to preserve the integrity of the state. There were frequent evidences of irresponsibility on the part of some of the disgruntled national groups. There were real threats from the revisionist powers, particularly from Bulgaria, which "allowed" the IMRO to administer Pirin Macedonia and engage in border warfare against Yugoslavia. [1]

But as Belgrade applied sterner measures, the Macedonians and Croatians went to further extremes. No effective moderating force appeared on the scene to seek a way out of the vicious circle. The Yugoslav Government was reinforced in its "unity" policy by the democratic powers of Western Europe. France, Great Britain, and Czechoslovakia in particular calculated that a stable Yugoslavia would insure stability in the Balkans and that only a strong government in Belgrade, a government catering to the "needs" of its strongest national group, could bring stability to the Kingdom.

The Communists, in pursuit of the opposite goal of bringing about the downfall of the bourgeois government, could hardly have evaded the exploitation of the ready-made nationality issue much longer and still remained good Communists. In the five years following the Second (Vienna) Conference, the CPY was gradually forced by domestic circumstances and by constant Comintern pressures to clarify its position against the extremes of

Great Serbism. The Third Party Conference in 1923 set the basic pattern for the subsequent evolution of the Party's nationality line. There followed a Comintern attempt to elicit CPY cooperation with the IMRO, and some gyrations in the Balkan Communist Federation's handling of the Macedonian issue. In the end, it was found necessary to purge the CPY of its persistently pro-Serb elements so that the advantages of the new nationality line could be maximized.

The Third Party Conference (December 17-26, 1923) was held in Belgrade. The national composition of the assemblage was not auspicious for the leftists. Of the sixty-five delegates, thirty-nine were from Serbia and Montenegro, eight from Croatia, five from Bosnia and Hercegovina, four from Slovenia, four from the Vojvodina, and two from Srem. Three Serbs, party leaders at Skopje, represented Macedonia. The left group took their characteristic anti-centralist position, calling for the rejection of the "unitary" Yugoslav idea and for the *recognition of the nationality of Macedonians.* The Party was asked to support the Macedonian and Albanian "national struggle" and to cooperate with the Croatian Peasant Party. There is evidence that "rightist" leader Marković was willing to compromise a bit, on a strictly theoretical basis, but generally he retained his old views. Repeating his thesis that the national struggles were a tool of the bourgeoisie and that the working class had nothing in common with these struggles, he held that the idea of a "unified" Yugoslavia was right and represented "tremendous progress." While admitting, for the first time, that the national movements in Macedonia, Kosovo, and Croatia were aimed against the "Great Serbian hegemony of the counter-revolutionaries," Marković insisted that the Party not aid such movements.

The Conference resolutions, however, indicated that the recent advice of foreign Communist officials had been digested. Although right-wing functionaries had again taken over key positions in the Party following Markovic's release from prison in late 1923, the pressure on their nationality position had become too great to withstand.[2] Because of their significance, the Third Conference's resolutions on the Macedonian issue are quoted in fair detail below.

The lengthy "Resolution on the National Question" gave the new key when, after calling for liberation from the influences of the imperialistic great powers, it demanded a "complete break with the policy .of national hegemony and internal oppression".[3] The centralistic Vidovdan Constitution was said to legalize Serbian bourgeois hegemony over the Croatian and Slovenian people and the "roughest national oppression, colonization, and forceful extermination and assimilatory Serbization in Macedonia. . . . Today the whole Croatian and Slovene people, as well as the peoples in Macedonia, are in the movements for their national self-determination. . . . the State of Serbs, Croats, and Slovenes cannot be considered as a homogeneous national state with some national minorities, but as a state in which the ruling class of one [the Serbian] nation is oppressing the other nations."

The Conference affirmed the principle of "self-determination to the point of secession" but added the vital Stalinist reservation, namely, "the recognition of the right of secession on the part of the Independent Workers Party of Yugoslavia does not exclude the right of its agitation against secession." Further, "In recognizing the right of secession, the IWPY does not agree that secession is always purposeful." It was stated that the Party would decide the purposefulness or inapplicability of the question of secession in each concrete situation. Of significant note is the fact that only Croatia, Serbia, and Slovenia were mentioned in the section on secession. There followed reaffirmation of the Marković contention that the "uniting of the Serb, Croatian, and Slovenian people in a common state lies in the direction of historical progress and the interest of the class struggle of the proletariat." Then, however, the Conference acknowledged that such a common state must be based on voluntary union and the full equality of each part. "Each people must have the right to arrange their relations with the other parts and with the state as a whole."

The Eighth Section of the Nationality Resolution dealt entirely with Macedonia. It opened with the following observation: "As no one of the nationalities which inhabit Macedonia has a majority, no matter what Balkan state rules over Macedonia, it means the oppression of most of the Macedonian population. The nationalistic regimes of all the neighboring bourgeoisie were established when the aspiration for independence was only just beginning among the Macedonian population." An "independent Macedonia is today the watchword of its entire population." The conferees called upon the Macedonian peasants to lead a struggle for the "establishment of worker-peasant rule in an independent Macedonia which will voluntarily enter the federation of independent Balkan republics."

The next section of the Resolution called attention to the "Serb bourgeois oppression of compact masses of Hungarians, Germans, and Rumanians in the Vojvodina and of the Turks, Arnauts,[4] Bulgarians and Kutso-Vlahs in most of Macedonia." The bourgeoisie of these minorities were accaused of collaborating in this oppression. The right of minorities to use their own languages and have their own schools was set forth. The Serbian people were reminded of the well-known Marxist maxim that they could not remain free while "strangling other people." Party members were urged to "expose constantly the class character of the slogans of self-determination, federation, and autonomy as mouthed by the opposition bourgeoisie."

As if this were not sufficient, the Third Party Conference, having taken counsel with the Comintern and the Balkan Communist Federation, also passed a "Resolution with Regard to the Macedonian and Thracian Questions."[5] This commenced with the geopolitical truism: "The possession of Macedonia secures, because of its geographical position, domination of the entire Balkan Peninsula." The observation made in the Nationality Resolution, in connection with the ethnic composition of Macedonia, was reworded as follows: "All the peoples who rule the neighboring lands are represented in Macedonia, but in such proportions that not one of them has an absolute majority. For this reason, whatever Balkan state rules over Macedonia means *national enslavement* of the majority of the Macedonian population and calls for a *national struggle*."[6] The Resolution recalled the struggle of the Macedonian population for liberation, and inculcation of hatreds among the peoples, and stated that the Turkish rulers "could not destroy the Macedonian peoples' consciousness that only a *united and autonomous* Macedonia will secure rights and freedom for all the peoples. The *Macedonian Revolutionary Organization* worked for the strengthening of this consciousness; it was the true organizer and leader of the revolutionary struggle of the Macedonian slavs without regard to nationality." Unfortunately, the Resolution went on, agents of the Bulgarian bourgeoisie had taken over the IMRO and diverted it from the path of the independence struggle. "Only *the establishment of autonomous Macedonia and Thrace and their union with the other Balkan countries in a federative Balkan republic will establish lasting peace among the Balkan peoples.*" Warning that some Macedonians were used by the Bulgarian counter-revolutionaries to suppress the uprising of Bulgarian workers and peasants, the Resolution continued: "*The conduct of these blind Macedonians, who masquerade as 'Macedonian revolutionaries' but who are paid gendarmes of the Bulgarian bourgeoisie and executioners of the Bulgarian working people, is a blow against the liberation of Macedonia itself and the Macedonian population must resolutely condemn it.*"

The Conference charged the "most harsh, terroristic" Serbian regime in Macedonia with driving into exile Bulgarians, Turks, and Arnauts and settling people from other parts of Yugoslavia in their place. The general oppression of all the non-Serb peoples, the closing of their churches and schools and the forbidding of their press and language was decried. The same situation was said to exist in Greek Macedonia, and the Bulgarian nationalists were accused of persecuting the Muslem Pomaks in Bulgaria. The Resolution ended with an analysis of the "class struggle" aspects of the Macedonian and Thracian situations. In an obvious attempt to profit from the popularity of the IMRO, the conferees held that "the proletarian parties do not even have anything against the organizations of the Macedonian and Thracian peoples, around which the working population group themselves in the name of their *national and cultural interests.* On the contrary, they are striving . . . to assure the prestige of the working masses over the bourgeoisie, large agrarian and adventuristic elements, who often use these organizations in order to attain their class aims and who at every possible opportunity betray the interests of the broad working masses."

Having reviewed the pertinent nationality resolutions of the Third Conference, it is rewarding to examine post-World War II Party appraisals of the Conference's decisions on Macedonia. First, Koliševski:

> From 1923 the CPY took the correct position on the national question and concretely, on the Macedonian question, underlining the fact that the Macedonian question in no way lags behind the Croatian and Slovene questions in its significance, recognizing the right of self-determination to the point of secession for the Macedonian peoples. Thus, our Party took the correct, basic stand on the national question, which was one of the strongest weapons in the struggle for attracting the masses of the Macedonian people to its line, as the Macedonian nation's right to equality, its right to self-determination, including even secession, was recognized. [7]

According to Tito: "At the Third Party Conference the correct stand on the Macedonian question was finally taken, that is that the Macedonian nation, and by this it was recognized as a nation, has the right to its own life and to equality." [8]

Tito's recapitulation of the Third Conference's decision on Macedonia, and Koliševski's to a slightly lesser degree, are somewhat disingenuous. In the examination of the two resolutions we have borne with the tribulations of the Macedonian population, the Macedonian peoples, the Turks, Arnauts, Bulgarians, and Kutso-Vlahs in Macedonia, the national minorities who comprise most of Macedonia's people. No mention whatsoever was made about *a Macedonian nationality.* The Macedo-Slavs, according to the CPY in 1923, were either Bulgarians or colonizing Serbs, neither group having an absolute majority in the whole of Macedonia. A Macedonian Republic was recommended to free, not a Macedonian nation, but a hodgepodge of nationalities. Such basic elements of Communist-defined nationality as a distinctive language and literature, a historically constituted community and a similar psychological make-up, were not definitively superimposed on the Macedonian issue by the CPY until two decades after the 1923 Conference.

While it is patent that the 1923 program gave Macedonia and other

Yugoslav Communists a platform infinitely superior to the Marković nationality line, it is no less obvious that the "correct basic" stand, i.e., the one taken in World War II, was something else again. After Tito's historical reanalysis, a prominent Macedonian Communist wrote that Tito "particularly emphasized" his claim that a Macedonian nationality was recognized at the Third Conference.[9] Thus, Tito's statement was not a slip of the tongue, but evidently an attempt to give the 1923 Party somewhat more credit for prescience than the record warranted.

Communist strategists, desperately seeking to recover the Party's lost momentum in Macedonia, saw that hatred of Belgrade was rife, pro-Bulgarian sentiment was strong, and the IMRO was widely viewed as the potential savior of Macedonia. The Comintern and the Communist Balkan Federation therefore endeavored to persuade IMRO leaders of the advantages of cooperation. As early as 1922 a Bulgarian Communist guerrilla band under one Pandurski attempted to take over some IMRO operations.[10] In their later attempt to capture the Macedonian Revolutionaries "from above," the Communists were frustrated by violently negative reactions on the part of a faction of the IMRO leadership and the rank and file. The Comintern's efforts to subvert the IMRO were not helped by the manifestations of continued Serb dominance in the CPY. The Marković faction, still in control, adhered neither to the letter nor the spirit of the Third Conference Nationality Resolutions.

In the early 1920's, the leaders of the traditional core of the IMRO were Todor Aleksandrov, Aleksandar Protogerov and Petar Chaoulev.[11] Their position on the question of Macedonian autonomy vs. Bulgarian annexation of Macedonia varied somewhat, but in general the advocates of the latter solution dominated the Organization. Against these "Supremists," in the period immediately following World War I, worked the pro-autonomy "Federalists," led by Philip Atanasov and Todor Panitsa.[12] There seems to have been a definite tendency toward Communism within the Federalist group.[13] Dimitar Vlahov and Hadji Dimov, IMRO veterans turned Communist, had connections with the Federalists. Negotiations, the details of which are still obscure, were conducted between the Supremists, Federalists and Comintern representatives in 1923 and early 1924. Two things are certain: the Comintern made every effort to reach a *modus vivendi* with the IMRO, and the CPY adamantly refused to support such collaboration.

After some preliminary discussions in Moscow between representatives of the three groups, serious negotiations were undertaken in Vienna in March and April 1924. It appears that Soviet Ambassador to France, Krustin Rakovski, a Bulgarian by birth, took part in the Vienna talks.[14] By early May the parties agreed on a manifesto pledging their united support to a new IMRO orientation for a Communist-flavored struggle towards an independent Macedonia. According to a Bulgarian (but pro-Yugoslav) source, Aleksandrov, Protogerov and Chaoulev agreed to the program in return for a large Comintern subsidy and the support of the CPY.[15] The May Manifesto's approach was in two key aspects similar to, and in one important regard different from, that which had been announced by the Communist Balkan Federation the previous March.[16] The Federation had acknowledged that Communists could not create an effective Macedonian revolutionary organization of their own but should seize control of the IMRO, "the real leader of the revolutionary struggle of the Macedonian slavs." It stated that the Serbian bourgeoisie was oppressing the Turkish, Albanian and *Bulgarian population* of Macedonia and called for the autonomy of that region.

The Vienna Manifesto came out for an independent and self-governing Macedonian state and announced the IMRO's cooperation with the "extreme progressive and revolutionary movements of Europe."[17] A fight was pledged for the "democratic decentralization" and federal reorganization of Yugoslavia and for a Balkan Federation. The Tsankov Government in Sofia, which had come to power in a bloody coup in which the IMRO was instrumental, was termed hostile to the *Macedonian* and Bulgarian peoples.

Shortly after the Communist success at Vienna the Fifth Comintern Congress passed a resolution on Macedonia and Thrace which implied approval for a united front IMRO.[18] It spoke of the "desire of the *Macedonian people in all parts of their shattered homeland for unification* and for the creation of a united independent Macedonia." The Comintern warned the CPY that it must "conduct a resolute and consistent struggle for the right of the oppressed nationalities to self-determination, up to political secession." Thus in the declaration of the Balkan Communist Federation, the reins of which the Bulgarians held, the Macedonian issue was one of liberating Bulgarians from the Serbian yoke. In the Comintern-inspired Vienna Manifesto and the Comintern's Fifth Congress resolution, on the other hand, there is the first intimation of the existence of a separate Slav Macedonian nationality. The three statements were alike in their espousal of the idea of an autonomous Macedonia in a Balkan Federation, and in omitting any reference to the theory that the right of secession does not infer the duty to secede.

The relative precision of the Vienna Manifesto's Macedonian plan made it difficult for the CPY to maintain ambiguity about its Macedonian policy. It was all very well, thought the Marković group, to cater cautiously to minority whims in Party resolutions, but the Manifesto was too much. It would have the CPY work hand in hand with the organization whose obvious aim was to detach Vardar Macedonia from Yugoslavia. It would thus undermine the faith of the CPY's basic national faction, the Serbs. Official CPY sources do not mention the fact that their Central Committee forbade Yugoslav Party organizations to support the united IMRO plan. The Balkan Communist Federation complained to the Comintern about the CPY's refusal to cooperate. Three members of the Yugoslav Central Committee were summoned to meet with a Comintern special commission in late May 1924. The Yugoslavs promised to reform their ways, but the CPY continued to drag its feet in implementing the Manifesto. The Greek Communists were naturally also against the plan.

On June 30, the prominent Cominform official Dimitri Manuilsky reproached the Yugoslav and Greek CP's for their attitudes on Macedonia, chastising Marković for the CPY's "passive attitude . . . to one of the most burning questions which is agitating the various Balkan nationalities at present."[19] The Fifth Comintern Congress' resolution on Yugoslavia included the following passage:

> The task of the Yugoslav Communist Party is to conduct an independent proletarian policy on the national question and to do so with such energy as to attract the Yugoslav peasant masses into becoming allies of the proletarian revolution. . . . The opinion of Miliokovíc [evidently a CPY delegate to the Congress] that the Communist Party must fight equally hard against any nationalism whatever, is not only opportunist, but objectively plays into the hands of Great Serb bourgeois nationalist policy. In their fight Communists must always bear in mind the differences between oppressing and oppressed nationalities.

The next month the Bulgarian chief of the Comintern's Balkan Section, Georgi Dimitrov, bluntly termed the standpoint of Marković and J. Milanović, who was another spokesman for the CPY's Serbian faction, as "rightist and liquidatory deviation."

However, the troublesome question of Communist collaboration with the IMRO was rendered academic soon after July 13, when the Vienna Manifesto was made public in the first issue of *Federation Balcanique*. The announcement stunned most of the IMRO-ists. It caused others to commence a rash of assassinations, the frequency of which did not abate for a decade. Although both Aleksandrov and Protogerov publicly denied having signed the Manifesto, IMRO agents in Yugoslav Macedonia evidently had been ordered by Aleksandrov to cooperate with the Communists. Aleksandrov was murdered in August 1924. Bulgarian army officers, holding that Macedonia should be an integral part of Bulgaria and fearful of the South Slav Federation ideal then being supported by Moscow, probably collaborated with chauvinist IMRO elements in this act. Ivan (Vančho) Mihailov, Aleksandrov's private secretary, seized the top IMRO position. There has been suspicion in some quarters that he was not guiltless in Aleksandrov's death.[20] Within the next few years, many other prominent Macedonian Communists and Federalists and some whom Mihailov may merely have feared as possible contenders for his job, met violent deaths. Hadji-Dimov, Aleksandar Vasilev, Atanasov, Chaoulev, and Panitsa were all tracked down and shot. Protogerov, who considered himself Aleksandrov's rightful heir, became the leader of the Federalists. He was accordingly dispatched by Mihailov's men in 1928.

This blood-letting, touched off by the Vienna Manifesto, thoroughly wrecked the Communists' united front IMRO operation. During the Protogerov-Mihailov feud, the IMRO gradually degenerated into what appeared to be a band of fanatic adventurers. The organization received funds and training facilities from fascist Italy and Hungary. There is no doubt that Mihailov's leadership was characterized by excessive trigger-happiness. It was, however, an exaggeration for a Yugoslav publicist to allege that Al Capone and Mihailov could easily have changed places. The perennial IMRO excuse for the perpetration of atrocities was their desire to "call the attention of the world public to Macedonia's enslavement." The applicability of this patriotic motive for murder lessened considerably during the reign of Mihailov. He has been pictured as representing the extremist annexationalists, but the events of the Second World War proved there was no definite meeting of minds between him and the Bulgarian nationalists. However, postwar IMRO efforts to depict Mihailov as having been a pure and consistent autonomist have a hollow ring.

The average Macedonian surely could not see the IMRO's internecine struggle in anything like a reasonable perspective, but the image of the organization as a "liberating" group did not disappear in Yugoslav Macedonia. Its anti-Serbian activities were consistent and sanguinary — and welcomed. Whatever its real aims may have been in this period, many a Macedonian household continued to pay its dues. Some of these IMRO supporters were likely prompted by fear of reprisals, but most were moved by loyalty to an organization that was *fighting* against oppression.

Almost two years after the original "united" IMRO fiasco, Dimitar Vlahov and several other Macedonian Communists in Vienna were to found "IMRO (United)," also called the *Obedinena,* which was patently a Communist front set up by the Comintern. Very few other Macedonians ever "united" with Vlahov. CPY history treats the abortive 1924 unification attempt as the actual beginning of Vlahov's equally unsuccessful IMRO (United) effort formed April 1, 1926. It is perhaps not surprising that contemporary Yugoslav Macedonian leaders attempt to read the present Party nationality line into their reconstructions of early Party activities, or that they claim for Vlahov's group the accomplishments of the original IMRO. Thus, Koliševski asserted:

> The establishment of IMRO (United) in 1924 [sic.] . . . was positively received in Vardar Macedonia in that the aim was the uniting of the whole Macedonian people in an independent state in the composition of a Balkan Federation which had to be tied to the working class and the revolutionary movement, especially to the Communist Parties in the responsible states. But, even in the beginning of the work along the line of the IMRO (United), a certain resistance was found among the members of the CP who were supposed to follow the line of the IMRO (United), and that resistance developed because the stand of the IMRO (United) on the national question was not in accord with the correct stand of the CPY on the national question. [21]

This somewhat factitious statement bears examination. As we have seen, in 1924 neither the CPY's nor the Comintern's position on the nationality question as it pertained to Macedonia was "correct," if one assumes, as do the Yugoslav Communists, that the post-1943 CPY policy is "correct." Koliševski would have been closer to the truth had he stated that: a) the then CPY leadership did not like the 1924 Vienna Manifesto because it could be interpreted to imply recognition of a Macedonian nationality; b) the 1924 Vienna Manifesto, however, made no mention of "the (whole) Macedonian people"; and c) the IMRO (United) was established in 1926, not 1924.

But perhaps Koliševski's interpretation was designed by implication to emphasize the sturdy CPY principle that any Macedonian policy which did not hold to a solution under Yugoslav aegis was incorrect. A vital factor in the CPY's consideration, aside from the then largely theoretical question of Macedonian nationality, was the escape clause. Yugoslav Communist leaders have consistently maintained that the Macedonians are not "obliged" to secede, if by such action they would be lost to a Balkan Federation not controlled from Belgrade.

With reference to the 1924 Vienna Manifesto, Koliševski admitted that it occasioned sharp quarrels between the Party's regional leaders in Macedonia and that "individual party organizations abandoned the line of class struggle and descended to a nationalistic position, for example, the Kavadartsi Party organization which even resisted the decisions of the CP." As positive aspects of the establishment of the IMRO (United) Koliševski listed: (1) its contribution in bringing out "political differentiations so as to isolate lying enemies of the Macedonian people, of the type of Vančo

Mihailov;" (2) its making known the "necessity for all sections of Macedonia, no matter to whom they belong," to struggle for their Macedonian state; (3) it correctly oriented itself on the nationality question and with that added a feeling of Macedonian national consciousness, especially in Pirin Macedonia and among the Macedonian emigres,"[22] and (4) the fact that it placed the Macedonian question before the world public.[23] Koliševski's interesting interpretation notwithstanding, Communist attempts to utilize the IMRO in the inter-war period were almost completely frustrated. The IMRO may have indirectly assisted the Comintern in that it contributed so much to the instability of the Balkans in the inter-war period, but the rugged terrorists remained the main obstruction to Communist success in Macedonia itself.

The Comintern's Balkan experts were not seriously phased by the 1924 setback vis-à-vis the IMRO. They continued to play upon national discontents with tenacity. As the need arose, of course, the Comintern made tactical concessions to the Balkan CPs. The pro-Bulgarian bias of the Comintern Macedonian resolution published in July 1924 was aimed at obtaining Macedonian support for the Bulgarian CP in its struggle for power following the bourgeois coup against Stambuliski. The united front tactics of the late 1930's gave the Serbian and Greek Communists a respite from their Macedonian tribulations.

As the Balkan Communists were not in power, their theoretical freedom of action on the Macedonian or any other regional issue was almost unlimited. They were not bound to support, as were the Balkan peasant parties (not to mention the nationalist governments), real or mythical "rights" of Greater Bulgaria, Serbia, or Greece. Observe the fate of Stambuliski who, with wide popular support, attempted to lead Bulgaria away from the sabre rattling policies of myopic extreme nationalism and to seek a rapproachement with Yugoslavia. Balkan Communist propagandists, most of whom were safely tucked away in Vienna or Moscow, could concoct appealing slogans about federation and self-determination without fear of being in the position of attempting to carry them out.

The Yugoslav CP leadership, however, could not bring itself to play the Comintern's nationality game with spirit. The CPY was under constant Moscow pressure to commence acting in accordance with its announced nationality line. Lest the Yugoslav comrades gloat over the Comintern's failure to capture the IMRO from above, fourteen members of the Yugoslav Central Committee were called to Moscow in February 1925 for lessons on nationality policy. Marković seems to have continued to insist that the Croatian and Macedonian nationality questions be soft-pedaled. He was criticized by Manuilsky, Radek, and Palmiro Togliatti. Then Stalin delivered his famous speech of March 30 at Sverdlov University. The crux of it was:

> As the starting point in the national program, we must postulate a Soviet revolution in Yugoslavia. . . . It is imperative to include in the national program the right of nations to self-determination, including the right to secession. . . . The program should include a special point providing for national territorial autonomy for those nationalities in Yugoslavia which do not find it necessary to secede from the country. . . . Under certain circumstances, as a result of the victory of the Soviet revolution in Yugoslavia, it may well be that on the analogy of what occurred in Russia certain nationalities will not desire to secede. . . . To avoid all misunderstanding, I must say that the *right* to secession must not be understood as an obligation, as a duty to secede. A nationality may take advantage of this right and secede, but it may also forego the right, and if it does not wish to exercise this right, that is its business and we cannot but take cognizance of the fact. . . . We must not confuse a right with an obligation. [24]

This pronouncement dovetailed nicely with the CPY's 1923 Third Conference nationality resolutions. It included the vital escape clause.[25] At the end of April 1925 the Enlarged Executive Committee of the Comintern passed a resolution recommending that the CPY give full support to all anti-Serbian national movements and use the slogan of the right of all peoples to secede from Yugoslavia. However, so that it would not appear that the CPY definitely advocated secession, the Committee proposed that Croatian and Macedonian Communists emphasize the necessity of common life with the Serbs, and throw the blame for oppression not on the Serbian people but on the Serbian bourgeoisie and on the minorities' capitalists. The CPY was also advised by the Comintern not to be too worried about the inciting of national hatreds, as these could be of benefit to the Party.

In June 30, 1925, article in the *Bolshevik,* Stalin criticized Marković for taking a "constitutional" approach to the nationalities problem. Marković was "divorcing the national question from the general international situation and from the right of self-determination (i.e., of changing the frontiers of Yugoslavia). For him it is virtually an academic question, not an actual question of the moment."[26] Marković, however, soon gave another example of his extreme reluctance to retreat. In August 1925 at Valandovo, the Serbian Cetnik leaders Kosta Pečanac[27] and Ilija Birčanin massacred a number of Macedonians who were accused of aiding the IMRO. The Provincial Macedonian CP organization reacted by calling for a campaign against the Serbs in Macedonia. The CC CPY condemned this suggestion as chauvinistic and deposed the entire regional leadership.

At Vienna during June 10-18, 1926, Yugoslav Communists appraised the Party's impotent condition with some candor. One resolution reproved the Serbs as being largely responsible for the factional strife. The Macedonian comrades were strongly attacked for their poor showing. The resolution about the Party in Macedonia read in part:

> The work of our Party is very weak from the point of view of the utilization of the exceptionally favorable conditions for successful work in the national question and the agrarian question. The non-utilization of differences and the fermentation in the IMRO and the failures to tie the fight against Serbian imperialism with a struggle against individual outrages (*valandovo*) . . . and the non-utilization of the great economic crisis in Macedonia, all have made the Party's tie with the masses weak. [28]

By this time it was not surprising that the members from Macedonia were in a state of rather complete confusion regarding the correct, or at least safe, nationality line.

The resolution imposed upon the provincial organization in Macedonia specific tasks including "the strengthening of work in national-revolutionary organizations, the building of party factions in them and the leading of campaigns and actions on the occasion of all concrete occurrences of the ugly outrages of the great-Serbian regime." Active support for the revival of national-revolutionary organizations on the basis of the May (Vienna) Manifesto of 1924 was ordered. Further, the Party "should not stop at abstract propaganda for the right of self-determination to the point of secession, but should take an active role in the everyday struggle against all concrete cases of national oppression (language, schools, political and civil rights, etc.)." [29]

The nationality resolutions of the Third Party Congress (at which the Party was officially renamed the Communist Party of Yugoslavia) indicated that the Central Committee's Moscow sojourn had been fruitful. However, bitter factional quarrels continued. The non-Serbs in the Party, particularly the Croatians, were incensed over the lack of correspondence between the Party's stirring resolutions and the "sit tight" policy of the Marković leadership.

Croatian Communist discontent finally led to open strife between members of the local organization in Zagreb. A rebel group of "anti-factionalists," so-called because they blamed factionalism on Marković's continued disregard of the approved nationality line, requested the intervention of the Comintern.[30] To their pleas, made outside the regular Party channels, the Kremlin responded with alacrity. At long last Marković was removed as Secretary General. Moscow ordered Djuro Djaković to take over the top job. Shortly thereafter, in April 1928, the Fourth Congress of the CPY was held in Dresden. The Party's fortunes were at low ebb. The conferees engaged in mutual recriminations about the signal failures.

The outstanding event of the Dresden Conference was a scathing attack on CPY factionalism by "Ercoli" (Togliatti), the Comintern's delegate. He made it clear that the CPY was to submit to Moscow in every detail. There were to be no more open declarations, or even clandestine maneuvers, which were not consonant with the Comintern's line of the moment. Togliatti stated, in effect, that the CPY's policy of turning out anti-Serb nationality resolutions while acting with a "realistic" appreciation of Serb dominance, was out. He said:

> [The Comintern requests] no declaration in words, no formal submission to decisions, no diplomacy, no kind thoughts. We can no longer be satisifed with any declaration on your side. In the history of the CP of Yugoslavia there are already too many declarations. [31]

Not only was Marković forced to write a humiliating letter of confession, but the left-wing was also attacked by Togliatti. He criticized Djuro Cvijić, an anti-Marković Serb from Croatia, for his expression of premature doubt as to the effectiveness of the new CC CPY and for his general attitude of opposition. Togliatti made his famous denunciation of "Balkanism," which he defined as fragmentation of the working class movement in the Balkans and the "continuous fight among those groups by means of intrigues and deceit."

Impressed by the vehemence of Moscow's expressions of displeasure, the Fourth Congress went to work with a vengeance on resolutions in favor of the rights of secession for almost every ethnic group in Yugoslavia except the gypsies and White Russians. Macedonian particularisms were acknowledged in a statement on "The Struggle against National Oppression." This decried the "great Serbian bourgeois denationalization policy, the colonization of Serb colonists, assimilation, (that is, the Serbization of *the Macedonian people*) . . . the recognition of the right to subsistence only of Serbian culture, language, etc."[32] At Dresden Mihailov's IMRO was described as having changed into a blind partner of the Bulgarian counterrevolutionary bourgeoisie. Another resolution claimed that "the very bourgeois strata who in the past were apostles of Great Bulgaria are helping the Serbization of Macedonia, and their 'national' aspirations do not go further than demands for an autonomous Macedonia within the borders of Yugoslavia."[33] Vlahov's IMRO (United) was given the green light to struggle for an *independent* and *united* Macedonia. The escape clause was lacking. The Congress passed a lengthy resolution about the Party's duties in the struggle against war among imperialist states, pointing out that the danger of war with Bulgaria was being increased by conditions along the Macedonian borders. However, the methods of transforming an imperialistic war into a revolutionary war were expounded in considerable detail. [34] Thus the chastened CPY went further than it had before, or has since, in its stated policy with regard to concessions to the non-Serb Yugoslav nationalities. The Comintern was directly responsible for the changes in the Party leadership and the Party line.

Why had Marković, who seemed to oppose his Moscow mentors regularly, been allowed to remain as Secretary General of the CPY until 1928. Regardless of its propaganda tactics of the moment or of longer-range "for the record" considerations in nationality and minority problems, the Comintern actually sided with the stronger of the contending elements. This policy of expediency was manifest in its allowances for Marković and the Serbian faction of the CPY. The calculable adverse effects on the dominant Serbs of real concessions to the Macedonians and Croatians were, until 1928, too great to be risked.

The approach of the CPY to the Macedonian question was a relatively minor aspect of its gradual evolution in treating the general internal nationality problem. But the Macedonian issue was unique in that it alone of the CPY's nationality problems directly involved foreign Communist parties. The Bulgarian and Greek CPs did not have such complexes of nationalities with which to deal. But the Comintern's united and autonomous Macedonia concept was disruptive, in varying degrees, to all three of the Communist Parties directly concerned. Because of its "antipatriotic" propaganda effect, the Comintern's Macedonian routine was played down by the three Parties, with at least tacit Kremlin approval, when it suited them to do so.

In its campaign of disruption in the Balkans, Moscow endeavored to exploit every societal weakness. Basically oriented to the strategy of using any dissatisfied group as an instrument in its struggle for total control, the Comintern tried to mobilize all such groups and to build among them a solidarity on new bases, with new prospects. Regarding Macedonia, the CPY *and* the Comintern were perfectly aware of the difficulties to which support of the Macedonians would bring them with the Serbs.

The reason the dilemma was more apparent than real was that resistance to the Croatian and Macedonian autonomy line *on the part of the Serbian groups in which the Communists were interested,* i.e., those Serbs who for whatever reason were already basically dissatisfied with the regime, was quite limited. So, while the CPY nationality approach was gradually geared to have broad appeal in the oppressed provinces, the Communists calculated that the reaction to this approach among their Serbian target groups would not be severely negative. They knew that in any case they could not persuade a majority of the Serbs willingly to sanction Croatian and Macedonian autonomy. All the same, the Comintern recognized, as did Marković, that the Serbs were the dominant element in the CPY and in the country as a whole, and that the support of key Serb elements was therefore essential to the attainment of eventual Communist power. Thus, while publicly supporting the leftist group in the CPY, Moscow had allowed the Marković faction to retain control of the Party, gradually pushing it to the "correct" nationality position.

The Macedonian Party organization was too weak to assist much in this reorientation activity. It was largely the efforts of the Croatian members and the leadership's marked failure in general organizational work that led to Marković's removal. He was discarded when it was no longer considered necessary openly to coddle Great Serbian leanings in the Party. He was publicly identified with the incorrect stand, and may have been at heart really incapable of accepting the federative line.

It is notable that in the entire process of shifting to its new nationality position, the CPY never agreed to support the extreme "nationalistic" movement in Macedonia, as the Comintern wanted in 1924. The 1928 Fourth Congress nationality decisions marked the temporary peak of CPY concessions. As the Party settled down under its new leadership it began to adhere consistently to the nationality line which it was to employ throughout its successful struggle for power. As this line pertained to Macedonia, it called for a combination of Macedonian autonomy and "unity and fraternity" with those Serbs and other Yugoslav peoples who were in resistance to the regime.

Thus the CPY ended the first stage of its evolution with a clear nationality program and without the encumbrance of Marković. It was to face even greater tribulations in the 1930's. Due to other factors the new nationality line was not used to good advantage during the next decade. However, it was kept in the Party arsenal and later proved to be a valuable weapon indeed.

CHAPTER 3
COMMUNIST FAILURE IN MACEDONIA
(1929 — 1941)

By the time the CPY adopted its new nationality policy and replaced Marković, the chief advocate of the "constitutional" approach, it was too late to utilize the new look effectively. In 1926, the Croatian leader Stjepan Radić had accepted the existence of Yugoslavia and renounced separatism. Macedonia had been forcibly pacified. Non-Serb national consciousness was largely present in such groups as the Croatian Peasant Party, where there was emphasis on peasant and social reform as well as on autonomy as such. In early 1929 King Aleksandar's dictatorship commenced. Try as it might to gain support for its program, the CPY found it difficult to exist under the subsequent conditions of police repression. When the Government relaxed some of its strictures in 1935, the CPY was forced to de-emphasize its nationality line in accordance with Moscow's Popular Front and collective security tactics. The net result of the CPY's inter-war efforts in Macedonia was failure.

Shortly after the Dresden Congress "purification" of the Party, the basic problem of the Kingdom erupted again. Radić was fatally wounded on the floor of the Skupština on June 20, 1928. King Aleksandar was unable to work out a satisfactory compromise with the inflamed Croatian political leaders. On January 6, 1929, the King dissolved the Skupština and rescinded the Vidovdan Constitution. Stern measures were taken to preserve public order. In April the new Party leader, Djaković, was arrested. He passed away in the Zagreb prison. The next Secretary General, chosen as usual by the Comintern, was Jovan Martinović, who soon fled to Vienna with the remaining Party leaders. Martinović ordered an ill-timed armed rebellion against the royal dictatorship and thereby caused the almost complete destruction of the weakened Party. "Only scattered, individual groups existed. Almost the entire leading party cadre, both high and low, were in prison, had been killed, or had emigrated."[1] The appointment of a new leader, Milan Gorkić (born Čižinski) at the end of 1932, did not pull the Party out of the doldrums. In fact, Party history has it that Gorkić was a provocateur, saboteur, and sectarian deviationist.[2]

In December 1934 the Fourth Conference of the CPY convened secretly in Ljubljana. There was little mention of the national problem. The Party confined itself largely to generalizations, going on record against fascism, great Serbism, the Monarchy and imperialistic war. However, the national line adopted at Dresden was maintained in the Congress' call for "worker-peasant power in all the countries of Yugoslavia."

Meanwhile, the Communist Balkan Federation had renewed its maneuvering on the Macedonian question. In May 1929 it published a resolution enlarging on its March 1924 proclamation. It read, in part:

> The Balkan Communist Federation has the special task of coordinating the activities of the Communist Parties of the Balkans in the sphere of the national revolutionary movement, of securing the connection and cooperation of the Communist Parties of the Balkans with the national revolutionary organizations which, as the Macedonian I.M.R.O. . . . stand for the cooperation of the oppressed nations with the revolutionary proletariat.[3]

The Resolution did not mention Vlahov's ineffectual IMRO (United). However, a few weeks later the Croatian fascist-revolutionist Ante Pavelić visited Sofia, where he was enthusiastically received by the public.[4] At this point, the Communist Federation made a rather complete switch. It condemned the "Fascist Macedonian organization of Ivan Mihailov" and supported the "real national-revolutionary movement with the IMRO (United) at its head." It gave another indication of recognizing Macedonian nationality in speaking of the "Macedonian fascists who keep the Macedonian population of Bulgarian Macedonia under the most cruel of regimes . . . and who are a tool of the Bulgarian bourgeoisie for the capture of Macedonia."

Another new factor resulted from the strong measures taken by the Georgiev Government in Sofia against the IMRO in June 1934, reducing its power to almost nothing and causing Mihailov to flee to Turkey. This made it possible for Bulgaria and Yugoslavia to regularize their relations. The Balkan Communist Parties opposed all moves towards such cooperation, for the last thing they wanted was the maintenance of the *status quo*. By this time the CPY's transformation from a Yugoslav-oriented group to a small clique of foreign-based agents taking orders from Moscow was complete.[5] As was evidenced at the Ljubljana Conference, the CPY now considered that there were a number of "countries" in Yugoslavia. It joined the Bulgarian CP and the unhappy Greek Communists in denouncing the Balkan Pact of 1934. There is no evidence, however, that the CPY in fact ever favored the revision of boundaries implied in the Comintern's attacks on the Balkan Pact. It was not long before the Kremlin's line changed altogether and the Yugoslav Party was again caught with a nationality approach which was inappropriate for the situation as analyzed by Moscow.

The Bulgarian Government's action against the IMRO was a shock to those Macedonians in Yugoslavia who counted on IMRO for deliverance. For generations Bulgaria had been looked upon as their best hope for liberation from the Turks, the Greek church, and now from the Serbs. The perfection of their faith in Bulgaria was destroyed. Certainly Mihailov and the other IMRO leaders could not, after 1934, have been wholehearted annexationalists. From positions of great behind-the-scenes power they had been driven into exile by their brothers. From that time the Bulgarians must have seemed more like unreliable cousins to the IMRO operatives and supporters.

With the assumption of revisionist leadership by Nazi Germany and the Communists' turn to united front tactics, "national-revolutionary" opportunities such as Macedonia presented became fascist, not Communist, causes. All efforts concentrated on the building of an European anti-fascist coalition. As European peasant and social democratic parties were deemed essential as temporary partners, Communists necessarily took a more traditionalist stand on the inflammatory minority problems. Of the three Communist parties directly concerned with Macedonia, the Greek naturally profited most by the dropping of the independent and united Macedonia slogan. The Greek CP took opportunity to point out in 1935 that as a result of the exchange of population between Greece and Turkey in the early twenties, Greeks predominated in Greek Macedonia.

The CPY's national tactics reverted back in the direction of the old Marković line. In the summer of 1936 the CC CPY, meeting in Moscow, resolved to oppose the breakup of the country at that time. "The CPY has made many mistakes on the national question," the CC confessed:

> *Until the Seventh Congress* [of the Comintern, which had passed the new word], the CPY understood and propagated the slogan of self-determination, including secession, in a completely sectarian manner. Secession was not considered as a right of the oppressed peoples, but as a basic necessity. About political territorial autonomy, for people who do not desire separation, nothing at all was said. The change in the world situation . . . impels the CPY to change its tactics on the national question but not, by this, to abandon the principle of the right of all peoples for self-determination to secession. [6]

Thus, the enforced change in the CPY's nationality approach was clearly identified as a temporary expedient. The Resolution went on to condemn the Mihailov and Pavelić organizations as being made up of fascist agents "who are now demagogically calling for independent Croatia and Macedonia." The Party admitted that it had been sorely mistaken in standing aside from the Croatian Peasant Movement, now headed by Maček.

Neither the new nationality line of 1928 nor its revision in the mid-thirties were of real usefulness to the Party until the Second World War. The democratic opposition parties, whose approach to national problems was essentially moderate, had the advantage of being legal and therefore respectable. The IMRO and Ustaši drew support from those inclined to extreme nationalism and fascism. The CPY was thus hard put to employ its brand of nationalism as a tool with which to move the Yugoslav public. As a result of the Government's studied catachresis in labeling all who favored autonomy as Communists, the traditional opposition parties were forced to demonstrate that they had nothing in common with the Communists. Actually, CPY aims were probably more effectively exposed by the popular anti-Great Serb groups than by the Government itself.

During the late 1920's and early 1930's the CPY was nowhere more shattered than in Macedonia. There was no local Macedonian political party to absorb pent-up nationalistic fervor. By late 1934 the IMRO, its former bases denied it by the Georgiev Government, was almost inoperative except for occasional assassinations outside Yugoslavia, such as the assassination of King Aleksandar in Marseilles. Yet the Macedonian Communists were unable to take advantage of their opportunity. The vagaries of the CPY's nationality line had much to do with their failure. It had become clear to many Yugoslavs that the Communists were playing with national questions for tactical purposes. The establishment of the dictatorship did not render the Communist endeavors more efficacious, as it did those of the Croatian Peasant Party to which Serb extremists had given a potent martyr.

Koliševski has painted a sombre picture of the "heavy blows" of the police on Macedonian Communists.[7] In April 1929, "the most powerful and most active party organizations (Skopje, Veles, Štip, Tetovo, Prilep)" were broken up. This blow caused a great diminution in all Party activity. The following August, police raids on the Kumanovo party organization resulted in the cutting of connections between local party organizations and certain members not caught in the previous roundup. For the next three years "all attempts to tie together the isolated organizations and groups in various towns in Macedonia were unsuccessful." In 1933 a few renovated local organizations established connections among themselves and with the CC CPY. A Provincial Committee for Macedonia was set up and began to print a paper, *Iskra* (Spark). But, "one after another of the provincial leaderships fell into the hands of police during 1933 and 1934." At a Party Conference in Skopje in February 1935, another regional committee, with headquarters at Kumanovo, was formed. "After the decisions of the Seventh Comintern Congress, the party organization in Macedonia attempted to build a united front for the struggle against facism with certain figures and representatives of the bourgeois opposition parties." This effort failed because of the "incorrect stand of certain of these on the Macedonian national question and because they did not want to fight against fascism." In late 1935 the police again fell upon the Provincial Committee and a part of the Skopje and Kumanovo locals.

With little in Macedonia to which a Communist could point with pride, Koliševski spoke of the "significant" role played by the Vardar Society in Belgrade and Zagreb, as well as by other student societies which were founded in "all towns of Macedonia." In early 1936, according to Koliševski's sad recital, "an attempt was made to create a mass movement of the Macedonian people, called the Macedonian Peoples Movement, MANAPO, on the basis of a solution of the Macedonian national question by full national equality of the Macedonian people within the borders of Yugoslavia, a united struggle with the progressive forces in Yugoslavia for a democratic country, against fascism and for the establishment of diplomatic relations with the USSR." In the 1936 county elections MANAPO was "moderately successful." (By this Koliševski indicates that its showing was poor.) In the 1938 elections MANAPO, not permitted to operate openly, "entered its candidates on the list of the Serbian Agrarian Party in Macedonia as it was the weakest and least compromised bourgeois party in Macedonia . . . Despite the terror MANAPO had great success and in a number of towns and districts received the greatest number of votes." (This is another way of saying the Party's success was limited.)

In analyzing the reasons for MANAPO's failure, Koliševski pointed to the weakness of the Macedonian CP leadership, its lack of organizational work and its failure to embrace such dissatisfied elements as the Albanians, Turks, and some of the poorer Serbian colonists. Thus, when the Comintern named a Croatian metal worker turned revolutionist to replace Gorkić as Secretary General, the new leader's legacy in Macedonia was a poorly organized, small group of Communists whose previous experience with the Party had been anything but happy.

The CPY is justified in regarding the dismissal of Gorkić and Josip Broz Tito's assumption of leadership in 1937 a major turning point in the fortunes of the Party. Moscow found in Tito an able organizer, an intelligent but non-intellectual conspirator, a brave man with incredible drive. There had been too much ideological hairsplitting among the expatriated CPY leadership. A man of action was needed. Tito was such a man.

Prior to Tito's taking over, the prison terms of many of the middle-level Party stalwarts had expired. Their dialectics had been much fortified at such "universities" as Sremska Mitrovica Prison, where Communism was the daily diet. With the exception of Tito, the entire Central Committee, made up of the old "factionalists," was purged in 1937. The Spanish Civil War provided the opportunity for a thorough purging of the rank and file, as well as an outside outlet for revolutionary fervor.[8] Tito's pre-occupation with organization and operations paid off in the development of strong cadres of young but well-trained conspirators. "At every level of Yugoslav society and in every nationality the Party had a group of supporters which, in a crisis, could be relied upon to provide the elite of a revolutionary movement."[9] Party membership increased from about 2,500 in 1937 (after the purges) to about 5,000 in 1939 and about 12,000 in 1941. There were about 30,000 in the first line of reserves, the Union of Communist Youth of Yugoslavia (SKOJ).[10]

Tito's success in building a tight, disciplined organization seems to have reduced open "nationalistic" factionalism in the Party to almost nothing. In 1937 "separate" Slovene and Croatian CP's finally were organized. By 1939 all of the old factionalist leaders, left and right, had been removed from the Party. With the lifting of some of the severe pressures of the Belgrade Government, Party recruitment climbed steadily in the years prior to the war.

In its public proclamations the Party tried to adhere to its liberal nationality line, and yet to remain within the framework of the USSR's instructions to fight those sympathetic to, or frightened by, the rising power of Nazi Germany. Milan Stojadinović, the Yugoslav Premier from 1935 to 1939, was characterized by the CPY as a Hitler agent and his Government as anti-people and hegemonistic.[11] When war appeared certain the new Government of Dragiša Cvetković finally agreed to some of the concessions demanded by Maček, and Croatia was granted a degree of autonomy by the *Sporazum* (Agreement) of 1939. The CPY denounced the *Sporazum* as a "maneuver, the aim of which is to postpone giving people their democratic and national freedom." A "people's government, which will ensure the people all democratic and national rights . . . which will rely on the democratic powers in its foreign policy, in the first place on the Soviet Union" was demanded by the Party.[12] A CC CPY proclamation of May 1, 1940, included the following:

Has this [Cvetković-Maček] agreement brought peace? No, because a furious struggle is being waged between the Serbian and Croatian gentry for division of those regions which should decide their fate for themselves. These are Bosnia and Hercegovina, and the Vojvodina. Serbian and Croatian chauvinism is being fanned. And they are not paying any attention to the national rights of Montenegro, Macedonia and Slovenia at all. Have these been given their democratic rights? No.[13]

That the Party was able to keep its ever-present internal nationality problems largely submerged was due to increased organizational efficiency and to effective purges. The role of national dissatisfactions as a motive for Party recruitment became negligible during the 1930's, according to former Party members. The CPY was mainly effective among industrial workers and intellectuals who considered themselves economically or socially under-privileged. The Spanish Civil War and the Party's conspiratorial aspects appealed to members of the frustrated middle-class youth. In Croatia the Peasant Party and the Ustaši absorbed and used national discontent. In Macedonia the discontent continued to fester.

The élan given to the CPY by Tito's workmanlike efficiency did not permeate to the Macedonian comrades in the immediate prewar years. By 1937 police action had again led to "the liquidation of the [Macedonian] party organization as such."[14] Aside from the abortive MANAPO effort, little was even attempted. In February 1940, Svetozar Vukmanović-Tempo appeared in Skopje to investigate the situation for the CC. He was accompanied by Miha Marinko and Sretan Žujović-Crni. As was the usual practice, a new leadership was chosen for the Macedonian organizations.[15] On August 2, according to Koliševski, the Party organized Ilinden demonstrations and "several thousand" participants took part in the one at Prilep.

A Macedonian Regional Party Conference was held later in August 1940 to review past mistakes and set new tasks. Crediting this Conference with having "tremendous significance for the further work and strengthening of the Party organization," Koliševski has called attention to weaknesses in one of its resolutions relating to the colonists and to the establishment of a national front in Macedonia.[16] The weakness on the touchy matter of the treatment of Serbian colonists was indicative of fundamental differences between the Macedonian Communists and the CPY leadership on the whole Macedonian question.

With most of Europe at war, the Fifth CPY Conference was held in Zagreb, October 19-23, 1940, six months before the German attack on Yugoslavia. Although this Conference is barely mentioned in most treatments of Yugoslavia, it cannot be passed over in a study of Macedonia. It was there that Tito must have realized his Macedonian Party members would be very hard to handle. According to an official Party account, the Fifth

Conference resolved that one of the most important tasks was the struggle for national equality of the oppressed peoples and national-minorities in Yugolsavia. This resolution, *inter alia,* called for:

> A struggle for the equality and self-determination of the Macedonian people against oppression on the part of the Serbian bourgeoisie, but at the same time, and stubbornly, for the unmasking of the Italian and Bulgarian imperialists and their agents, who, using the same kind of demagogical promises, wish to subjugate the Macedonian people;
> A struggle for the freedom and equality of the Arnaut [Albanian] minorities in Kosovo, Metohija, and the Sandžak . . . [There was no promise of self-determination for these Albanians];
> A struggle against the colonizing methods of the Serbian bourgeoisie in these regions and for the exiling of all these colonizing elements who are helping the Serbian bourgeoisie to oppress the Macedonian, Arnaut, and other peoples. [17]

Of the one hundred and five delegates to the Fifth Conference, six were Macedonians, including Metodije Šatorov (known as Šarlo), Bane Andrejev, Mirče Acev, and Cvetan Dimov. Satorov and Andrejev were to play important roles in later events.[18] In his review of the Fifth Conference, Koliševski singled out Šatorov for particular criticism, for the latter represented the then apparently widespread pro-Bulgarian sentiment in Yugoslav Macedonia. Šarlo was not in agreement with certain decisions of the Conference. Koliševski accused him of openly defying orders to organize strikes and strengthen the working class struggle, and of being "completely incorrect" on the question of the Serbian colonists.

> Taking a national-chauvinistic position, he took the view that *all* colonists should be exiled from Macedonia, without regard to whether these colonists were supporters of the great-Serb regime, various former gendarmes, *Solunci,*[19] national workers, and the like, or whether they were poor peasants from Serbia and Lika, who . . . not only felt an affinity with the Macedonian people, but were active fighters against the oppression of the great-Serbian bourgeoisie and actively assisted the CP in its struggle against reaction. [20]

Šatorov was criticized for having kindled national hatred against the Serbs, his stand being "completely congruent with the line of the separatist Vančo-mihailovist elements." With regard to the united front stand of the CPY, Koliševski continued, all of Sarlo's proclamations and articles in the year before the war indicated that he rejected the correct anti-fascist line, "the solution of the national question . . . within the borders of one Yugoslavia." Instead, Šatorov favored the creation of a national front with all opponents of the great-Serbian regime. He was guilty of using slogans about "the secession of Macedonia at any price." The national-separatist elements, aiming to break up Yugoslavia and to join Macedonia to Bulgaria, collected about Šatorov. Koliševski concluded his review of the prewar situation by admitting that because of Šatorov's treachery "the wide masses of the people were left [exposed] to the uncontrollable hatred and defeatist propaganda of the anti-people's, fifth columnist, and fascist elements."

That Šatorov's recalcitrance on the problem of Serbian colonists was not unique was confirmed by the fact that the other five Macedonian delegates to the Fifth Conference gave full support to his presentation. The Party leadership desired *no* resolution about expelling the Serbs from Macedonia, although there was willingness to again condemn the "colonizing policy" in general. The Macedonians persisted in their view that *all* the Serbs should be removed, insisting that this plank was necessary to gain popular support. It was only after Tempo and Marinko "convinced" the Macedonians of the correctness of the Party's line that they agreed to a compromise resolution calling for the expulsion of only the "bad" Serbs. The CC CPY was by then a body not prone to compromise with "incorrect" members. It must be assumed that the Party's position in Macedonia was so poor and the CC's control over the Macedonian Communists so weak that the leadership was forced temporarily to yield a bit in order to retain at least a facade of authority over the Provincial Organization.

It is probable that Tito was not overly dismayed by the lack of unequivocal support for the current nationality line from the Macedonian delegates. The total Macedonian membership at that time was 300, with about 400 youths in SKOJ. The CPY, since 1920, had not been at all successful in Macedonia, and other problems were more pressing in 1940. The Nazi-Soviet Pact made it even less possible than before to appeal to genuine national aspirations. Macedonians had no reason to trust the CPY to lead them out of the wilderness. Party resolutions about the right of self-determination to secession had never been emphasized — they appear more significant in (possibly touched-up) retrospect than they were at the time they were circulated. The vital question of whether the CPY really recognized the existence of a Macedonian nationality was still in doubt. It is reasonable to assume that other Bulgarian Communists besides Šatorov had commenced operations in Yugoslav Macedonia before the war. The CPY knew its position in Macedonia was tenuous, but it is doubtful if the Party was cognizant of its absolute powerlessness there.

At the outbreak of hostilities in 1941 then, the Serbs had succeeded in suppressing any open manifestation of opposition in Macedonia. It is exceedingly difficult to ascertain the "national" sentiment of the Macedonians at that time. They were certainly anti-Serb, and to them Yugoslavia meant Serbs. In the 1920 elections, the Macedonians' sole inter-war opportunity to express themselves, they voted overwhelmingly against Belgrade. The continuing process of forced Serbization, which had started in 1913, had only stiffened their resentment. With police repression and Serbian monopoly of local administrative jobs, the Macedonians were sufficiently antipathetic to it to be willing to accept almost any change. Yet there was police terror and Serbian civil service monopoly in Croatia too, and the Croatian Peasant Party still rocked the Kingdom to its foundations. Admittedly, Belgrade would not have tolerated even a patriotic (to Yugoslavia) Macedonian nationalist party, whereas the Government was powerless to prevent the Croatian Party. The failure of the Macedonians to organize a mass, active underground organization might be attributed in part to the deadening effects of five centuries of foreign occupation, and to the amorphous character of Macedonian national consciousness. Also, there was lack of support for the Macedonians on the part of Yugoslavia's other dissident elements. Croatian Peasant leaders, who presumably should have been sympathetic to the idea of Macedonian nationalism, if only for its troublemaking potentialities, did nothing to encourage anti-Belgrade sentiment in Macedonia.

From analyses of available materials it appears that most Macedonians were desirous of union, perhaps with some measure of autonomy, within the framework of Bulgaria. Had that country not been most active in freeing Macedonia from the Turks? Were there not great similarities in language and cultural background? The existence of Macedonian (not Great Bulgarian, but Macedonian) organizations in Bulgaria implied Bulgarian acknowledgement of Macedonian particularities. The Yugoslav Macedonians' only recent experience of Bulgarian rule (1915-1918) had been satisfactory. A number of local men, like Vlahov, had been given important administrative jobs.[21] However, the Bulgarian Government's 1934 "treason" to the Macedonian cause must have left its mark. It was characteristic of the Macedonians that they usually insisted on their Bulgarian qualities vis-à-vis the Serbs and Greeks but on their Macedonian qualities vis-à-vis the Bulgarians. Events after 1934 surely increased the intensity of the latter distinction.

For what did the IMRO stand and what was its power to inspire and lead the Macedonian people on the eve of World War II? Here too clarity is lacking. But at least after 1934 the IMRO leadership desired some kind of autonomy, rather than outright annexation by Bulgaria. And regardless of the disrepute into which Mihailov's group had fallen in the minds of gentler and less frustrated men than those populating Macedonia, the magic of

Ilinden, of heroes like Delčev and Aleksandrov, was still meaningful. The fact that CPY proclamations and resolutions in the inter-war period cast the IMRO and the openly covetous Bulgarians in roles of the utmost villainy indicated the Party's keen recognition of the danger from those quarters.

In contrast to the lack of specific knowledge with regard to Macedonian aspirations before the war, it can be stated with certainty that one solution not wanted by most of the people was Communism, despite the CPY's interest in the nationality problem and its resolutions on Macedonia. The minuscule Party enrollment in Macedonia on the eve of the war speaks more eloquently than the Party's postwar attempts to idealize its prewar role. But the new CPY leadership was not upset by the dichotomy between the Party's nationality principles and its actual handling of the Macedonian issue in the late thirties. It had done what it could.

In this confused situation there were, after the Balkans were engulfed by World War II, many possibilities for action by interested national and political groups. The CPY was convinced that in its recognition of the existence of Yugoslav nationalities, in its idea of a federative organization of the country, it had a program corresponding with the desires of many Yugoslavs. The chief danger to the Party's riding to power on such a program was the possibility that effective democratic elements might espouse the same principle.

By the time war came to Yugoslavia, Tito had transformed the CPY into a tightly organized network of tough, loyal cadres. Even in Macedonia a small core of young Party members had been newly organized. The Macedonian leadership, however, was viewed with reservation. It appeared not to comprehend the CPY's major organizational tenet; the need to operate in a thoroughly monolithic, pro-Yugoslav fashion.

PART II
STRUGGLE FOR MACEDONIA
DURING WORLD WAR II

CHAPTER 4
MACEDONIA AFTER THE
DISINTEGRATION OF YUGOSLAVIA

The test of the CPY's nationality policy came during World War II. The long-smoldering national dissatisfactions, unleashed by the disintegration of the Yugoslav state, resulted in a bloody civil war. Although the party's policy on Macedonia had not been fully elaborated, its major concepts had been outlined. When the opportunity came to utilize that policy, it proved amazingly effective despite defection and weakness in the ranks of the party organization in Macedonia. Macedonia, the vortex of so many conflicting interests where psychological and diplomatic warfare supplemented the clashes of arms, was one of the most critical tests of the Yugoslav communist nationality policy.

World War II had been underway for a year and a half before it descended in full fury upon Yugoslavia. After the failure of Mussolini's 1940-41 winter campaign against Greece, Germany, needing bases for operations against the Middle East, sent flanking troops into Bulgaria, which had adhered to the Axis on March 1, 1941. In an attempt to secure Yugoslavia's "neutral" support and acquiescence in the passage of German troops, the Nazis promised Belgrade long-coveted Salonika. When this bribe was refused, dire threats were made. The pressure on Belgrade, particularly on the Regent, Prince Paul, led to Yugoslavia's signing the Three Power Pact with Germany and Italy on March 25. Thereupon, angry mobs of Belgrade Serbs (not "the Yugoslav people," as is sometimes alleged) demonstrated against the Germans and the Government of Cvetković and Maček which had compromised with them. In the outburst of patriotic indignation, it was possible on March 27 for a group of army officers to install air force General Dušan Simović as premier and young Petar as king.

Although the March 27 putsch was a moral defeat for Hitler and was interpreted abroad as primarily an anti-German act, the new Government's most obvious characteristic was Serbian nationalism and mistrust of the

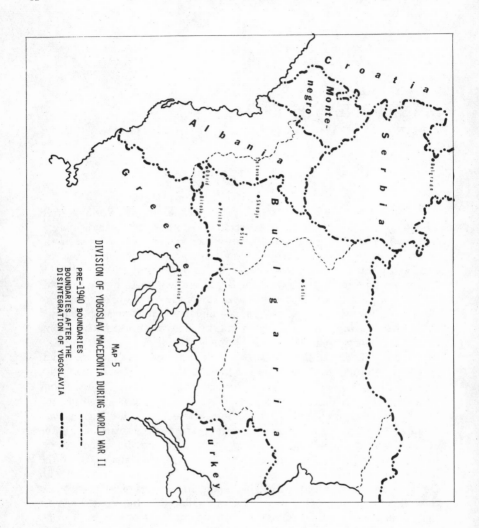

MAP 5

DIVISION OF YUGOSLAV MACEDONIA DURING WORLD WAR II

PRE-1940 BOUNDARIES

BOUNDARIES AFTER THE
DISINTEGRATION OF YUGOSLAVIA

Croats. The new leaders "may have been more interested in undoing the concessions made to the Croats by Prince Paul than in resisting the Axis."[1] But Maček was called to join the new Government.

Belgrade needed a breathing spell and desperately wanted to avoid war. On April 3, Momčilo Ninčić, who had replaced Cincar-Marković as Foreign Minister, informed Yugoslav diplomatic representatives that the Government would respect the agreement of March 25 and that "it will be the principal care of the Government to pursue a policy of good and friendly relations with Germany and Italy."[2] Logically, a treaty of friendship and nonaggression was signed on April 5 with the USSR, which had a nonagression treaty with Germany. Hitler, however, decided to take no chances with the Simović Government. On April 6 German forces commenced the invasion of Yugoslavia, with Greece the ultimate objective of the operation. The Italians and, on April 10, the Hungarians joined the German attackers. Bulgarian troops joined in a week later, after Yugoslavia and Greece were, for all practical purposes, defeated.

The highly vaunted "Yugoslav" Army, in which nine out of every ten officers were Serbs and only two of the one hundred sixty-five generals were Croats, was completely routed. Attacked from all sides, beset by widespread desertions and mutinies, especially in units where Croats predominated, Yugoslavia capitulated after ten days of confused retreat. According to one source, shortly before the invasion Tito had directed that "all elements, regardless of their ideological outlook" should be assisted in overthrowing the monarchial regime and in dissolving Yugoslavia "into its several component parts." There are other indications, however, that the party consistently supported the continued unity of the Yugoslav state.[3]

In the subsequent division of the Yugoslav spoils, Germany, Italy, and Hungary took over segments of the north and west. An independent Montenegro was established under Italian protection. Albania, also under Italian control, was extended to the east. A greatly diminished Serbia was made a "Protectorate" with General Milan Nedić as the puppet ruler. The Independent State of Croatia was proclaimed. Yugoslav Macedonia, with the exception of the Albanian-populated western fringe and northwestern corner which went to Albania, was placed under Bulgarian occupation. Bulgaria also occupied portions of Greek Macedonia, although the Germans insisted on retaining Salonika and the lower Vardar valley under their own direct military control.

The Bulgarian troops were enthusiastically hailed as liberators by the Yugoslav Macedonian Slavs. Although details about the reception are lacking, there is every reason to believe that the manifestations of joy upon being freed from the Serbs were similar to those which occurred in Croatia. In the latter province there had been complete apathy to the March 27 putsch and mass desertions to the German invader. A student at Zagreb University at the time recalls that only two students there evinced serious reservation about being "liberated" by the Germans. Croation reaction was rather a protest against old Yugoslavia than a willing acceptance of German and Italian occupation or even of genuine enthusiasm for the "independent" fascist Croation state proclaimed on April 10.[4]

The warm Macedonian welcome of the Bulgarian forces (the IMRO organized many of the reception committees) may be attributed in part to the fact this was the first opportunity since 1920 for popular protest against Great Serbism. It was not necessarily an indication that the Vardar Macedonians wished to be transformed in every respect into Bulgarians. Evidently there was no attempt by the Macedonians to proclaim an independent or autonomous state, as the Croations did. If Ivan Mihailov and the remnants of the IMRO made any attempt at this juncture to fight for Macedonian separatism from Bulgaria, and there is no evidence that they did, they were completely ineffectual.

The Bulgarians' welcome in Macedonia gradually wore thin, due to the manner in which the occupation was carried out. The Germans, whose ethnic geographers had recently differentiated the Macedonian Slavs and the Bulgarians, did not allow Sofia formally to annex Yugoslav or Greek Macedonia. The Bulgarians were not deterred by this technicality from treating the Macedonians as wayward children needful of stern reorientation. The Bulgarians simply took it for granted that the Slavs in Vardar Macedonia were Bulgarians. Bulgarian officials and a very few Macedonian emigres were appointed to administrative positions. Eight hundred Bulgarian schools were established. Bulgarian teachers and priests were called upon to do service in the "New Lands."[5] In July 1942 a citizenship law provided that all inhabitants were held to have acquired Bulgarian nationality unless they opted for Serbian or Greek nationality.

Thus there were no indications of Bulgarian acceptance of the principle of regional autonomy.[6] That the Bulgarians conducted themselves more like masters than tolerant liberators was especially frustrating to the Macedonian intellectuals, the social group in which a conscious desire for some form of autonomy had traditionally been strongest. With the incorporation of Macedonia into the Bulgarian war machine (army recruitment and later, conscription, requisitioning of food, transport and buildings) dissatisfaction deepened. As the Germans squeezed Bulgaria for more food and supplies, Bulgarian rule in Macedonia began to seem almost as oppressive as the Yugoslav had been. While there was no popular reaction in favor of the previous regime, there was gnawing discontent with "Great Bulgarian" chauvinism. And it was only in March 1944 that the Bulgarian Commissioner of "redeemed" Macedonia, Dr. Konstantin Partov, announced that the reclaimed Macedonians would participate in Bulgarian parliamentary elections.

Another consequence of Bulgarian occupation was the virtual elimination of the "pure Serbian" element from Yugoslav Macedonia. At least 43,000 and perhaps as many as 120,000 Serbs were forced to emigrate and resettle in Serbia.[7] Thus the ethnographic jumble was unscrambled to the extent that, in 1945, the Šar mountains and the Crna hills could reasonably be acknowledged as the southern limits of Serbian settlement. The 1948 Yugoslav census found only 29,752 Serbs in Macedonia, 2.6 per cent of the population. In the Bulgarian-occupied portion of Greek Macedonia the ethnic composition was more drastically affected. Considerably more than half of the Greeks were driven out and partially replaced by former inhabitants of Bulgaria. Thus a major impediment to Communist and IMRO plans for a Greater Macedonia, the overwhelming Greek ethnic character of Greek Macedonia, was removed.[8] That such a Greater Macedonia was not achieved must be attributed partially to the inflexible refusal of the Bulgarians, including the Bulgarian Communists, to cater to Macedonian separatist inclinations.

One may ask, if the Macedonians were disappointed in Bulgaria's brand of liberation, why did they not do more about it? First, relief upon being rid of the Serbs was enormous, and Macedonian gratitude to the Bulgarians was correspondingly great. Then, as the process of Bulgarization progressed, and the Macedonians realized that perhaps there were significant differences between them and their traditional redeemers after all, no democratic alternative was offered them. So they continued to grumble quietly about their wartime privations and the rulers who seemed increasingly foreign. Their illusions about the Bulgarians were, however, slow to dissipate. In its early acceptance of Bulgaria's claim over Yugoslav Macedonia, the tiny band of Macedonian Communists was in tune with the attitude of its own people.

CPY records claim that the Party took the lead in resistance soon after the Axis forces attacked. Tito no doubt did make plans for guerrilla and military operations. But in 1941 the CPY leader was still beholden to Moscow, and therefore he did not order *active* resistance against the occupiers of Yugoslavia until after the June 22 German attack on the USSR. According to CPY versions, during the crucial period from March 27 to June 22, 1941, Šatarov (Šarlo), the Secretary of the Macedonian Provincial Committee, consistently sabotaged all CPY directives which reached him. Thus, when the CPY came out against the dismemberment of Yugoslavia, Šatarov ig-

nored the appeal and failed to communicate some of the CC's directives to
the other Macedonian Party members.[9]

The occupation rendered regular communication between the CC
CPY and the Macedonian Communists very difficult. The latter, although
regarded as unreliable by the CC, were perforce left mostly to their own
devices and to the direct influence of the Bulgarian Communists. It is odd
that Tito, the thorough organizer, had not set up emergency liaison channels. For the next two years the development of the Macedonian situation
was out of the CPY's control. Those directives which did get through to the
CPM were openly defied. It appears that the entire Committee supported
Šatarov's disobedience and turned without any qualms to the Bulgarian
Workers' Party (Communist) for direction. During these two years Tito was
occupied with more urgent problems than those posed by Macedonia. The
CPY first concentrated upon the development of resistance and revolution
in Serbia and, after defeat there, in the Bosnian mountains.

It was significant that the Macedonian Communist leaders made no attempt during the upheavals of the first part of the war to establish an independent party in the spirit of the Comintern and Balkan Communist Federation line of the 1920's. Perhaps more of the Macedonian Communists
would have been willing to string along with the CPY but for the fact that
the attitude of the Macedonian people made the prospects for local Yugoslav success appear exceedingly remote. In any case, the CPB encountered
no difficulty in dominating the Macedonian Committee. However, as later
events made evident, such autonomist tendencies as the Macedonians had
in 1941 were sharpened as disenchantment with the Bulgarian occupation
increased.

The CPB set up a commission to take over the organization in Vardar
Macedonia, adopting the view, "one territory—one party." The resulting
dispute between the Bulgarian and Yugoslav Parties over the right to operate
in Macedonia was superficially a jurisdictional disagreement. The Bulgarians insisted that the occupation justified their action. The CPY insisted
on its legalistic position; its right on the basis of the territorial integrity of
prewar Yugoslavia. It was patent that the motivation of each party was to
establish operational claims to Macedonia for the purpose of ultimate retention. The CPY's open hostility to Bulgarian involvement accorded with
its consistent aim to have at least Vardar Macedonia inside Yugoslavia.

Much time was to elapse before Tito's operatives in Macedonia could
compete with the Bulgarian Communists on anything like an equal footing.
At the end of April 1941, Šatorov, having dissolved the existing Macedonian Provincial Committee,[10] went to Sofia where he declared his adherence to the Bulgarian CP. He refused to attend a meeting of the CC CPY in

Belgrade in May or to carry out the CPY's directive to conceal arms from the occupiers.[11] In late May, Lazar Koliševski, a Macedonian Communist whose devotion to Tito and the CPY was steadfast, and Dragan Pavlović, a Serb, were sent to Skopje to combat Šatorov's line and to take over the Macedonian organization. For the next six months there was bitter maneuvering between Koliševski, a few local Serbian and pro-Yugoslav Macedonian Communists on the one side, and Šatorov, his relatively numerous Macedonian Communists, and the CPB agents on the other. In September 1941, Koliševski selected a new Provincial Committee composed of himself as Secretary and Mara Naceva, Borko Taleski, Blagoj Minkov, and Vera Aceva. Later, Bane Andrejev, who had supported Šatorov at the 1940 Zagreb Conference, was co-opted to the Committee. Koliševski also organized the first Macedonian Partisan units at Kumanovo and Prilep. Besides Koliševski, the Headquarters Staff consisted of Cvetko Uzunovski, Mirče Acev, Strašo Pindžur, and Mihajlo Apostolski.[12] On October 11, the Partisan detachments engaged Bulgarian occupation forces with no success. The failure of the first Partisan military action in Macedonia was exploited by those who favored the policy of passive resistance and of awaiting "more appropriate conditions."

A few days after the German attack on the USSR the CC CPY formally relieved Šatorov of his duties, read the "Old Bulgar" out of the Party, and called for active partisan resistance. Šatorov reacted by issuing a leaflet favoring only a boycott of the German and Bulgarian fascists (not an armed struggle against them) and calling for a "free Soviet Macedonia." Tito protested to the CC of the Bulgarian Party, but that body declined to censure Šatorov. It pointed out that conditions for an armed struggle did not exist in Bulgaria, of which Varder Macedonia was now a part. In the meantime, Tito had referred the dispute over Macedonia to the Comintern. According to the CPY version, Moscow replied in August that the Bulgarian CP had erred in trying to take over the Macedonian organization and that an active partisan struggle under the leadership of the CPY should be developed in Macedonia.[13]

An explanation given by some sources for this and subsequent Comintern support for the CPY position on Macedonia is that Tito won out simply because he had adopted the Stalinist policy of the partisan war. However, this explanation relies more on the later reputation of the Yugoslav partisans and their dispute with the Bulgarian communists over methods of resistance than on actual events before August 1941. Although the CPY under Tito's direction did issue a proclamation calling for armed struggle against the German occupation on June 22, 1941, when the Comintern returned its verdict in August the Yugoslav resistance had amounted to only sporadic acts of sabotage and actions of a few relatively unarmed bands. In determining which party would operate in Macedonia, both the Yugoslav Communists and the Comintern took the legalistic stand that the prewar boundaries would mark the limits of jurisdiction.

The Bularian CP, despite the Comintern's reply to Tito, continued successfully to jockey for control of the Macedonian Communists.[14] In the meantime, the Bulgarian CP sent Petar Bogdanov and later, Bojan Balgaranov to Skopje with others to counteract the influence of Koliševski and Pavlović. The CPY's analysis of Pavlović's reports to the CC indicated that even his position was "incorrect;" that he did not grasp the fact that the basic cause of the dispute was "the conflict between the revolutionary line of the CC CPY and the opportunistic line of the CC CPB."[15] Koliševski was arrested by the Bulgarian police suspiciously soon after the arrival of Balgaranov in Macedonia. From November 6, 1941, until the end of the war the CPY's most effective Macedonian operative remained in Bulgarian prisons. Apparently none of the prominent pro-Bulgarian Communists working in Macedonia were so apprehended.

After Koliševski's arrest, Bane Andrejev took over the leadership of the Provincial Committee.[16] Unbeknown to the Yugoslav Party, Andrejev already had connections with Balgaranov and was under the latter's influence. According to the Yugoslav account, Andrejev went to Sofia, where he received instructions from Traičo Kostov, the Secretary of the CPB, in December. Upon Andrejev's return he took an "opportunistic position," characterizing the few pro-Yugoslavs as factionalists. Consequently, from November 1941 until February 1943, the CPY was unable to make any headway in Macedonia. Andrejev proved to be as unreliable as most of the other leading Yugoslav Macedonians, with the exception of Koliševski, insisting that conditions for mass resistance did not exist and at least tacitly supporting Bulgarian claims to the region.[17]

In reviewing this period, Tito stated that the pre-1943 Macedonian Communist leaders committed "the biggest mistakes" of any Party organization during the war. He bitterly attacked the Šatorov-Balgaranov leadership, under which "the partisan movement . . . vegetated, was stunted and misled, isolated from the masses." Tito admitted that the members of the Provincial Committee "sabotaged the uprising in Macedonia, for, in their opinion, Macedonia was not occupied but was liberated by the troops of Tsar Boris while the German troops played a 'positive role' because they helped 'liberate' Macedonia."[18] Ranković underscored Macedonian resistance to CPY overtures by saying that the intervention and constant aid of the CC CPY was successful only with "great difficulties and a stubborn struggle against the remains of the inimical work and conceptions of Šatorov, supported by various opportunists and liquidators from Bulgaria." [19]

Under the influence of the Bulgarian Communists the Macedonian Committee condoned mobilization of Macedonians for the Bulgarian Army in early 1942. The Balgaranov-Andrejev leadership issued proclamations which did not acknowledge any tie to the CPY. The Executive Committee of the CPB, in a telegram of February 26 to Tito, pointed out with feigned sadness that "for about three months the Macedonian comrades have had no ties with the CP Yugoslavia," that the Macedonian leadership often turned to the CPB for advice, that the Party had only 700 members, mostly youths, in Macedonia, and that it seemed wise to form an independent CP there. Tito replied that reorganizing the CP in Macedonia as an independent Party was "incomprehensible" and that he was sending a representative "for liaison with the Bulgarians and for assisting the comrades in Macedonia." [20] The new representative, on whom the CC CPY pinned its hopes of salvaging something in Macedonia, was Dobrivoje Radosavljević, a Serb whose Party code name was Bobi.

It took Radosavljević six months to reach Macedonia and make contact with the CPY's few supporters there. [21] Even before his arrival resistance to Andrejev's line had developed on the part of some of the local Macedonian Communists. Radosavljević faced a tremendous challenge nontheless. In time he was criticized by the CC for wanting to compromise too much with the still strong anti-Yugoslav feeling of the Macedonian people. However, he capitalized on small advantages and laid much of the groundwork for eventual CPY success for which Vukmanović-Tempo has received most of the public credit. The transition of the Macedonian Communist operation from the pro-Bulgarian line to the Tito line was gradual. There is considerable evidence that the CPY had to exert constant pressure to prevent the Macedonian comrades from wavering back into the clutches of the Bulgarians.

In early June 1942, prior to Radosavljević's arrival, a Provisional Provincial Committee had been formed by the pro-Tito faction. The Committee, composed at first of Mirče Acev, Cvetko Uzunovski, Cvetan Dimov, Mara Naceva, Ljubčo Arsov, Kuzman Josifovski, Borko Temelkovski, and Strašo Pindžur, set as its aims the establishment of contact with the CC CPY, the organization of partisan units and the formation of a national liberation front. [22]

The Provisional Committee began to organize partisan units, complete with political commissars. It set up a Regional Military Staff which later developed into the Headquarters of the National Liberation Units for Macedonia. However, even this anti-Andrejev faction was subsequently deemed by the CPY to be somewhat under the influence of the Bulgarians. In a Macedonian language proclamation of June 22, 1942, the Provisional Committee was not specific as to the national CP with which it was aligned. It did call on Macedonians to take as an example the struggle of the other Yugoslav peoples. The proclamation included an appeal to develop the traditions of the Ilinden Uprising and ended with, "Long live the struggle of all peoples of Yugoslavia and of the brotherly Bulgarian people! Long live the national liberation struggle in Macedonia! Death to Fascism—Liberty to the people!"[23]

Soon after the formation of the Provisional Committee, four of its expressly pro-Yugoslav members fell into the hands of the Bulgarian police "under very suspicious circumstances." The pro-Bulgarian group thus regained formal control but their dominance was now clearly threatened. A few pro-Yugoslav leaders remained at large. It appears that for the next month or two there were two independently operating segments of the Provincial Committee, one representing the CPY and the other the CPB. The CPY's records do not indicate the precise time at which the Yugoslav faction gained the ascendancy nor the methods by which this was achieved, but it seems that shaky control of the Provincial Committee was in the hands of essentially pro-Tito elements well before Vukmanović-Tempo came on the scene in early 1943. The trend can be seen from the Committee's proclamations. In a Macedonian-language proclamation of July 9, the Provincial Committee protested the police killing of Cvetan Dimov, a Skopje laborer who had been a member of the Provisional Committee, but there was no call for armed struggle against the occupiers. Later the same month, however, the Committee proclaimed that a general uprising was necessary to kindle the national liberation struggle in Macedonia. Another proclamation urged the peasants to join the Partisans and "to drive out the fascist occupiers—Germans, Italians, and Bulgarians" in the name of "Free Macedonia."

When Radosavljević finally arrived on the scene in late August 1942, he sent a number of situation reports to the CC CPY, describing the shambles in which he found the Macedonian organization. He outlined the state of the Party cadres and leadership and noted the danger of Mihailov's IMRO. In working against Bulgarian influence, he commenced the extremely significant public disassociation of the pro-CPY Macedonian Communists from "Great Serb chauvinism". On September 24 Radosavljević wrote the CC that after a month of investigation "the situation is clear to me." The Party organization and the leadership cadres were very weak and opportunistic (*viz.* pro-Bulgarian). Many of the party units existed only on paper. Mirče Acev and Strašo Pindžur were sent out to reorganize local partisan units. The Provincial Committee sent to all district, local and provisional committees and partisan units an analysis of past mistakes in Macedonia. In outlining its plans for a general uprising, the Committee suggested the use of the name "Macedonian National Committee," a relic, the CPY archivist points out, of the "terminology and conception of the CC CPB."

A short time later Radosavljević wrote that the greatest drawbacks were the lack of communications and "the position of Del [a code name for Andrejev] toward the most responsible comrades, who are now returning from prison without any practical sense for leadership." The comrades who know Andrejev well, Radosavljević continued, "fully understand that Andrejev has not been able to orient himself . . . in this fateful moment. And all the other comrades could not orient themselves without the [aid of the] CC CPY". After all the arrests, there remained only ten of the leadership cadre from the pre-war days.

Of special note were Radosavljević's observations about the activities of Ivan Milailov's men. He wrote that Mihailov, "who is capitalizing on the indisposition of the people against the Bulgarian rulers, with the protection of the German Consul, is openly and legally agitating against the Bulgarian rulers (and at the same time he is connected with the most reactionary clique and team of Hitler in Bulgaria—Krapčev and company) and their terror in Macedonia, their policy of bringing in Bulgarian civil officials to the detriment of Macedonia . . . and preparing, with the aid of Hitler (Pavelić is the mediator), for the 'autonomous Macedonia.'" According to Radosavljević's information, the IMRO-ists were saying that the Partisans would be easy for them to handle, that they had no quarrel with them and that "if the Partisans still do not agree with us when we come to power, we shall use the counter-četas to annihilate them." [24] Radosavljević designated the Mihailov maneuvers for an antonomous Macedonia as "the chief danger in the struggle of the Macedonian people."

In an October 1942 proclamation directed to the Bulgarian occupation forces, the Headquarters of the Macedonian National Liberation Committee (which was under the guidance of the Serb representative of the CC CPY) emphasized that the Macedonian Partisans had "nothing whatsoever in common with the Great Serbian chauvinists." Stating that "Nedić, Pečanac and their new partner Draža Mihajlović are allies of the German and Italian occupiers and their Bulgarian, Croatian and other agents," the proclamation warned that "these chauvinists and traitors are sending their agents into Macedonia . . . to establish a base among the population." Claiming that only the Macedonian Partisans were working against "these foreign aspirations." the proclamation closed by asking the Bulgarians not to shoot their Macedonian brothers.

In response to some of Radosavljević's observations, Blagoje Nešković, a Serb on the CC CPY, wrote in a letter of November 6 that the Communist International did not leave the Macedonian Party organization in the framework of the CPY "only for formal reasons." He insisted that Macedonia be treated as an integral part of Yugoslavia and threatened that the right to freedom in the new Yugoslavia would be enjoyed *only* by those peoples who fought the occupiers and their servants. Such a slogan as "Free Macedonia," divorced from the slogan "Free Yugoslavia," could damage the liberation struggle not only of the Macedonian people but also of all the other peoples of Yugoslavia. Nešković also criticized the suggestion that, "because of the hatred which exists among the Macedonian people against old Yugoslavia" the name of the Party organization in Macedonia be changed.

The Provincial Committee's next Proclamation was duly signed in the name of the CPY. It accused Mihailov of assisting Hitler's aims by "carrying on a struggle against the Bulgarian rulers, while singing a eulogy to Hitler who is supposedly 'fighting' for the unity of the Macedonian people." The proclamation also condemned the agents of Kosta Pečanac, "that most reactionary Great Serbian chauvinist and German agent, who is attempting to attract the 'Serboman' population of Macedonia to his traitorous aims." The Yugoslav Government in London was also criticized: "Up to now they have not said one word about guaranteeing the freedom of the Macedonian people. Such are the agents of Draza Mihajlović of the type of Trbić, who are . . . separating the Macedonian Partisans from the general struggle, excusing themselves on the basis of conserving their strength, of not giving unnecessary victims." The proclamation condemned "Great Bulgarian reactionaries" as well as Great Serbism.[25]

Radosavljević was beginning to implement the CC's tactical pattern in Macedonia, but neither the Bulgarian Communists nor the Macedonian people in general were impressed with the new propaganda line. In late November Radosavljevic complained to the CC CPY that the CPB had not answered any of his appeals for a proclamation clarifying their position on Macedonia. He implied that the Bulgarian Communists might be excused, for they were "having trouble on the Macedonian question with some groups in the Fatherland Front."

It was significant that in the calculated employment of anti-Great Serb propaganda in Macedonia Tito saw to it that Serbian Communists were the propagators. One aim was to give the denunciations of Great Serbism a ring of conviction. This must have surprised and pleased the Macedonian Communists. The other aim was to make it perfectly clear to the Serbian Party members in general that they were not to press any "natural advantages" they might have by reason of numbers of leading positions.

Having bridged one part of the gap separating the CPY from the Macedonians by denouncing Great Serbism, Radosavljević undertook to build the second span—across the formidable obstacle of residual Bulgarophilism. Through his efforts the CPY had moderate success in reclaiming some of the Macedonian Communists. In the process, an even greater potential danger became apparent to the CPY. This was the gradual coalescence of support for Macedonian autonomy, in reaction to the rigors of Bulgarian occupation. Sentiment for autonomy among the Macedonian Communists was confusing the Party's "jurisdictional" dispute with the CPB. The CPY had to convince the Macedonians (and the other non-Serb Yugoslavs) that it really meant to implement some of the concessions promised by its nationality propaganda line.

CHAPTER 5
GAINING THE INITIATIVE

To enhance his frail but growing psychological and military initiatives, Tito drew up and publicized the Party's plan for the future framework of Yugoslavia at the earliest opportunity. It was to be one of the Communists' basic weapons against their domestic enemies. The Congress of Bihač (Bosnia) in November 1942 was of great significance to Tito's subsequent exploitation of Yugoslavia's nationality problems. The Congress elected the Anti-Fascist Council of National Liberation of Yugoslavia (AVNOJ) to act as the central organ of government for the "liberated territories," which at that time were by no means extensive. The key point of the Bihač program was the guarantee of equal national rights to all "peoples of Yugoslavia." The Macedonians were listed as one of the five nationalities.

In this effort to tap the springs of the several national dissatisfactions, the CPY was compelled to take a concrete stand on the recognition of the Macedonian Slavs as being distinct from the Bulgarians and the Serbs. In the Party's expressions of the vital corollary to this line, that the Macedonian Slavs are specifically a separate *Yugoslav* people, not only in the ethnic sense but in the sense of belonging to the country of Yugoslavia, the practitioners of the Yugoslav revolution emphasized features of the approach which had a loosely federative sound.

Bihač was also important in that Tito found, probably to his surprise, that foreign reaction to the implied usurpation of the powers of the legal Yugoslav Government was not particularly negative. The USSR had already advised him to be circumspect in his relations with the representatives of the Government-in-exile; that it would be ill-advised to shock the Allies into discovery of his aims. But the Soviet-controlled "Free Yugoslavia" radio station located in Tiflis broadcast the six-point Bihač program.[1] Admittedly, the decisions of the First AVNOJ Assembly did not appear blatantly revolutionary. Private property was to be respected and radical social changes postponed until after elections could be held.

After Bihač, according to the Party account, Tito wrote the Macedonian Provincial Committee a letter which confirmed this final, "correct" approach.[2] This communication, dated January 16, 1943, is particularly interesting as a delineation of Tito's tactics on the Macedonian national question. Undoubtedly Svetozar Vukmanović-Tempo, the CC's next "instructor" in Macedonia, was given instructions in harmony with the letter prior to his departure for Macedonia. But whether Tito's letter "paved the way for the arrival of Tempo at the end of February 1943" seems doubtful.[3] At least the *Arhiv* claims the letter did not reach the Macedonian Committee until August 1943, six months after Vukmanovic-Tempo arrived. In any case, the letter merits close attention, for related evidence indicates that it accurately outlined the situation as seen by the CC CPY. For one thing, it made evident that Tito was more pleased with the outlook of the Radosavljević-Acev Committee than he had been with that of the one headed by Andrejev. Tito wrote, in part:

> From the material you have sent, it is clear that you have insufficiently and incorrectly understood the character and aim of the present national liberation struggle and that you have therefore made big mistakes. . . . The main characteristics of the Party organization in Macedonia are . . . vacillation in the question of the application [of the Party's political line] in practice, organizational confusion and weakness, indecisive relations with the vacillating, squabbling, opportunistic and un-Partylike elements inside the Party, a narrow-minded conception of the question of the struggle for freedom and independence of the Macedonian people. . . . liberal relations with "autonomous" tendencies of organizational-Party character, as with "autonomous" tendencies of national character. . . . It must be clear to you that the national liberation struggle is the significant form through which will be decided the question of the existence, freedom, and independence of all the peoples, and equally of the Macedonian people. . . .
>
> The raising of the question of "autonomy" or of "possible specifically Macedonian conditions" falls outside the framework of our position and line and those who bring up this question are, in the final analysis, essentially identifying themselves with those, who because of the term "Yugoslavia," isolate the Macedonian people from the unified struggle of all the peoples of Yugoslavia. The "problem" of Yugoslavia today is not a problem of the regime of former Yugoslavia, which character some Macedonians, willingly or unwillingly, objectively or tendentiously, wish to give to this question. . . . It is obvious that your opinion about the political utility of separation from the frame of the CPY means that you have been taken in by such [automomist] tendencies and by misunderstandings of the perspective of today's struggle and the role of our Party in it. . . .
>
> With the correct stand in the national question . . . with organization and participation in this battle . . . our Party can raise all of the Yugoslav peoples to an armed uprising . . . preparing the conditions for the solution of other subsequent problems. . . . Our CPY is the guarantee that the brotherly unity of equal peoples with the right of self-determination, which

must not be abused, will in essence be completely in contrast to former Yugoslavia and her hated, reactionary, oppressive, and hegemonistic regimes.

The change of party labels which seem to you to be the reason for the alienation of the masses from our Party, would not really change anything, but would mean an opportunistic retreat toward the enemies or the future oppressors of the Macedonia people and the secret or open agents of fascism. ... The change of name of the Party ... [would allow] the vacillating, bourgeois and opportunistically orientated elements ... constantly to attempt to dominate the party organizations and the young and inexperienced membership, and would lead to the duping of honorable party members so that they would be subject to foreign and mistaken influences.

Tito's letter went on to give instructions concerning the organization of partisan fighting units and the role of political commissars therein, advising that "insofar as possible, all members of the staff should be members of the Party, but the commanders may be from outside the Party."

Several conclusions may be drawn from this letter. First, Tito was justifiably disturbed about the danger from those favoring a pro-Bulgarian autonomist solution, for by this time the Bulgarian Communists had been forced to cater to public reaction against Bulgarian absorption. Secondly, Tito stipulated that a vaguely defined measure of self-determination for Macedonia would be forthcoming only with the *active* involvement of a considerable portion of the population in partisan warfare. Thirdly, Tito recognized that popular support of the Yugoslav Communists was still at such a low ebb and that there was such a paucity of Macedonian Communist leaders that he sanctioned the utilization of non-Communist "front" men as commanders of Partisan detachments.

After the arrival in Skopje of Tempo on February 26, 1943, there ensued radical changes in the activities of the Macedonian Communists and a general improvement of the CPY's power position in Macedonia. Tito had complete faith in Tempo, who had done excellent work in preparing for Partisan activity in Bosnia and who, a Montenegrin and a Sremska Mitrovica graduate, could be counted upon to avoid any compromise in the CPY's struggle against still powerful pro-Bulgarian influences. Tempo had two immediate, related tasks: the organization of Partisan fighting units and the clarification of the CPY approach to the Macedonian question.

Tempo announced the innovations in the Party's approach to Macedonia as soon as he arrived in Skopje. In a February 28 letter to all CPY organizations and members in Macedonia, he disclosed the decision of the

CC to organize a Communist Party of Macedonia, within the framework of the CPY and under the leadership and control of the CC CPY.[4] The members were ordered to cleanse the Party of "all fence-sitting, factionary, undisciplined" elements and to fight against "the Hitler mercenary and traitor, Vančo Mihailov, the Great Bulgarian mercenaries and the Great Serbian mercenaries like Mihajlović." Macedonians were to be urged to unite "in common struggle with the other brotherly peoples of Yugoslavia, the brotherly Bulgarian people of the Fatherland Front, the Albanians and the Greeks." Bulgarian Communists, Tempo assured the comrades, had "nothing in common with the Great Bulgarian imperialist rule in Macedonia." Macedonians should wage partisan warfare "for full national freedom and equality, . . . for the right to decide their own fate." The closing "long lives," so indicative in Communist pronouncements, favored longevity for "the national-liberation struggle of the Macedonian people, the glorious CPY and the Communist Party of Macedonia."[5] Another letter of the same day to all Macedonian Partisan units had much the same message, but ended with praise for the "supreme Commander Comrade Tito."[6] This was probably the first use of Tito's name in a Macedonian Communist instruction. It was signed by Tempo in the name of the National Liberation Army. A few days later Tempo issued specific instructions about the creation of operational zones, and the duties of zonal Partisan staffs and other units. The first detachments which saw action were those in the Debar, Tikveš, and Kumanovo districts where "large areas" were allegedly liberated during the summer of 1943.

The formation of the CPM marked the beginning of the last stage of the CPY's evolving wartime Macedonian policy. The creation of a local Party did not work immediate miracles, but it was an essential element in the formula for the CPY's eventual success. First there had been the insistence on the CPY's legal rights vis-a-vis the CPB. Then the "instructors" from the CC had come to combat and purge pro-Bulgarians from the Macedonian organizations and to initiate partisan warfare. These operations were conceived and carried out on the initiative of the CPY and implemented by its delegates, not by Macedonian Communists. The exception was Koliševski, but his endeavors had been brief and fruitless. By early 1943 the CPY realized that platitudinous declarations about Macedonian rights would not suffice to capture the hearts of the Macedonian Communists, to say nothing of those of the general public. There was need for convincing proof that the CPY would not follow a policy of "Serbianizing" Macedonia. Also, later events indicated that at this time there was a trend in favor of an independent Macedonia among the Bulgarian as well as the Macedonian Communists. The formation of a CPM was an act resulting not from a position of local strength but rather from a mixture of desperation and hope. Tito perceived that a CPM had to be formed, for psychological effect in the first instance. This was acknowledged by Koliševski at the Macedonian Party's First Congress in December 1948:

> The formation of the CC CPM tore from the hands of the reactionary and the autonomous elements the last arguments that the Party Organization in Macedonia and the national liberation movement supposedly were blindly subservient to "Serbs" and to some kind of "Serbian" leadership, and thereby cut through the roots of autonomist tendencies.[7]

After March 1943 there was a great increase in CPY propaganda relative to the recognition of the Macedonian nation as one of the members of the future federative Yugoslavia, rather than an independent or autonomous Balkan state. This concept was vaguely and gradually extended to include Bulgarian and Greek Macedonians.

In early March at Tetovo, Tempo formed the Central Committee of the CPM, picking men and women who had gone on record against the Bulgarian Communists. It consisted of Koliševki (still in prison), Cvetko Uzunovski, Strahil Gigov, Kuzman Josifovski, Borko Temelkovski, Vera Aceva, Mara Naceva, and Bane Andrejev.[8] Four of these had been leaders of the essentially pro-Yugoslav Provisional Committee of June 1942. Andrejev's retention in a position of some importance was proof of the paucity of experienced "name" candidates whom the CPY could trust, as well as of Andrejev's fast political footwork. However, his past ideological suppleness was recognized in that he was not made a Politbureau member of the CC, but only a member of the Plenum.[9]

By this time the influence of Balgaranov was greatly reduced[10], but Tempo soon expressed serious reservations about the new Party's prospects. The almost total lack of effective organization, the fact that only ten "old hands" were left in the higher ranks, the stubborn persistency of anti-Yugoslav sentiment—these factors led Tempo to caution the CC CPY that the creation of the Macedonian CP was "premature" and that it would need constant "assistance" if it were not to stray from the CPY line.[11] It took several months to cure the Macedonian leadership of the habit of using slogans of autonomy for "practical purposes." Even though the CPY's Macedonian efforts were now being carried on under the immediate direction of a hand-picked CC, the Macedonian Party soon evidenced the deep-rooted tendencies Tempo had feared. While Tempo was engaged in drumming up support in Albania and Greece, those tendencies were enunciated in a June 1943 CPM proclamation.[12] In this document the new CC CPM followed the "correct" line up to a point, denouncing Great Bulgarianism and Great Serbism.

However, future Macedonia was treated as a separate Balkan state; nothing at all was said about its being in the framework of Yugoslavia. The Committee proclaimed that it was working to create "the unity of all Macedonians, without regard to whether they were earlier 'Bulgarophiles,' 'Serbomans,' or 'Grecomans.'" The statement included the following:

> The Fascist occupiers . . . want to separate [the Macedonian intelligentsia] from their people. . . . They forbid the Macedonian language and banish all that is Macedonian. . . . With the doctrine of Marx, Engels, Lenin, and Stalin, develop still further the struggle of our people for the realization of their centuries-old ideals. . . . Long live the Macedonian National-Liberation Front! . . . Long live the brotherly National-Liberation Armies of Yugoslavia, Albania, and Greece! . . . Long live our mighty allies, Soviet Russia, England, and America! Long live the Fatherland Front and the insurrectional detachment of the brotherly Bulgarian people! Long live the brotherhood of all Balkan Peoples!

. A note in the *Arhiv* states that this Proclamation "provided an opportunity for the clarification of the political line of the CPM on the question of the unification of the Macedonian people," but quotes Tempo as characterizing it as "a tremendous political mistake in that in it Macedonia was treated outside the framework of Yugoslavia." The lack of any reference to Tito in the Proclamation, the jumbling together of the Yugoslav Partisans with the Albanians and Greeks, while the Bulgarian Fatherland Front rated its own "long live," and the appeal to fight for "centuries-old ideals" (which could not, by any stretch of the imagination, have included the ideal of Yugoslav rule)—these were naturally disturbing to Tempo, who realized the need for more work among the Communists in Vardar Macedonia.

By August 2, 1943, the CC CPM was sufficiently reindoctrinated to publish an Ilinden Manifesto crediting the "precious sacrifices of the Yugoslav peoples . . . and the strength of the National Liberation Army with Supreme Commander Tito at its head" with being the guarantees of national freedom and equality of the Macedonian people. The list of "long live's" was in proper order for a CPY proclamation, with Tito and his Partisans topped only by the Red Army, and the Bulgarians lumped together with the Greeks and Albanians. Both Tempo and Radosavljević attended the meeting at which this manifesto was drawn up. At this gathering, on the shores of Lake Prespa in the less dangerous Italian-occupied zone, it was decided to organize armed units of battalion and brigade strength,[13] formally to launch a National Liberation Front, and to prepare for an anti-fascist assembly of National Liberation of Macedonia (ASNOM). The CC CPM took note of the fact that much progress had been made in military and political education in the Partisan units, but that "in the rear" (i.e., in all of Macedonia except the small "liberated" pockets), such educational work had been neglected. Kuzman Josifovski was dispatched to Skopje to direct a group of special Party agitators whose aim was to "gather the masses in the cities around the Front, prepare for the ASNOM assembly and also to *revive* the Party organizations in the rear."[14] In September, Josifovski formed an Action Committee for Skopje.

The Party's situation in Macedonia was summarized by Tempo in a rambling report of August 8, 1943, to the CC CPY.[15] He indicated that the CPY would have to go to greater lengths in compromising with elements still basically antagonistic to anything Yugoslav, before victory could be assured. Thus, after claiming that "a large number of Old Ilinden fighters and political representatives" (IMRO-ists) had oriented themselves to the CP because of the new surge of battle, Tempo wrote that steps had been taken to include some of them in the coming anti-fascist assembly. It was "necessary to gather respectable patriots and old Ilinden leaders." Balgaranov had succeeded in convincing the "entire provincial leadership, Andrejev, Mara Neceva, and Pindžur . . . that in Macedonia the conditions for partisan warfare do not exist, that is, that the conditions for putting the CPY line into practice do not exist." Regarding the CPB policy of allowing only limited guerrilla action by small bands, Tempo claimed that during 1942 there were only six such units, with from ten to fifteen men apiece, and that there was no disposition on their part to fight against the Bulgarian occupiers as such, but only against "the reactionary government of Filov." All of these units were shattered. Draža Mihajlović was "spreading his net among the Serbo-man masses around Skopje, Kumanovo and Kičevo, through his agent, Bojča Tribić," but his influence was not great, according to Tempo.

The report went on to review Tempo's accomplishments in giving the Macedonian Communists some momentum. Some significant excerpts:

> I formed the CC CPM from the best activists, those who through all the difficult times remained faithful to our Party. . . . Naturally I managed this whole movement in the direction of union with the other peoples of Yugoslavia. . . . I undertook measures to free some comrades who were in concentration camps.[16] . . In the course of these 3-4 months the conditions of the Party organizations improved-significantly. . . . To the leadership have come new, young cadres, who are still without experience, but who are therefore devoted to our Party and the national liberation struggle. . . . Strong fighting groups have been created . . . numbering from 70 to 80 partisans. . . . The influence of our Party has spread, especially in the territory under Italian occupation.[17] In the Kavadarci region [Tempo described a successful Partisan stand there against a heavy Bulgarian attack], our units have the

full support of all of the people. In vain did the Bulgarian occupiers carry
out terrible acts of repression on the people, killing and slaughtering women
and children, burning villages, etc. . . . . In vain did they give large sums of
money for the organization of counter-četas, as they did not collect even one
man. The Partisans are always on the offensive. . . . Naturally, great dangers
have arisen . . . on account of the young and inexperienced cadres and the
great terrorism carried on by the Bulgarian occupiers.

Tempo recognized the IMRO as the greatest impediment to the achieve-
ment of CPY objectives in Macedonia. His letter continued:

> The Macedonian people have begun to realize that in the place of Great
> Serbian hegemonists have come Great Bulgarian hegemonists with the same
> aim, that of suppressing the national consciousness of the Macedonian peo-
> ple. Thus the Bulgarian mercenaries from the ranks of the Macedonian peo-
> ple have begun to isolate themselves from the masses. . . . The agents of
> Vančo Mihailov are working throughout the whole of Macedonia. They are
> coming out for the unification of the Macedonian people and for their na-
> tional independence. The Germans are helping and supporting them to keep
> in check the Bulgarians in whom they have no confidence. . . . The danger
> from Vančo Mihailov is quite great . . . because he is calling for the uni-
> fication of the whole Macedonian people, among whom national conscious-
> ness and the idea of unification is awakening today. . . . It is most difficult
> with the agents of Vančo Mihailov, but there too the process of decay is
> sensed, especially in connection with the ever greater indication of the fall
> of the German fascists. Within the ranks of the IMRO differentiations have
> begun. One side is declaring for Russia and is gradually approaching our
> views, while the others are openly uncovering themselves as open agents of
> the Gestapo . . . .
>   A special problem is introduced by the slogan for the unification of the
> Macedonian people. . . . The entire Macedonian people demand unification.
> . . . The Greek Partisan movement has not reached the great majority of the
> Macedonian people [there] who, under the influence of the IMRO, are ser-
> ving the occupiers and fighting against the Greek Partisan Army. At the
> request of the Greek Staff our četas from the Bitolj region crossed over into
> Greek Macedonia and there accomplished great political penetration of the
> Macedonian masses. . . . The Macedonians want to be under the command
> of our Headquarters for Macedonia. We rejected this because of the posi-
> tion of the Greek Party on the Macedonian question . . . .
>   But this question is also very acute with the masses of Macedonian peo-
> ple in our own Macedonia. Therefore, I wrote a letter to Comrade Ljuba
> (Radosavljecić) asking him to employ, in our Macedonia, slogans about the
> unification of the Macedonian people. [Tempo then recounts how Radosavl-
> jević used these slogans in the proclamation which was such a "tremendous
> political mistake, in that it treated a united Macedonia outside of Yugo-

slavia18] I met with Ljuba and three members of the CC CPM in the field and, after long discussions, we agreed that it was necessary to correct the line. It took an especially long time to convince Comrade Ljuba. Finally we agreed on the following: since the National Liberation Movement has developed most strongly in Yugoslav Macedonia and because this movement is the center for gathering the whole Macedonian people, it is necessary to employ the slogan of the liberation and unification of the Macedonian people in brotherly cooperation with all the Yugoslav peoples. The Macedonian people have most secure guarantees that our National Liberation Armies . . . are fighting against every national subjugation on the part of the Great Serb hegemonists. It was remarked that Comrade Ljuba was mainly responsible for the deviation in the proclamation. Nevertheless, he is very well-oriented in the field and is a good leader.

Thus, Tempo clearly perceived that the reaction against Bulgaria had taken the form of sentiment for Macedonian unification and autonomy. His instruction to Radosavljević about the use of unification slogans was an example of the CPY's ability to turn obstacles into steppingstones. The propaganda campaigns against Great Serbism, then against Great Bulgarianism, were going well. Now the IMRO-ists were demonstrating that they still had appeal. In Greek Macedonia a Communist named Goči (or Gočev) was having some success in stirring the embers of the Greater Macedonian idea among the Slavs there. Bulgarians of various persuasions were beginning to realize that they could salvage Macedonia only by some sort of an autonomy gambit. Manifestly, the momentum for Macedonian autonomy could get out of hand. Tempo took steps to counter it.

He wrote the CC CPM on August 10 that in the view of the CC CPY, the Macedonian Party had not done well in its task of carrying the Party's principles into practice and that its stand on the question of the struggle for freedom and independence of the Macedonian people was "narrow."

> We have not been sufficiently energetic in striking at these "autonomist" tendencies which have to a certain extent spread through our Party Organization in Macedonia. . . . expressed in efforts to get out from the framework of the CPY and to isolate the struggle of the Macedonian people from the struggle which the other peoples of Yugoslavia are waging. . . .
> It is necessary to carry on an unsparing struggle against these "autonomist" tendencies. . . . I fear, comrades, that we were premature in founding our CC CPM. . . . We must with our work and our successes show our CC CPY that we shall be able with its constant control and assistance, which it has until now always extended, to lead the struggle of the Macedonian people for their national liberation.

Tempo closed this letter by ordering the establishment of a Provincial Committee of SKOJ (Communist Youth) in Macedonia.

Italy's withdrawal from the war in September 1943 gave a boost to the Macedonian Partisans who acquired large quantities of sorely needed arms and ammunition from the Italians. A number of troops serving with the Bulgarian occupation forces deserted to the Partisans.[19] The Partisans took what bits and pieces of territory they could before German and Bulgarian troops replaced the vacating Italian forces.[20] Macedonian Communist units, under their newly created "General Staff of the National Liberation Army and Partisan Detachments of Macedonia" (NOV and POM),[21] took over a considerable area of "liberated territory" in Western Macedonia. A "Mirce Acev" Battalion had been formed on August 18 and a "Strašo Pindžur" Battalion on September 24—the first "regular" Partisan units in Macedonia. In the region around Debar on the extreme western border of present Macedonia which was then annexed to Albania, the Partisans set up local administrative bodies in the area they occupied.

An early October Manifesto of the General Staff, NOV and POM, is considered by the Party to be one of the most significant documents in the development of the Macedonian revolution. The Manifesto made public the CPY's intention to ride the swell of popular support for the united Macedonian idea. It called for a general uprising against all enemies of the liberation of Macedonia, in "brotherly unity" with Yugoslavia. Macedonians were urged to fight the "still many difficult and severe struggles" against the Bulgarian occupiers and the "Great Serb hegemonists headed by traitorous General Draža Mihajlović." The Četniks were accused of uniting with "Great Albanian hegemonist circles" against the Communists in the Gostivar-Tetovo region, while "in the Kumanovo region, by attacks on mosques, they are trying to create quarrels and throw the Macedonians, Skiptars and Turks into mutual, fratricidal war."[22] The "Great Albanian fascists and hegeominists" were warned against their attempts to divide Macedonians and Albanians over the question of the boundary between them. The enemies last pinpointed by the Manifesto were the "Macedonian fascists, the traitors of the Macedonian people, the servants of the German fascist occupiers, headed by Vančo Mihailov on the one side and Kitinčev, Džuzelov, Čkatrov, Kosta Cipušev on the other."[23] Although the Manifesto stated that these groups were "decaying," it warned that a long, united and bold struggle was needed against their efforts to divide the Macedonian people. Then came the bombshell: "Never before have the Macedonian people had such a good position and so many allies for the establishment of your age-long ideal—united Macedonia."[24]

Although Tempo, in his August report to the CC CPY,[25] had explained the necessity of using the united, i.e., Greater Macedonia slogan, it is not certain that its utilization in the October Manifesto signified specific approval on Tito's part. The CC's reaction to Tempo's united Macedonia idea may not yet have been received. Tito's first response to Tempo seems to have been a letter written October 9, and it made no mention of the idea.[26] In any case, for a time the CPM played the unification theme for all it was worth. In the name of the CC CPM Strahil Gigov sent a circular letter to all Party organizations stating that the "particular question is the introduction of the new slogan which we shall use, and that is the UNIFICATION OF MACEDONIA, Macedonia which is dismembered and divided among Balkan imperialists."[27]

The new line evoked prompt reaction from a dangerous quarter. Shortly after the distribution of the General Staff Manifesto a group of Skopje intellectuals, who had been drawn into the work of Josifovski's Action Committee of the National Liberation Front (ANOK), published a letter contending that the General Staff had no right to make any pronouncement on Macedonia's self-determination. The authors held that freedom and equality for Macedonia could be won only in the framework of a Balkan Federation, i.e., not as a part of Yugoslavia. This approach to the Macedonian question was the same as that then being crystallized by the Bulgarian Fatherland Front. It was obvious that the Skopje group had sympathy for, and probably connections with, the Bulgarians. Among the participants were Lazar Sokolov, Blagoj Hadji Panzov and Kiro Petušev.

The CPY considered the letter opposing the General Staff Manifesto an "indirect reaction of the CPB leadership to the political line of the CPY on the Macedonian national question" and a new attempt of "bourgeois, nationalistic, chauvinistic, autonomist" Macedonians to subvert the CPM. The commentary on the intellectuals' letter in the *Arhiv* charges that the essence of their demands was that "they reserved for themselves, as men who had been invited to the anticipated first meeting of the Anti-Fascist National Assembly of Macedonia, the right to determine the line of the national liberation movement, and held that without them nothing could be undertaken." The "nationalist-chauvinist stand" of the group's letter was evidenced, "by 'small' but characteristic remarks" such as criticizing the Manifesto's use of the word *položaj* (position) which is not used in the Macedonian language, and making much of "the names of some members of the General Staff, which are supposedly 'Serbian'." On December 20, Josifovski wrote to the CC CPM with reference to ANOK's rebuke to the General Staff.[28] Noting that he had written earlier that ANOK did not comprehend the line of the Manifesto and that they were preparing a reply thereto, Josifovski remarked:

> The ANOK members and other invitees to the projected assembly,
> . . . approached the question of Macedonia narrowly and nationalistically.
> . . . Comrades, all these men are, in the main, intellectuals from the cities,
> who were least affected by the occupation . . . and who therefore do not com-
> prehend that now is the time for the realization of our aims in general, every-
> day battle . . . but who considered the Macedonian question abstractly. As
> our influence was weak, they, without really wanting it, accepted the posi-
> tion of Vančo Mihailov and other traitors . . . this chauvinism is advocated
> to such an extent that today it is injurious and dangerous to the national
> liberation struggle.

In a footnote added three days later, Josifovski reported that further conversations with the ANOK dissidents had revealed their demand "that the
rear must be organized in such a way that greater precedence be given to
them than to the front. . . . There are city slickers for you!"

It was natural that this anti-Yugoslav expression of Macedonian nationalism, however permeated it may have been with Bulgarophilism, should
have been voiced by urban intellectuals. That social element had traditionally
been in the forefront of the movement for recognition of Macedonian individuality. Its relative deprivations under Serbian rule had probably ex-
ceeded that of any other class. The opposition of the Skopje intellectuals
indicated that while Tempo may have succeeded in persuading the new
leaders of the CPM to go along with the CPY line, the roots of anti-Serbian,
anti-Yugoslav hatred and of autonomist or pro-Bulgarian leanings were
still deeply imbedded in Macedonia. The more the CPM widened its front
organizations, the more care it had to exert to prevent such roots
from sprouting. This incident was, however, the last recorded instance of
overt Macedonian Communist or Communist front opposition to the CPY's
program for Macedonia. Macedonian aversion to Yugoslavia did not, of
course, suddenly disappear, even in the CPM. But the Partisans were expanding their areas of direct control, and it was becoming increasingly in-
advisable for Macedonians to voice such differences as they may have had
with the Yugoslav Communists.

Tempo's assiduous work marked a consequential turning point in the
struggle for Macedonia. He set up the organizational framework which was
to utilize the Italian surrender and other windfalls in the interests of CPY
aims. The basic obstacles had been removed. The conditions indispensable
to the Party's "positive" action had been created. A crucial stage of "contradiction" had been attained with regard to the relations between the groups
of the CPY's domestic enemies, and within each of those groups. Now it
was time to secure the commitment of the passive masses to the struggle.
That commitment, the extent of which sufficed to enable the Party to seize

power, was achieved by the combined application of threat and promise. The "liberation" struggle underwent a more rapid transmutation in its revolutionary form all over Yugoslavia once the Communists were strong enough to carry out the final phase of their plan. However, it was not until mid-1944, when Axis power was beginning to disintegrate and when Allied victory was probable, that large-scale Partisan activity developed in Macedonia.

Our review of the preliminary stages of CPY success in Macedonia, much of it necessarily in the form of summarization and analysis of Party source material, has dealt largely with the "mechanics" of the process. It is appropriate here to examine more closely what the Communists accurately call the "dynamics" of this process. [29] The major field of battle in Macedonia, as elsewhere in Yugoslavia, was not in the barren hills and in the forests where the Partisan units operated, but in the minds of the people. This is not to imply that because the Partisans won their revolution a majority, or even a large minority, of Yugoslav Macedonians were persuaded to acknowledge the rectitude of the evolving CPY line. The degree of willing acquiescence was minor. The role of external developments and circumstantial factors, and the use of force and threats of force as stimuli to Macedonian "acceptance" of Tito's revolution, were no less important than in other Communist revolutions.

In comparison to the CPY's manipulation of political, sociological, and psychological factors, the relative inflexibility of contending Yugoslav and Bulgarian groups stood out in sharp relief. The comparative passivity, ideological and physical, of non-Communist elements deserves no moral condemnation. But it is a poignant fact that narrow nationalism often obscured the outlook of the main anti-Communist Yugoslav resistance leaders; their myths did not correspond to changing reality. The persistence of those myths of "Greater Our Nation-ism," their reinforcement in the darkness of defeat, make it all the more imperative to attempt to understand the *modus operandi* of the Yugoslav Communist revolutionists.

Tito's growing prestige in the world, and the material support he received in late 1943 and 1944, resulted from his incessant military activities. For his Yugoslav opponents it was a vicious circle. The more the Partisans fought—or were believed to have fought—against the Axis occupiers, the more material assistance and moral support they received from abroad, and the better the CPY could persuade or coerce additional Yugoslavs to join the fight against the domestic and foreign enemies of the Party. Then the cycle repeated itself. Activism and reckless conflict were pitted against passivism and conservation, although, of course, not in black-white extremes. The Serbian Četniks were not at all passive at times, especially in the early stages of the war. The IMRO leadership appears to have been consistently passive, although this condition was partially an enforced one. The Četniks, at least, soon realized who their ultimate enemy was. But apparently neither of these groups perceived that the bells were tolling for them *all during* the occupation; that while they conserved their strength for the post-occupation showdown, debilitating forces were gnawing at their rigid sinews. They reasoned that they could contribute little to the struggle against the vast power of the Axis; let the great Allied Powers take care of that phase of the war. The real enemy was at home. So they readied themselves for the final battle, the one against the Communists.

The CPY also knew its chief enemies were domestic ones. The vital difference was in the means and timing applied to the end. The nature of the Communist approach was not fully understood by their opponents. This was due partly to ignorance of the fanaticism of the CPY's drive toward power. It was also due to the inability of the anti-Communist Serbian groups to recognize that their traditional ethnocentrism was now far too static a concept. Such recognition would have required a basic revision of their sincere and tenaciously held faith in the essential superiority of "we." The Communists endeavored to sharpen the negative, divisive characteristics of ancient chauvinisms, and to force the opposition into further extremes, working for its separation from the aspirations of the people.

It is axiomatic that Communists, in the period before and during revolution, attempt to create conditions of conflict if none exist. They try to create "contradictions" between their real and declared adversaries,[30] contradictions within the ranks of each opposing group, and contradictions between their adversaries and those people who have not chosen sides. In Macedonia the conditions of conflict did exist. The Communists needed only to canalize and exploit them. Obviously there could be no meeting of minds between the Četniks and the Bulgarian nationalists, between the Bulgarian nationalists and the IMRO, or between the IMRO and the Četniks. The CPY was the ostensible friend of all victims of these irreducible national rivalries, and the outlawed and the dispossessed in any society have tremendous latent dynamism.

The CPY strategists divided the people of occupied Yugoslavia into three general categories: those who were palpably victimized in some way, those who were "privileged," and those who did not suffer substantial privation and hence were undecided and waiting. For the Communists, the victims were relatively easy prey *unless* they believed they could fight their oppressors more effectively under different banners. In considering this "victim" approach, it is useful to examine how it was applied to the Serbs, for that application helped to seal the fate of the legal Yugoslav Government.

The Serbs were in a sense all victims, and they were ready to be led to revolt against the occupation. To an extent they did revolt. However, for long and exhaustive warfare they needed to know for what they were fighting, with whom, and how costly the fight might be. In this respect they split. Nedić, proclaiming his loyalty to the King, served the Protectorate Government to save the Serbs from extermination. His supporters became the "privileged" group and were very vulnerable to CPY propaganda exploitation. Mihajlović and his Četniks, although actively hostile to the occupation, overdid retaliations and claimed retaliations against the non-Serbs. Mihajlović, the Minister of War of the Government-in-Exile, became the symbol, perhaps somewhat to his dismay, of the concept of old Yugoslavia so unacceptable to the Macedonians and Croatians. The tragic "whirlpool of events" about which he spoke at his trial was in essence his identification with the struggle for former Serbian privileges, and ultimately he had no choice but futilely to wait in the hills for liberation. He was joined mainly by victimized Serbs in Croatia and Macedonia who saw in him the most effective protagonist of the "chosen people" image of the Serbs' mission, an image which from Ilija Garašanin to Nikola Pašić to Konstantin Fotić had shown remarkable obduracy.

While in Serbia many of the peasants could and did stand on the sidelines, the minority Serbs in Macedonia and Croatia could not. Eventually, as the Partisans began to acquire international support, the CPY seemed to offer them better opportunity than did the Četniks for wreaking vengeance on their oppressors. Mihajlović, unacceptable to the non-Serbs, could not long offer the protection the CPY did to the Serbs outside of Serbia. Thus his most likely adherents began to slip out of his grasp. The Communists seemed to side with the majorities in the regions of former Serbian oppression (Macedonians and democratic Croatians) and yet appeared to defend those Serbs who had been oppressed in retaliation.

The immediate objective of Tito was to exploit all such contradictions, all victims, and to induce and force the uncommitted to commit themselves. There were of course gradations of victimization. As more and more people became dissatisfied the Communists first concentrated upon those whose victimization might be only temporary. Thus, when the Macedonian intellectuals were becoming disillusioned over the method and extent of their Bulgarian "liberation," they were considered a crucial target group for CPY nationality propaganda.

The Party did not push the "sharpening of the opposition" until late 1943, when its strength and prestige became formidable. With the growing intensity of warfare, no effort was spared in forcing the undecided to take sides. If, as a result of the CPY's efforts to dichotomize passive elements, most of a target group went over to the domestic enemy, it was still considered a net gain in the long run. There would always be a number who would join the Četniks or the scattered IMRO bands, but those who fled to wait were no match for those who were committed to unremitting warfare. Naturally, everything possible was done to dissuade the undecided from going over to the enemy. Partisan persuasion teams and strong-arm squads informed bystanders that they could not remain home; they must fight. They told passive elements that if the latter joined a non-Communist resistance group no mercy would be shown upon their inevitable capture. No mercy was shown; no allowance made.

Constant conflict, the creation of new tensions until all had taken sides — this was the program. Numerous villages, innocent of any active resistance, were attacked by the occupation forces or by non-Communist native units because the Partisans deliberately provoked the attacks by ambushes. Most of those who escaped the ravaged villages joined the Partisans. The Party's enemies were provoked into making tragic mistakes. Fighting the Četniks and the IMRO bands in such a way as to push some of them into first insignificant, then major compromises with the occupiers and the quislings, was part of the pattern. If the ultimate enemy apparently were voluntarily connected with the Axis, as was Mihailov, so much the easier to compromise him ruinously.

That the CPY had been so long unsuccessful in Macedonia resulted, according to the Agitprop approach, from the paucity of existing victims and the difficulty in creating new ones. Very few Serbomans remained. Most of the Albanian minority in the northwest was enjoying its incorporation into Albania. Chagrin over the nature of Bulgarian occupation was not intense enough to erase memories of Serbian deprivations. However, the growing resentment against conscription and stringent rationing, and the intelligentsia's disappointment that its capabilities as administrators, school teachers, etc., continued to be largely ignored by the Bulgarians, finally resulted in enough depreciation of enthusiasm to make it possible for the CPY to manipulate some sullen Macedonians into angry, personal involvement against the occupation.

The Communists' concessions to Macedonian nationalism may have been distrusted by the average man, but what were the alternatives? The representatives of old Yugoslavia did not even pretend to concede anything. The Bulgarians had not conceded enough. Ivan Mihailov, portrayed as hiding out in Zagreb on the sufferance of Pavelić and the Germans, began to appear ill-matched against Tito, whose prestige was fast rising and who repeatedly assured that prewar Yugoslavia would not be rehabilitated. Among the new, young Macedonian Communists and among modest numbers of other Macedonians, mostly disoriented idealists, a new type of "nationalism" began to evolve. Gradually the bandwagon climbers and the professional revolutionaries, to whom inaction was anathema, joined the Partisans. The calculated destruction of competing groups went on apace.

At the Fifth Congress of the CPY, Milovan Djilas touched upon the flexibility of the Agitprop approach:

> Was the national question in Yugoslavia to be a lever for the liberation struggle or a lever for the occupiers and their allies? In the individual areas of Yugoslavia the question was put differently and therefore the tasks of our propaganda, even though in essence the same, were to a certain measure specific for individual areas.... Among the masses of the Macedonian people it was necessary to direct propaganda activity as much against Great Serbian as against Great Bulgarian conceptions. . . . It was necessary for the CP in Macedonia to strike with equal sharpness against Great Bulgarian hegemony and the policy of denationalization. . . . and especially to popularize the struggle of the Serbian Partisans against the Great Serbian Četniks. [31]

At the local level every wile was employed to present the Communists in the most favorable light. When in a village known to be pious, Partisan guests were instructed solemnly to cross themselves as the church bell rang.

Thus, while the Četniks and the IMRO agents were attempting to conserve a major portion of their strength for use against the Partisans, Tito risked everything throughout the war in order to increase his potential power. Knowing that the CPY's chances would be slim if it were to emerge from the war as one of several resistance groups with relatively equal records, he diligently employed the classic Communist strategy of creating a popular image of the CPY as an "acceptable" group, destroying competing "acceptable" groups, and subsequently seizing power as the most powerful remaining group. A vital component in this strategy was his anti-Axis guerrilla activity, which was sufficiently effective to win Allied recognition and commendation. The prestige he thus acquired was very valuable in his campaign to destroy opposing reistance groups.

It is also pertinent to examine some of the CPY's wartime problems vis-a-vis the USSR and the CPB with regard to the "type of resistance" issue as it was related to the Macedonian question. An understanding of the differences between the CPY and the CPB approach to the question of Partisan activity—basic to an appraisal of Tito's Macedonian success—is instructive also with regard to the reasons for his success in general. Why did these two CP's, both then loyal to Moscow, employ such divergent policies? It was a case of revolutionary, militantly Communist, partisan warfare and of attempts to force mass participation therein, as against the Bulgarian approach of infiltration, caution, and "waiting for the appropriate time." We have noted previously that to ascribe Moscow's support of Tito on the Macedonian question chiefly to the latter's policy of armed resistance and partisan warfare may be too facile an explanation. Full examination of the USSR's attitude toward independent communist resistance groups in Yugoslavia and other East European countries must await the availability of considerably more Communist source material, but analysis can be employed to outline the main components of that attitude.

The Comintern's endorsement of Tito's right to control of the Party in Macedonia came in August 1941, *before* Tito had distinguished himself in partisan warfare. The Secretary-General of the Comintern was the venerated Bulgarian Georgi Dimitrov, certainly the dominating figure in international Communist circles insofar as Balkan affairs were concerned. It is not surprising then that, although Tito did win formal Comintern sanction in this and subsequent wartime jurisdictional disputes with the CPB, Moscow followed a decidedly cautious and opportunistic policy with regard to Tito's "national" revolution. The Comintern's support for the CPY in Macedonia was something less than all-out. What part, if any, Bulgarian nationalism may have played in Dimitrov's directives can only be conjectured. That Moscow was for a time extremely wary of Tito's adoption of the policy of armed resistance and partisan warfare and repeatedly scolded him for being too revolutionary, is a matter of record.[32]

The Bulgarian Communists' policy of passive resistance and infiltration of the army and governmental institutions, followed in occupied Macedonia as well as in Bulgaria proper, aimed at the creation of a Fatherland Front which was in due time to seize power. This line was consistently followed by the CPB, apparently without reprimand from the Comintern or the Kremlin. Further, when the Bulgarian line was applied in Macedonia, despite contrary directives of the CPY, with which contender the Comintern had on legalistic grounds ostensibly sided, there was no evidence of Moscow criticism of the CPB.

Was Moscow fearful of an organized, indigenous armed resistance movement in Bulgaria, a movement which it could not at the time supply and completely control? At the time Tempo turned the tide in Macedonia with the channeling of some "nationalistic" revolutionary inclinations into armed revolt, the UK and the USSR had already laid the groundwork for the subsequent Big Three Moscow agreement on the division of postwar influence in the Balkans. Stalin therefore counted on Bulgaria as a bird almost in hand; large-scale resistance by coalition forces was the last thing he wanted there. Moscow probably speculated that in the event of significant Bulgarian armed revolt, the Western Powers might find themselves leading Bulgarian (and other Balkan) anti-Axis efforts. The United States and the UK both were in liaison with several resistance groups in the Balkans. They were in a position to supply those groups with materiel. Churchill was itching to have British and American troops liberate the Balkans, a plan which Stalin tenaciously opposed. The calculated pattern of later Soviet moves in Bulgaria — the short, technical "state of war" in September 1944 after the evacuation of German troops; the Societ occupation for the period needed firmly to establish Communist power, to "legalize" that power and to frustrate the holding of free elections—could not have been woven so artistically had there been effective native resistance groups in Bulgaria. Stalin was keenly aware of this danger. He overcame essentially the same danger elsewhere, notably in the Warsaw and Slovak uprisings.

In Yugoslavia, Stalin was faced with a somewhat different challenge. Early in the war Moscow could not reasonably hope for a preponderant share of postwar influence there, and later its share was fixed at fifty per cent. The USSR therefore favored active resistance in Yugoslavia and, greatly underestimating Tito's potentialities, pressed for cooperation among the resistance groups. Soviet interest in partisan warfare in Yugoslavia probably came from a desire for "safe" anti-Axis activity which would relieve pressure on the Eastern Front and from the consideration that Tito might possibly come out on top in the long run. Moscow was not at all happy about his too open espousal of Communism and his refusal to join with Mihajlović in common action. To the Kremlin this appeared dangerous; the time was not yet propitious to bring the Communist cards out of the sleeve.

Until late in the war the Russians apparently failed to realize that the CPY was the group in Yugoslavia most capable of developing a resistance movement appealing to the malcontents of *all* the country's nationalities. It was Tito's very independence from the almost purely Serbian Četniks that constituted one of his main elements of appeal in Croatia and Macedonia. However, until at least late 1943, Moscow's approach was based on the assumed necessity of recognizing the legal Yugoslav Government in London, and on the corollary necessity of Tito's collaboration with that Government's representative in the field. The Comintern's support of the CPY's rights in Macedonia was thus consistent with its legalistic approach to, and with its understanding of, the whole problem of Yugoslavia. To have seemed to presage the dismemberment of prewar Yugoslavia by acknowledging that Macedonia was properly in the Bulgarian Communist Party's sphere would not have been consonant with that approach.

Tito's assessment of the CPY's potentialities in the struggle for power was much more perspicacious than was Moscow's. He felt that the USSR was unduly circumspect in its relations with the Government-in-Exile.

Observing Moscow's promises to the West, including the promise of free elections, Tito concluded that the fate of the Communist revolution had to be determined *during* the war, by the annihilation of all other resistance groups to which popular enthusiasm might accrue. He realized that any resistance organization not under the control of the CPY would be a rallying point for anti-Communists. He knew that the overwhelming majority of Yugoslavs would not willingly accept a Communist Government. Tito was aware that Mihajlović had genuine support among some Serbian elements and that, if the CPY was to capture the hearts of the persecuted Orthodox minority in Croatia, it had to act quickly. He also realized that increasing Croation opposition to the Pavelić government might well lead to the organization of pro-Western resistance groups there. And lastly, the significant danger to, and opportunity for, the CPY's aims in the reservoir of pro-autonomy and pro-unification sentiment in Macedonia was evident to the Yugoslav Communists.

CHAPTER 6
TITO'S GROWING AMBITIONS
AND SUCCESSES

After selecting new leaders for the Communists in Yugoslav Macedonia and starting them off on a pro-CPY line, Tempo turned to the next phase of his charge. He diligently strove for the development of collaboration between Tito's Partisans and the Communist military bands in Albania and Greece, to lay the groundwork for later cooperative political action of which Tito would be the "natural leader." Concurrently, Tempo discussed with other Balkan Communist leaders the possibility of establishing a Balkan staff to coordinate partisan activities. Tito, of course, was to be the leader for he had built a unique record as master of partisan warfare.

Albania, its Drin valley one of the two potential outlets to the sea for southern Yugoslavia (the other being the southern Vardar valley and Salonika), had excited the ambitions of Belgrade expansionists since the 1870's. The CPY's attempts to dominate the Albanian resistance movement were in the tradition of long-standing Yugoslav designs on its weak neighbor. After Albania had become an Italian colony, the CPY sent Miladin Popović there in 1939 to attempt to found a Party organization.[1] In the fall of 1941, Dušan Mogoša of the CPY's Regional Committee for Kosovo and Metohija (which region had been annexed by Albania) was ordered to Tirana as an "instructor."[2] A year later another instructor from the CC CPY, Blažo Jovanović, played a role in the Albanian CP's First Conference.[3] The Yugoslav delegates had a difficult task. The former Yugoslav Albanians had no inclination to fight their way back into the Yugoslav state; quite the contrary was true. The Albanians as a whole had little inclination to assist in the Communist revolution. Resistance gradually coalesced around a non-Communist front and the Communists were getting nowhere. It was to subvert this front, the Bali Kombetar, and to organize Partisan fighting units, that Tempo had in mind when he left Macedonia.

In April 1943 Tempo conferred near Elbasan with the Albanian Communist leader, Enver Hoxha. He assured the Albanians that the frontiers had become anachronisms; that the one million ethnic Albanians living in Kosovo, Metohija, and western Macedonia would present no problem in the federated Soviet Republics.[4] On his second mission to Albania, in late June, Tempo attended a meeting of the CC CPA. It was there that he got down to cases. According to the CPY account, Tempo, "on the demand and with the assistance of Koci Xoxe" (who was to be purged by the CPA following the Cominform break), aired his view that the CPA must "actively work to create differences in the ranks of the Bali Kombetar, and to destroy those openly collaborating with the occupiers."[5] Tempo complained that some, Hoxha included, "considered it necessary to wait for the differences in the ranks of the Bali Kombetar to come about by themselves." But the CC CPA, inspired by the presence of the special emissary of Tito, adopted the "correct" position of Xoxe and Tempo.

While Tempo thus reinforced the CPY's influence over the CPA, his immediate objective with regard to the Albanian problem was to gain control of the situation in Albanian-populated areas of Yugoslavia, where the legacy of prewar Serbian rule was as bitter as it was in Vardar Macedonia. The support of Bali Kombetar for "ethnic Albania" compounded the CPY's difficulties. Tempo's report of August 8, 1943, to the CC CPY revealed the extent to which Tito's agents believed it necessary to compromise with the Albanians, so antagonistic were the Škiptars to anything Yugoslav.

> In Kosovo and Metohijo I found myself in a really difficult situation. The Party organizations have a too sectarian position on the question of drawing all groups into the National Liberation Front of the people of Kosmet. The sectarians were especially concerned about the nationalist Škiptar groups which were in truth chauvinistically disposed toward the Serbs, but at the same time were hostilely inclined toward the Italian occupiers. . . . It is essential gradually to organize Party units which could successfully cope with the great chauvinistic hatred which indeed exists between the Škiptars and Serbs. . . . I selected the best Party activists from the field and formed a Temporary Regional Committee. . . . The extent of chauvinistic hatred of the Škiptars, against the Serbs is made clear by the fact that one of our units, which was composed of Škiptars, was surrounded by over two thousand armed Škiptar peasants and the battle went on for several hours until the Škiptars saw that it was a Škiptar unit. Then they departed and left the Italians holding the bag. All Škiptar villages mobilize as soon as any kind of a unit appears. . . . The Škiptar masses as a whole seek annexation to Albania and there is real danger of the reactionary mobilization of these masses by chauvinistic groups of old Albania—"The Bali Kombetar" . . . .
>
> I had to send additional instructions in which I foresaw the establishment of separate Škiptar units and separate Serbian units, with Fadilj Hodža at the head. . . . But these measures will not be enough. . . . therefore, I decided that this instructor, Dušan [Mugoša], be sent from Albania to the Kosmet; thus, I am strengthening the Regional Committee. I sought help

from the Albanian Party in the work of mobilizing the Škiptar masses in the Kosmet. The CC CPA and Milo [Miladin Popović] are proposing that the Škiptar masses be under the command of the Headquarters Staff of Albania, while the Serbs be under the command of our Headquarters. Milo even thinks that it is necessary that a party incorporated in the framework of the CPA also be organized in Metohija. I think that both these measures would really make easier the gathering of the Škiptar masses into the National-Liberation struggle, but on the other hand we would lose many of the Serbian people. Therefore, I cannot give any sort of a decision on this question without asking you for advice. With the Serbian masses the situation is generally favorable; . . . the majority are under our influence. But we must not lose sight of the hidden danger. Namely, that with the slogan of "Revenge against the Škiptars" the Great Serbs would be able to mobilize the Serbian masses in the Kosmet (in view of the organizational-party weakness of our organizations).

[The Albanians] agreed with all my proposals [including that of a Balkan staff]. Several Albanian *četas,* which were organized by the Italian occupier for fighting against the Macedonians, have disintegrated due to the correct work of our Party organizations. The process of unification of the Macedonians and Skiptars is going along. . . . I dept in mind that all of the Škiptar masses who are mobilized on the territory of Yugoslavia be under the command of our staffs. Naturally, I announced that in this regard it was not necessary to be severe, that is, those fighters, Škiptars, who by no means would agree to be under our command, should temporarily remain under the command of the Škiptar *četas* which are operating on our land. Later they must gradually come under our command.[6]

By the time Tito's reaction to Tempo's comments was forthcoming, the CPY's domestic and international position had improved so much that further drastic concessions to nationalism were not deemed essential. In any case it is doubtful that Tito would have assented to an acknowledgment of CPA jurisdiction over the Yugoslav Albanians. He was aware of what the consequent antagonism on the part of the Serbs might mean. It might well destroy the delicate balance of power he was trying to effect among the Yugoslav nationalities. The Field of Kosovo, symbol of the fall of the Serbian Empire to Turkey in the fourteenth century, and Peč, the old seat of the Serbian Patriarchate, are situated in Kosovo and Metohija. The fact that Albanians had largely replaced the region's Serbs, most of whom went north in two great migrations (1690 and 1737) made these symbols of past glory even more dear to the hearts of Serbs.

Tito's recognition of the dominant Serbs as the main key to power was fully as acute as that of Marković and the Kremlin two decades before. He did not want to jeopardize the potential support of his Serbian target groups

by precipitant concessions to minority elements. ˎ
rush in his direction in late 1943, Tito felt he could ˎ
CPA and make it desist from troublesome interference witℎ.
ling of the Albanian minority in the Kosmet, southern Serℓ
donia. In November 1943 Tito made his position clear. Pointiℎℊ
"various reactionary cliques are attempting to . . . represent our moˎ
as a Great Serbian one," the CPY informed the CPA that it was necessarˎ
develop among the Yugoslav Albanians "brotherly love toward the heroic
peoples of Yugoslavia." The Albanian people had to realize that the Yugoslav Partisan movement "is not and cannot be their enemy, but their friend
and cofighter in the struggle for a beautiful future. . . . The new Yugoslavia
. . . will be a country of free peoples, and consequently there will be no place
in it . . . for the national oppression of the Albanian minorities." Thus, the
CPY again insisted on the legality of Yugoslavia's prewar boundaries in a
case where such insistence was to its advantage.

In early May, 1943, Tempo made contact with the Greek Communists
in an attempt to establish CPY predominance in Aegean Macedonia. Antagonism between Greeks and the Slav minority in western Greek Macedonia,
simmering before the war because of the Metaxas dictatorship's repression
of the Slavs, had been inflamed by the Italian occupiers' organization of a
special Slavic gendarmery force which engaged in raids against the Greeks.
Bulgarian agents were given free rein and, since their influence was dangerous to the CPY's Macedonia-within-Yugoslavia plans, Tempo suggested
that it would be well to let Tito's agents organize and lead the Slavs
of Greece.[8] The Greeks refused. But Tempo did induce the High Command
of the Greek National Liberation Army (ELAS) to permit the organization
of Greek Macedonian Slavs into a Slav National Liberation Front (SNOF).
Although the ELAS Command readily agreed to join in military action
with the Yugoslav Partisans it could not have been enthusiastic about having
separate Greek Slav units, for this move seemed to portend Yugoslav efforts
to create a Greater Macedonia. The question of Greece's possible loss of
Aegean Macedonia was the chief *bête noire* of the Greek Communists. Acquiescence in such a proposal, however disguised by plans for some sort of
a Balkan Communist Federation, would severely shatter their popular support.[9]

In his August 8 letter to the CC CPY, Tempo related the Greek Communists' insistence on discretion in this matter:

> The Greek Party has the following stand on the question of Macedonia:
> Macedonia, that is the Macedonian minorities, will receive in Greece free-
> dom and security from all national subjugation. They do not recognize any

sort of right of self-determination of these people. In the course of long discussions I succeeded in convincing them of the need to recognize this right of the Macedonian people in Greece, but they consented only to the extent that the Balkan Staff publish a declaration of principle in which it will be said that all questions between the Balkan States will be resolved in brotherly cooperation, recognizing the right of self-determination of peoples . . . .

I consented to the demand of the Greek delegate that the Balkan Staff rotate between four commanders, one from each of the Balkan countries, thus manifesting the unity of the Balkan countries. In doing that I had in mind that reactionary elements, especially in Albania and Bulgaria, would conduct a big campaign against the partisans of the respective countries if [their partisans] would accept a "Serbian" command, for that is how it would be construed if a single commandant were appointed.[10]

Tempo closed his report by summarizing his advice to the KKE: to render ELAS-EAM more openly Communist and to take more offensive military action.

At a later conference the Yugoslav and Greek Communists agreed that their respective guerrilla groups would operate within their respective old national boundaries and that SNOF would be an integral part of the Greek Communist forces. Andreas Dzimas, a Greek Slav from Kastoria and the recognized leader of the Macedonian autonomy movement in Greece, was despatched to Tito's headquarters as representative of ELAS. In the fall of 1943 Goči (or Gočev), a Slav from Florina, took over the leadership of the SNOF units. As noted earlier, Goči favored a Greater Macedonia. His bands had a strong autonomist coloring from the start and he openly advocated an *independent*, united Communist Macedonia. Thus his line was a dangerous one from the CPY point of view. It was partly to weaken Goči's position and to minimize the effects of his manipulation of the popular slogan of unification that Tempo gave the green light to the CPM to play with the same slogan. Tempo complained that "there was no mention (by EAM-ELAS) of any right of the Macedonian people—not even so little as a declaratory admission of such a right—to a claim to self-determination . . . by reason of its participation in the people's liberation struggle."[11]Tempo claimed that the fault for the strained relations between the SNOF and the Communist Party of Greece lay in the "un-Marxist nationalistic political leadership of the KKE on the Macedonian national question. The CPY can only be 'at fault' for having made a correct solution of the Macedonian national question in the framework of Yugoslavia, and thereby having indeed given the whole Macedonian people a picture of the only proper way of solving the question of national liberation." The Greek Communists were cognizant of the CPY's maximal Macedonian aims in 1943. It is small wonder that subsequent relations between Yugoslav and Greek Communist leaders were often strained.

When Tempo returned to Skopje in the autumn of 1943 from his tour of Albanian and Greek Communist-held areas, he discussed matters of mutual concern with representatives of the CC CPB. Tempo did his best to encourage the Bulgarians to undertake all-out partisan resistance. Failing in that, he told them that their delegate for Macedonian Party affairs (presumably Balgaranov) was *persona non grata.* According to Tempo's account:

> I proposed that they use our territory in the Vranje District[12] for the formation of their *četas* and that they take action in the direction of Trun and Sofia from there. Similarly I proposed that they form partisan *četas* in Bulgarian Macedonia and that they connect with our *četas* around Štip for united action. I also gave them our opinion that they would one day really have to get into the struggle. There were stormy discussions. . . . Finally, they agreed with my proposals about joint cooperation but as yet they still have not done anything.[13]
>
> I have informed the Bulgarian delegate in Skopje that according to the decisions of the Communist International it is no longer necessary for him to collaborate with the Party leadership in Macedonia. He no longer has any influence at all in Macedonia. I don't know if I was mistaken in this matter. The Bulgarian Party has decided to take part in the Balkan Staff.[14]

Throughout his lengthy report to the CC, Tempo mentioned his discussions with Albanian, Greek, and Bulgarian Communists about the creation of a Balkan staff. It is improbable that he would have commenced negotiations on so far-reaching a proposal on his personal initiative; apparently he was sent on the mission as the official delegate of the Partisan Supreme Staff.[15] Yet Tempo's successful preliminary work with regard to the Balkan Staff idea, a task which must have been given him by the CC CPY, was sharply criticized when Tito answered his letter of August 8. Among the significant developments in the intervening months was an increase in the acerbity of Moscow-CPY relations. The CPY's eventual reversal of position on the Balkan Staff was, in the main, in reaction to the Kremlin's lack of enthusiasm for unrelated instances of CPY initiative.

In a postscript to his illuminating report, Tempo made some general suggestions with regard to Macedonia. He deemed it essential that the Party make a "special declaration that Macedonia will receive full freedom and equality with the other peoples of Yugoslavia." He wrote that it was necessary that radio "Free Yugoslavia" make special broadcasts to Macedonia in the Macedonian language. The special declaration on Macedonia would be "widely popularized and would tie the National Liberation Movement of the Macedonian people still more strongly to Yugoslavia." Tempo's suggestions were in harmony with Tito's next psychological warfare move, for the historic Jajce Assembly, meeting in November 1943, did precisely what Tempo had proposed.

The most significant political event in Tito's revolution was the Second AVNOJ Assembly in late November 1943. Foreign reaction or lack of reaction to the Jajce program had much to do with Yugoslav Communist success over their last effective opposition. At Jajce the Anti-Fascist Council for the National Liberation of Yugoslavia was declared the "Supreme Legislative and Executive Representative Organ and the Supreme Representative of the sovereignty of the nations of Yugoslavia as a whole", thus denying the legality of the London Government-in-Exile. With regard to the constitution of AVNOJ as the new Assembly of Yugoslavia and to the Provisional National Liberation Committee as the executive body of the Government, Tito did not run a great risk, for he had already acquired the support of the Allies for his Partisan activities. He correctly calculated that any dismay about his usurpation would be outweighed by their appreciation for his military contributions. On November 8, the Commander in Chief of the Mediterranean Theater of Operations, General Maitland Wilson, had warned Četnik collaborationists to desert the Nazi cause or be regarded as traitors to the United Nations.[16] Brigadier Fitzroy MacLean at Tito's Headquarters was sending Churchill reports of Četnik passivity, of their descent down the "slippery slope which leads to collaboration," of the Partisans being "more numerous, better organized, better disciplined and better led than the Četniks."[17]

According to the Yugoslav version, Tito in October had asked Stalin to inform the British and American representatives at the Moscow Big Three Conference that the Yugoslav Communists did not acknowledge the King or the London Government and that AVNOJ was "the only legal government of the people." The USSR did not place this statement on the Conference agenda.[18] Moscow was still unwilling that Tito rush into action which might arouse Western suspicion. The lack of previous Soviet approval seems not to have moderated the Jajce decisions. King Petar was forbidden to return until and unless he was asked to return. The Anti-Fascist Council resolved, "on the basis of the right of all nations to self-determination, including the union with or the secession from other nations," that Yugoslavia be "build up on a federal principle which will insure full equality for the nations of Serbia, Croatia, Slovenia, Macedonia, Montenegro and Bosnia and Hercegovina."[19]

There were no Macedonians on the supreme executive body of the new provisional government, the seventeen-member "National Liberation Committee," but one of the five vice-presidents of the Presidium of the Central Anti-Fascist Council was the aging Dimitar Vlahov. Vlahov had appeared with regularity as a "Macedonian publicist" at war-time All-Slav Congresses in Moscow. In August 1941, calling for a fight against German fascism, he described Macedonia as "the nation which in conjunction with the Bulgarian nation waged a prolonged war for national and cultural regeneration . . . which for half a century has been waging a revolutionary struggle for the political liberation of our martyred country . . . which gave the Bulgarian and Macedonian people a number of popular educators and revolutionary fighters."[20] It was no mean success for Tito that Vlahov, a redoubtable figure in Balkan Communist Circles, consented to participate in the incipient Yugoslav Government. He gave the CPY a much needed Macedonian "name" figure and strengthened its position vis-a-vis the still hopeful Bulgarian Communists. Properly reoriented, Vlahov could be very useful should the opportunity arise for the Yugoslav Communists to utilize to their own ends the "Independent Macedonia within a Balkan Federation" concept.

Three Macedonians were among the fifty-six ordinary members chosen for the Central Anti-Fascist Council: Mihajlo Apostolski, the Partisan military leader in Macedonia; Vladimir Poptomov, a Pirin Macedonian who less than a year later sided with the CPB and who became Bulgarian Foreign Minister in 1949; and Metodije Antonov-Čento, who in 1946 was accused of having been a member of the IMRO and convicted for having worked for a "completely independent Macedonia."[21]

In January 1944, Churchill announced that of the resistance forces in Yugoslavia only Tito's Partisans would receive Allied supplies. Two months later the Soviet Union sent its first military mission to Tito. Although Moscow gradually exhibited more hostility towards the exiled Yugoslav government, it took some time for Soviet ire about Tito's independent action at Jajce to die down. In retrospect, Jajce appears to have been one of the first indicators to the Kremlin that Tito would be difficult to manage. According to Dedijer's account:

> Tito did not notify the representatives of any of the big powers in advance of the concrete decisions at Jajce. . . . Moscow's first reaction was furious. The "Free Yugoslavia" radio station had orders not to broadcast the order prohibiting the King's return; Yugoslavia's representative in Moscow, Veljko Vlahović, was reprimanded. . . . Manuilsky delivered Stalin's message: "The *Hazyayin* [Stalin] is extremely angry. He says this is a stab in the back of the Soviet Union and the Tehran decisions." Stalin's reaction took the Yugoslavs by surprise. It was not clear to them at the time. They recalled Stalin's opposition to [the Bihać Assembly.][22]

The USSR did not publicly recover from its shock at Tito's drastic action until it was manifest that the Western powers were unmoved by Jajce. On December 14, Moscow announced: "The events in Yugoslavia which have already met with understanding in Britain and the United States are considered by the Government of the Soviet Union to be positive facts . . . These events also bear witness to the remarkable success of the new leaders of Yugoslavia . . . " [23] Thus the Kremlin, observing that Tito had convinced Churchill of the value of the CPY's efforts, at last began to realize that through Tito its share of control in postwar Yugoslavia could perhaps be increased. Also, there was a meeting of minds between the Soviets and the Yugoslav Partisans in opposing any Western invasion of the Balkans. At Tehran, "Operation Overlord" was scheduled but Stalin was fearful that his plans for political domination of the Balkans might still be upset by a "soft under-belly" attack. He was therefore now prepared to render Tito more moral support, to let the Partisans do all they could to make an American-British invasion appear less necessary. [24]

Jajce, having given more distinct form to the CPY's promises of a federative state, provided a much needed fillip to the Party's work in Macedonia. Kuzman Josifovski, the head of CPY operations in Skopje, wrote the CC that the Second AVNOJ decisions, particularly the promise of self-determination to the point of secession, had made a very positive contribution. [25] Vlahov's participation in the new government and the USSR's "recognition" of the Partisans had also helped a great deal, he wrote. Josifovski's report showed use was being made of foreign approval of the recognition of Macedonia as a nation. All Macedonians accepted Jajce, he claimed, except "the fascists and part of the city people and the intelligentsia." He attributed Bulgarian preparations for Macedonian participation in elections for the Bulgarian National Assembly to their realization of Jajce's threat to their position.

If the Bulgarian Government feared Jajce's effect in Vardar Macedonia, the Communist-dominated Fatherland Front was no less concerned. In December the Front issued a statement on Macedonia directly opposing Tito's line. It proclaimed, in part:

> Macedonia is an apple of discord among Balkan peoples [where there has been] mutual extermination of Bulgarian, Serbian, Greek and Albanian bands. . . . It is the cradle of the Bulgarian renaissance. . . . After the establishment of the free Bulgarian State (1886) the fate of enslaved Macedonia was always near to the heart of the Bulgarian people. . . . To give Macedonia lasting pacification the Fatherland Front proclaims the watchword "Macedonia for the Macedonians" neither a change in the present division of Macedonia among its enemies [one of whom, since Jajce, was Tito's "gov-

ernment"] nor the annexation of all of it to any one of the Balkan States. The only saving solution is an integral, free, and independent Macedonia. The Soviet Union and the democratic powers will guarantee a free and independent Macedonia.[26]

Bulgarian Communists subsequently claimed they had been compelled to agree to this startling affront to Tito to preserve the unity of the Fatherland Front.[27] Although the Yugoslavs did not accept this explanation, it was quite possibly true. To have acquiesced in Tito's primacy in Macedonia would have been one of the least popular acts the CPB could have devised. The reference to USSR backing of this Bulgarian proposal for Macedonia was probably pure wishful thinking. The CPY's coup in acquiring such a personage as Vlahov, who had been Dimitrov's right-hand man in the Communist International, gave evidence that Moscow approved of Tito's retention of Yugoslav Macedonia, at least.

The CPY later characterized the Fatherland Front's December proclamation as being in the "typical style of Great Bulgarian propaganda" in that it included no mention of the fact that "the Macedonian people exist as a separate nation, but speaks only of the 'population' of Macedonia." [8] A note in the *Arhiv* alleges that Kiril Dramaliev, one of the authors of the declaration and a CPB representative in a leading Fatherland Front position, had written in the October 1943 issue of a Front organ that the Macedonians were Bulgarians, that Macedonia was "holy Bulgarian soil," and that San Stefano Bulgaria should be restored. Further quoting Dramaliev: "There is no other region in the Bulgarian country which is dotted with so many sacred historical and national monuments of our ancient past as is Macedonia." The stand of the Fatherland Front and the CPB leadership is "the only logical result of their earlier Great Bulgarian and nationalistic references to the Macedonian people."

The Bulgarian Communists were on the defensive in the Macedonian imbroglio, but Tito was not yet certain that all of the CPY's Balken eggs would hatch. In fact, he had come to the conclusion that discretion was in order. The cautious trend was evident even before the Jajce Assembly. A Tito letter to Tempo of October 9, which may have been en route for as long as a month, indicated that the Balkan Staff plan was something less than perfect. Tito wrote that a group from the Communist International was on its way to Tempo to "discuss generally with you all questions of cooperation between ourselves and the other neighboring Balkan countries." This was a group of CPB leaders headed by Blagoi Ivanov, sent from Moscow to inspect Tito's operations with the aim of "helping to strengthen the national-liberation struggle in Bulgaria." Tito continued:

In relation to the question of the establishment of a so-called Balkan Staff, for which you became so enthusiastic; in the present situation, the creation of some sort of United Staff would be a mistake, and even harmful. I do not know whence this idea came; I fear that our allies smuggled it in through some indirect channel. We have our General Staff for the whole of Yugoslavia, which can in every respect extend aid to the Bulgarians as well as to Greek Partisan units. . . . Within their respective national boundaries there should exist leading military centers, which can effect the collaboration of allied relations, whether by way of military representatives or political representatives working for the coordination of operations and the exchange of experience from their struggles. Yugoslavia in every respect has the leading role in the Balkans. . . . In our opinion, and also in the opinion of Djeda [the Communist International] we must be the center for the Balkan countries, militarily as well as politically. . . . Our armed strength and the ever more powerful ambition of the popular uprising . . . can play a more decisive role in the national liberation movement in all Balkan countries . . . .

It seems to us that our Greek comrades have also gone too far. They have left the leadership of partisan units to uncertain officers, who have made it possible for the whole of our national-liberation movement in Greece to fall under the influence of the English. . . . We also have an English mission at our Headquarters. With our General Staff is an English general, with a whole staff of English officers, but we by no means allow them to mix in the pulse of any of our internal affairs. . . . It is understood that they still maintain connections with Draža Mihajlović and I know they have sent an English general to him, which is completely absurd, but consistent with the policy of England. But in any case the coming of a representative of the English Army to our Staff and the recognition of our National-Liberation Army as a belligerent power has had great political influence not only in our country but also abroad . . . .

The local English representative has asked me to permit the landing of one of their missions in Macedonia at our Partisan Headquarters. Until now I have refused, but one day he informed me that one of their missions had landed in Albania and that one member of that mission had departed for Macedonia. . . . Don't give him any military secrets at all, but only the generalities which they need to know as allies. You may give him approximations . . . but nothing completely precise. . . . Your task in Macedonia is: to establish more solid connections with Bulgaria and Greece, but especially with Bulgaria, so that events there will not leave us out and somebody else take the initiative, which would not be in the interest either of the Bulgarian people or us. You will discuss this in detail with the comrades who are coming.[29]

The reputed approval by the Communist International of Yugoslavia as the "center" for Communist military and political endeavors in the Balkans fit in well with Tito's ambitions. His omission of any reference to Tempo's United Macedonia proposal may have resulted from his desire to preserve the "legality" of the CPY's improving position in Vardar Macedonia. An overt overstepping of the legal framework of old Yugoslavia would have brought negative reactions, particularly from friends of Greece. At this stage, Tito appears to have been satisfied that Balkan partisan coordination, "guided" from his Headquarters, would effectively serve his ends. A Balkan Staff would have necessitated real deference to the comrades in Albania, Bulgaria, and Greece and would have invited more direct control from Moscow. Although Tito wished to keep a relatively free hand, he was sensitive, to a degree difficult to ascertain, to probable reactions from the Kremlin.

The change of pace—albeit largely tactical—called for in the next directive to Tempo must have resulted from Stalin's blast against the initiative and independence displayed by the CPY at the Second AVNOJ Conference. Written on December 6, 1943, a week after Jajce, this fascinating instruction was more definite on several crucial issues:

> It is most important that we speak about certain mistakes, and only those of a political nature, which can have very great consequences not only for the development of the movement there and for future movements of the Yugoslav people, but also for the movement in the whole of the Balkans.
>
> First: The formation of any kind of a Balkan staff is basically wrong. There is no reason whatever for it in the present situation—international— and also here in the Balkans, all reason is against it . . . We must pay strict attention—with regard to the international position—to Yugoslavia as a whole, as a state which existed and still is recognized abroad as such, taking care that we do not formally or legally overstep that framework in our slogans, and that in fact we do not, in various phrases, help the reactionary cliques, who want to depict the movements of the Balkan peoples—in the Balkan countries—as some kind of Balkan Bolshevism . . . .
>
> Second: With regard to Macedonia, from the information at hand we see that neither you, nor the comrades there, the Greeks and Bulgarians, have correctly approached that problem. The Macedonian people have the right to self-determination, even to the point of separation. . . . It would be good at some meeting of the Territorial Anti-fascist Assembly of Macedonia . . . to affirm this right, in principle, in the name of the Macedonian people. But it would be wrong to treat that right as a compulsory one. . . . In the present situation of the struggle of the whole people against fascism it would be harmful to emphasize that right too much. . . . The Macedonian people, being sovereign in their rights, have the right to unite in a federative community with other peoples, this it has to do today and join in common struggle with the other peoples of Yugoslavia.
>
> . . . The question of Kosovo and Metohija should be met in a similar

way. Slogans about the union of Kosovo and Metohija with Albania today, which Miladin [Popović] supports, also the position on the command of the Albanian General Staff over Metohija, would in fact play into the hands of the enemies . . . who are trying to slice off, piece by piece, the democratic movement of the people of Yugoslavia and who are putting in the first place not the question of the struggle against the occupiers, but the delimitation of boundaries between antagonistic nationalities, etc. I have written in this vein to Comrade Miladin and the CC in Albania.

Third: We call your attention to a very important fact—to cooperation with the comrades of the Greek and Bulgarian parties. In this regard you must be tactful and take into account that they are independent parties. But, by this we do not mean to say that in political questions you should be hesitant. You are now in a place which is of primary importance, and your work has enormous importance for the development of the national-liberation movements in the Balkans and for rendering impossible the isolation of the liberation struggle of our peoples.

Fourth: in the light of all this it should be clear to you that our actual slogans cannot be either for Balkan Federation or for unification with the Bulgarians; however, in "general" propaganda [*opštepropaganda*]³⁰ we are stating and stressing the wish of the peoples of Yugoslavia that the Bulgarians march with them into one united future federative community, and in "general" propaganda we are also talking about the brotherhood and unity of the peoples of the Balkans. You see from the radio news that now in England and America combinations are being made with the most varied federations of Central Europe, the Balkans, etc. . . . You must pay attention to international circumstances and must hold strictly to our slogans and positions, and not get into big and abstract combinations.³¹

So, while Tito had not been deterred from his Balkan ambitions by Moscow's rebuke over Jajce, he realized the need to be more careful. Being in a commanding position in the Yugoslav situation, he deemed it wise ostensibly to go along with the Soviet policy of caution in the rest of the Balkans. He shared the Soviet fear that open "Bolshevization of the Balkans" might occasion Western countermoves. Tempo was not to desist from his efforts to widen the area of CPY influence; Tito acknowledged that Tempo's work was of "enormous importance" to the liberation movements in the *Balkans.* The implication was clear that this work was not to be confined to mere support operations to the military benefit of the Partisans in Yugoslavia.

Tito was not, however, prepared to be bland about the Bulgarian Fatherland Front's December declaration on Macedonia. On January 24, 1944, he sent Georgi Dimitrov a radiogram, the available section of which gives no evidence of fawning. Complaining that the declaration, in demanding "the unification of a Macedonia which did not need to be connected with anyone, but be completely independent," was contrary to the AVNOJ decisions. Tito stated that the Front's approach coincided with "German policy, i.e., the grooming of Vančo Mihailov as the leader of an independent Macedonia." Then with abrupt frankness: "In our opinion the Fatherland Front would be better advised to address themselves to the Bulgarian soldiers in Yugoslavia, asking them to cease the war against us."[32]

By the beginning of 1944 the goal was in sight for the CPY in Yugoslav Macedonia. The Macedonian comrades were in general following the party line. The CPY had in its fold Vlahov, probably second only to Mihailov as a Macedonian notable. Jajce had given at least a limited number of Yugolav Macedonians reason to believe that the "new Yugoslavia" might not be unacceptable. Bulgarian influence in general, and that of the CPB in particular, was fading. The revolution in Vardar Macedonia had yet to be consolidated, but Tito and his strategists were keeping an eye on a larger Balkan picture in which they saw Yugoslav Macedonia as a springboard.

During the first months of 1944, Partisan activity in Macedonia secured increased areas of "liberated" territory. As it became apparent that Bulgaria was seeking a way to withdraw from the war, additional Bulgarian gendarmerie units joined Tito's forces. The extent to which active participation in the Macedonian Partisan Movement grew is indicated, assuming the CPY figures are reasonably correct, by the stated Party losses. During the war eleven members of the Regional Committee and the CC CPM were killed and six were interned. Another 539 CPM members, including ninety-four members of various committees, were killed "in action". Of the 1,600-odd Party members who were arrested by the occupation authorities, thirty-four were condemned to death. Although the number of Macedonian Party members killed or imprisoned was small, it was roughly proportional to such losses elsewhere in Yugoslavia. It attested to a growing willingness to sacrifice for what they believed to be the CPY solution. These losses, however, hit the leadership cadres especially hard.[33]

Through the spring of 1944 the CPY gave substantial aid to the Bulgarian Partisan units which were being organized, mainly in those parts of Bulgarian Macedonia contiguous to "liberated" territory in Vardar Macedonia. In his position as contact man for the "military and political center of the Balkans", Tempo got in touch with members of the Bulgarian Partisans' General Staff and of the Central Committee of the Fatherland Front. He noted that "our coming into this area has brought about a complete change in the [Bulgarian] Party."[34] The Bulgarian Partisans in the "Hristo Botev" Battalion were put under Bulgarian command, and a "Georgi Dimitrov" Brigade was formed.

The Bulgarian and German occupiers made desperate attempts to wipe out the snowballing partisan units in Vardar Macedonia. In January and February of 1944 the Bulgarians and Germans under General Marinov launched their first large-scale offensive against the Macedonian partisans. According to CPY account, the 15,000 Axis troops were joined by the "Vardar Corps" of Mihajlović. The Partisans had some success against the Četniks who then commenced their fruitless trek to the north. Tempo led the bulk of the Partisan forces in retreat to the eastern extreme of Vardar Macedonia. On April 30, the Germans and Bulgarians started their second and last military offensive against the Yugoslav Partisans. In this campaign, which lasted almost two months, the Macedonian Partisans managed to retreat without great losses.[35]

Thus the Partisans were only negatively successful against the two major offensives in that they escaped destruction.[36] But with Axis military power on the wane, it did not matter how much "liberated" territory the Partisans were forced to evacuate as long as they maintained the major portion of their units intact. As had been the Partisans' practice throughout the war, they retained what they could of easily defensible territory for purposes of foreign and local prestige. However, the other, smaller pockets of Partisan control were more vital to them. These "tactical" enclaves were vital as bases from which to carry out sabotage, agitation, recruitment, and supply missions. Characteristically, the Partisans utilized the sharp fighting and resultant deprivations to mobilize additional men. In September an alleged 66,000 Macedonian Partisans were organized into seven divisions and three corps.[37] With the disintegration of the Axis and the involvement of increasing numbers of Macedonians in active fighting, the CPY stepped up its propaganda campaign. The promise of self-determination made at Jajce was elaborated and widely publicized preparations were made for the "first Macedonian national assembly" in history.

The turning of the tide was summarized by Mošhe Pijade, the CPY's proficient publicist, in the May 15, 1944, issue of the journal *Nova Jugoslavija.* He used strong nationalistic phrases in appealing for Macedonian support. He called Jajce "the high point of [Macedonian] national individuality and political maturity." The Partisan struggle in Macedonia was described as the end of Macedonian "prehistory and the beginning of their true history." He toyed with such symbols as "the Macedonians as a separate Southern Slav nation . . . the struggle for national freedom . . . the birth of Macedonia and the Macedonian people as an independent national and state unit." The article which was given wide circulation in Macedonia, succinctly demonstrated the adaptability of the CPY propaganda approach, with the minimum goals explicitly expressed and without abandonment of the more grandiose schemes. Pijade's article is a monument of CPY psychological warfare tactics:

> The principle [of federative Yugoslavia] could have flowed *only* from the free will of all of our peoples, a will witnessed in brotherly armed struggle —that of equals among equals associated in one state community. But for the true achievement of these great democratic principles it was necessary to annihilate every trace of any kind of chauvinism—the *Serbian people* particularly have had to deliver the mortal blow to great-Serb chauvinism . . . . In Macedonia neither the primary or middle schools nor the seminaries were in the hands of the Macedonian people, but in the hands of propagandists of the neighboring Balkan States, who preyed upon every Macedonian child . . . The Macedonian intelligentsia were educated and shaped entirely outside of Macedonia in Bulgaria and Serbia, Greece and Rumania, where they became alienated from their nation, estranged. . . . On one's fingers one can count those Macedonians who, like Dimitar Vlahov, outside of their fatherland, consistently advocated the idea of an *independent Macedonia as an equal member of a federation of Balkan peoples.* . . . Thus the Macedonian people gave its intellectuals to other peoples, while it remained without its national intelligentsia, which would have contributed to the formation of the nation, the building and strengthening of the Macedonian national spirit, the development of the Macedonian culture and language. But, although in the most difficult straits, although a significant number of the urban population in Macedonia was under the influence of various propagandists the Macedonian peasantry preserved the national spirit, and it is also today the main bearer of the struggle for national freedom of the Macedonian people.
>
> The establishment of the modern history of the Macedonian people means . . . the resurrected right of the Macedonian people to direct their own destiny themselves. The Macedonian people did not receive this right of theirs as a gift. . . . They took up arms, formed their own national partisan units . . . and under the leadership of Marshal Tito took an *active role* in the liberation war together with the other peoples of Yugoslavia, Albania and Greece.[38] Thus with their own struggle, they established the basis of their national independence . . . .
>
> The decision of the Second Assembly of AVNOJ with regard to the federative construction of Yugoslavia, delivered a frightful blow not only to the chauvinists in Zagreb, Belgrade, and Cairo,[39] but also to the fascist clique in Sofia. Therefore, the Bulgarian rulers, after the Second Assembly of AVNOJ—after three years of terroristic rule and unrestrained plundering of the Macedonian people. . . . remembered to send Professor Turov as commissar in Macedonia and at meetings to promise elections . . . explaining theat Macedonia was a part of Old Great Bulgaria. It was late. . . . Macedonia and her people had become aware of themselves, of their rights and their strengths, aware of the value of its fraternal *community with the other peoples of Yugoslavia, with whom more and more Bulgarian and other Bal-*

kan peoples are associating. . . . The decision of AVNOJ had a particular echo abroad, in wide democratic circles as well as in official allied circles . . . Thus a Norwegian publicist, Brailsford, a connoisseur of Macedonians, speaking over the London radio, said, . . . "For me, who knows Macedonia well, the promise of Tito and his comrades, is the best guarantee that independent Macedonia will go as a member into the *South Slav Federation,* that is the sole way to assure victory and real peace." Similarly, there followed the favorable comments of the English press and the London radio, which have, after long practice in speaking only about the Serbs, Croats and Slovenes, began to speak also about the Macedonians and Montenegrins as national individualities. . . .

Who are those who are against the freedom of the Macedonian people? There stand the wrecked remains of the great-Serb hegemonist clique and its agents, like Vojvoda Trbić and the Četniks of Draža Mihajlović. . . . There stand the Great Bulgarian hegemonists and their Macedonian agents, like Vančo Mihailov, Spiro Kitinčev, the Čkatrov brothers, etc., whose traitorous anti-Macedonian role long ago became clear to the Macedonian people. . . . However, the Macedonian people have paid too much in blood both for Serbian and for Bulgarian "liberations." Faithful to the traditions of their revolutionary, national fighters and teachers, Goce Delčev, Damian Gruev, Dšorča Petrov and Sandanski, it has unfurled the banner of the struggle for its national freedom and is exterminating, beside the occupiers, traitors of both sorts. . . . Free and equal, (Macedonia) is even today certain that the brotherly society of *associated free people of Yugoslavia* will generously assist it in its economic and cultural rising. . . . Perhaps one day it can be said that free Macedonia in free, democratic, federative Yugoslavia is the most beautiful and most democratic acquisition of the common liberation struggle of the peoples of Yugoslavia. It will no longer be an apple of discord between the Balkan peoples, but the most beautiful pledge and tie of their friendsip and cooperation. [40]

Pijade's article was calculated to appeal to Macedonians of almost all persuasions. Nationalists were flattered, and the framework into which Macedonia would go was pleasantly vague to those who lacked experience in evaluating such CPY "programs." Macedonia was to have a definite position as a unit in some sort of a loose confederation, it seemed, of South Slav nationalities under Belgrade's egis. The references to Vlahov's views indicated that the idea of a Tito-led Balkan Federation had not been cast aside by the CPY. The decreasing viability of any alternatives to Communist domination and the skillful manipulation of propaganda produced qualified enthusiasm for the CPY's Macedonia program on the part of some Macedonians. The majority of the Macedonian population, however, accepted the CPY program with passive resignation.

As part of its program to consolidate its power in Macedonia, the first meeting of the Anti-Fascist Assembly of National Liberation of Macedonia (ASNOM) took place on August 2, 1944, the anniversary of the Ilinden Uprising. [41] The preparations had been troublesome, as the defection of the Skopje Front Committee of intellectuals indicated, but 122 delegates were rounded up for the meeting in the monastery of Saint Prohor Pohinjski. The Macedonian People's Republic was proclaimed an equal federal unit in Democratic Federative Yugoslavia. ASNOM was constituted the supreme legislative and executive body of the Republic. The national minorities in Macedonia were guaranteed "every right for a free national life." Freedom of speech, press, secret balloting, assembly and association were promised, with the important qualifications that all fascist or pro-fascist activity was forbidden. A commission was set up for "the establishing of the crimes of the occupiers and their helpers." The Macedonian language was decreed the official state language, effective immediately. [42]

In a proclamation accompanying the ASNOM Decisions, Macedonians were warned that Mihailov was preparing mercenary bands to take over Macedonia when the Bulgarian units withdrew and that Milan Nedić was also preparing to march into Macedonia to renew great-Serb slavery. In the name of the new Macedonian state, the populace was urged to take part in the Macedonian Front and to join the Partisan army. [43] At a concurrent meeting of the CC CPM, plans were elaborated for the establishment of "Organs of Peoples' Power" and the creation of a Central Committee of the United Liberation Front in anticipation of the breakdown of the Bulgarian regime before the advancing Soviet army. The day after the ASNOM meeting a Party consultation was held in the village of Ravno. Here the "chauvinistic-separatistic conceptions of some of the 'pretty-bourgeois elements,' members of the ASNOM, were subjected to severe criticism." [44]

The CC CPM issued another proclamation in connection with ASNOM on August 4. [45] The foundations of the Macedonian state were said, with considerable justification, to have been built "with the bones of thousands of your best sons and daughters," but then, "cemented by the precious blood of your best fighters, Orca Nikolov, Kuzman Josifovski, Strašo Pindžur, Cvetan Dimov, and Mirče Acev," all of whom were CPM casualties. Now that there was little question about the CPY's ability to hold Vardar Macedonia, it was considered safe to be somewhat more open about further aims. Accordingly, the proclamation urged:

> With the participation of the whole Macedonian people in the struggle against the fascist occupiers in Yugoslavia, Bulgaria and Greece, you will also achieve the unification of all parts of Macedonia, which were separated

> by the Balkan imperialists in 1913 and 1919. The Atlantic Pact and the
> Tehran Agreement . . . guarantee the right of self-determination. . . . And
> in the demand for the full unification of the Macedonian people, all the other
> people of Yugoslavia stand behind you today, as well as the AVNOJ and
> the heroic National-Liberation Army of Yugoslavia.

It was now manifest that the CPY accepted the Macedonian border of
prewar Yugoslavia rather as a working basis for further aggrandizement than
as the maximum delimitation it desired. This unveiled threat to obtain Pirin
and Aegean Macedonia, by armed force if necessary, was made at the time
the situation in Bulgaria was approaching chaos. The Greek government of
Papandreou was dead-locked with the Greek Communists, although the
latter were themselves seriously weakened by divisions over methods and
principles. [46] The proclamation, after reminding waverers that the Red Army
was advancing on Belgrade, went on to warn:

> The old foes of the Macedonian people, Vančo Mihailov and Stanišev,
> and in addition Čkatrov, Džuselov and Kitinčev, are forging a criminal con-
> spiracy against the Macedonian people. . . . Observing the imminent fall of
> fascist Bulgaria, they are preparing, with the aid of German units and some
> of their own armed groups . . . to take power in Macedonia in their bloody
> hands. Abusing the righteous demand of the Macedonian people for a free
> and independent life, they are preparing for it "autonomy" and "indepen-
> dence" similar to that in unfortunate Pavelić Croatia. . . . So as to avoid use-
> less sacrifice, the Macedonian people must immediately take all measures
> so as to frustrate these traitorous bands from again throwing [Macedonia]
> into new suffering and convulsions.

The proclamation of August 4 ended with "long lives" for all the new organs
of power in Macedonia and Yugoslavia, and for Tito (the USSR and Red
Army, Bulgaria, Greece and Albania were omitted), and with the hope that
the "People's Democratic Power, the Power of the New Macedonian State,
will spread over the whole of Macedonia so that the entire Macedonian people would be shown the benefits of the new sovereign power of Macedonia."

By this time, the IMRO and Četniks were eager to engage in struggle
against their real enemy, but the appropriate time had long since passed and
they were relatively enervated. Whether the CPM's prediction about Mihailov's preparations was based upon shrewd speculation or agents' reports, [47]
it was not long before the IMRO chief made his only wartime attempt to
affect the fate of Macedonia. Having thus far refused to take an active role
under German auspices (and it should be remembered that he was still officially considered a criminal by the Government of Bulgaria) Mihailov was in

early September 1944 pushed by the Germans to do what he could. According to the MPO, he was flown to Skopje in a German plane, after having promised the Germans only that he would survey the situation and see what might be done. Mihailov evidently had no precise plan of action and was quite naturally afraid of being left alone under attack from all sides—the Communists, Četniks, Greeks, and Great Bulgarians all opposed him. The obvious weakness of his position, together with his reluctance to take a course of action which would most certainly result in bitter civil war, persuaded Mihailov to leave Skopje after several days of conferences with his political friends. Many of the younger Macedonian patriots, particularly those of the intelligentsia who might well have followed him earlier in the war, were now eagerly scrambling for positions in the burgeoning Communist regime. As the CPM continued to stress locally popular aspects of cultural and political freedom, more and more of the formerly indecisive elements answered the party's appeals to "lead in the building of new Macedonia."

By mid-November 1944 the Germans were completely dislodged from Macedonia and organs of "People's Power" established on all levels of administration in Yugoslav Macedonia. The pattern of Party retribution used elsewhere in the country was followed, with large-scale purges of elements hostile to the CPY. There was stepped-up mobilization of men to take part in the fighting in the north. (It was not until May 10, 1945, that all of Yugoslavia was liberated.) The Macedonian recruits were subjected to rigorous Party indoctrination and were dispersed in various units, rather than organized in special Macedonian outfits. While the Party convinced a limited number of Macedonians that it had their interests at heart, it simultaneously spread a strong net of power throughout the region. As the probabilities of being entangled by this net increased, additional Macedonians found it expedient to go along with Tito's proposition and, at last, there seemed to be no space at all between the meshes. The CPY's solution was no longer a likely alternative; it was at hand. The Party intended, with the postwar implementation of its nationality-federalism line, to render the next generation more amenable, but it realized that it would be necessary to keep the vexatious Macedonians on short tether for a considerable time.

In retrospect, it must be acknowledged that the CPY played its cards with consummate skill in Vardar Macedonia. The arousing of resistance activities there, and the conversion of those activities into a thorough-going revolution, were probably fraught with more obstacles than was the case elsewhere in Yugoslavia. Even to those fully aware of the potentialities of tiny Communist revolutionary groups, it appears somewhat incredible that a political party having but 300 members in 1940, with 400 additional young cohorts in SKOJ, should have been the instrument by which control over a hostile people was gained and through which that people's "nationality" was recognized. This accomplishment was even more surprising in that of those 700 prewar supporters almost none followed the CPY line on Macedonia during the first two years of the war.

From the foundation of the CPY in 1919 until 1943 the Party had less success in Macedonia than any other of the contending groups there, vastly less than the pro-Bulgarian elements. The evolution of the CPY approach to the Macedonian problem, a hesitant but real evolution from the "Great Serb" position of Sima Marković to the final recognition of a Macedonian nationality, was the key element to its success. The Yugoslav Communists' contention that their program coincided with the aspirations of most Macedonians at the end of the Second World War is not persuasive. However, after more than twenty years of frustration, the CPY did enlist the active support of some Macedonians and, more importantly, managed to exploit the passivity of most of the others. In both of these accomplishments the CPY was given crucial assistance by the inflexibility of the traditional Serbian Bulgarian, and Greek approaches.

The Communists also were able to strengthen the suspicion that the IMRO's program did not differ essentially from that of the Bulgarian Foreign Ministry. The semi-internment of the colorful Mihailov may have contributed much to the IMRO's failure during the war. Yet his lieutenants in the field apparently did not attempt to activate popular support during the Bulgarian occupation. Assuming Mihailov favored autonomy and welcomed the occupation as the first step in that direction, his early lack of clarity and decisiveness, unavoidable as it may have been, contributed to the serious diminution of his popularity in the backwash of reaction against Sofia's occupation policies. Regardless of how much appeal the legendary IMRO may have had, its dormancy and its subservience towards the Bulgarians in the early stages of the war played into the hands of its Communist opponents.

There was no evidence of evolution in the Macedonian policies of the Serbian and Bulgarian nationalists. They consistently aimed at the integration and forced assimilation of the Macedonian Slavs with their respective nations, thus creating the atmosphere for the fermentation of Macedonian nationalism. There is no surer way to awaken and foster the national consciousness of an essentially anational people than to deny them the right to maintain cherished differences (e.g., dialect or language) and to refuse them basic elements of equality (e.g., proportionate power in administration). Belgrade's interwar economic and social policies also contributed much to Macedonian resentment. These policies, including unfavorable exchange of currency after World War I, Serbian colonization, heavy taxes without compensatory state investment in Macedonia, in addition to all the denationalizing measures, were counterproductive.

There was never any indication that the Serbs might consider for Macedonia an arrangement along the lines of the 1939 *Sporazum* with Croatia. That they would not allow to Macedonia what they belatedly allowed to Croatia was simply a matter of power; they were able forcibly to control the weaker Macedonians. During the war and revolution the exiled Government of Yugoslavia, including its representative Mihajlović, was unable to cast aside the stultifying mantle of intense Serbism. There is little doubt that Macedonian resistance to inclusion in Tito's Yugoslavia was much less violent than resistance to a reversion to their pre-war status would have been.

The Bulgarians dissipated their reservoir of good will in Macedonia by their unbending, nationalistic occupation. Their inability to attune their approach to a dynamic situation was confirmed by their static insistence on recovering their San Stefano Treaty boundaries. The Bulgarian nationalists could not bring themselves to admit that Macedonians might have other aspirations than that of being absorbed, as "pure Bulgarians" into the Bulgarian state. The Bulgarian Communists dawdled, as had the Serbian Communists before Tito's rise, and did not make the adjustment until it was too late for them.

Perhaps it is not too quaintly Wilsonian to observe that the democratic powers, unlike the Communists, for the most part neglected to appraise the Macedonian problem accurately, or on time, or from the point of view of the Macedonian people, and thus excluded themselves from the possibility of constructive action. Macedonia became "the Macedonian Question" in 1876. Since then, outside powers have treated it as a pawn in their power struggles, siding with their favorite contenders, or, of having no direct interest, treating the whole matter as a colorful curiosity. Although some dispassionate observers of Balkan affairs in the interwar period did make known the extent to which Macedonians were outraged at Belgrade's treatment, there is no evidence that the democratic powers endeavored by diplomatic devices to modify the implementation of the Great Serb concept.

It was left to the CPY to treat the problem outside of the framework of the conflicting traditional approaches and to generate the power to apply its treatment to at least a part of the patient. As we have seen, the greatest single factor in the CPY's success in Vardar Macedonia was its adjustment to the evolving situation, its moving as far as necessary in the direction of recognizing, and exploiting, and frequently stimulating Macedonian national aspirations. Theoretically and practically the Party accepted the thesis that a Macedonian nation did exist. Through its actual (and theoretical) engagement in the liberation-revolutionary struggle, that nation had acquired the right to self-determination as defined by the Party. The symbols of nationality were fruitfully employed and amplified. In offering this gift of national recognition, the CPY made its acceptance contingent on the Macedonians' "willingness" to be included in a new Yugoslavia. Therefore, while it became heretical for any Yugoslav to deny Macedonian nationality, it was a punishable heresy for any Macedonian in Yugoslavia to treat the new nation outside the framework of the new Yugoslavia.

CHAPTER 7
CONTINUING INTEREST IN
AEGEAN AND PIRIN MACEDONIA

The Macedonian policy adopted by the CPY had a twofold purpose. First, it was a means to gain control over the area and keep it within the new Communist Yugoslavia. Before the CPY's policy of recognizing a Macedonian nationality, there were only two possibilities: the Slavs of Macedonia were Bulgarians or Serbs. If the CPY declared the Slavs of Macedonia to be Bulgarians, and the vast majority before World War II considered themselves to be more Bulgarian than anything else, there could be no justification for keeping the Macedonians within the Yugoslav federation; the Bulgarians should be united with their co-nationals in a Bulgarian state. But if the CPY declared the Slavs of Macedonia to be Serbs they would revive all the old anti-Serb resentment produced by two and a half decades of Serbization and have difficulty in establishing control in Macedonia. Recognizing the Macedonians as a separate nationality was ideally suited to the CPY's domestic aims—the Slavs of Macedonia were not Bulgarians, hence the invalidity of any Bulgarian claim to Vardar Macedonia; they were not Serbs, hence no revival of resentment against Serbs. As a separate Slav nation, the Macedonians were rightfully joined with their brother Slav nations (Serbs, Croats, Slovenes, and Montenegrins) in the Yugoslav federation.

The second aim of the CPY's Macedonian policy was to expand the hegemony of the Yugoslav Communists. Tito's postwar aims were not modest. He requested and sought to secure through military occupation Venezia Julia including Trieste from Italy, almost half of the Austrian province of Carinthia, inclusion of Albania in the Yugoslav federation, and the Greek and Bulgarian portions of Macedonia. Since the Macedonian Slavs were now a nationality, the Macedonians in Pirin and Aegean Macedonia should, it followed, be united with their more numerous Yugoslav Macedonian brothers and become part of the Macedonian Republic in the Yugoslav federal state. The Bulgarians had long been the sponsors of Macedonian unification; now the Yugoslavs seized the initiative and became the patron saint of unification. The Yugoslav's new Macedonian policy gave them the ideal tool to use in achieving this end. Playing up Macedonian cultural distinctiveness would certainly appeal to the Slavs of Aegean Macedonia who had been subject to Hellenization. The Bulgarian Macedonians—recognizing that Bulgaria was on the losing side in another war and seeing the increased prestige of Tito's new Yugoslavia—would realize that currently Macedonian unification was possible only under Yugoslav egis.

The drive for Macedonian unification was begun by the Yugoslav partisan leaders during the war, even before they had secured control of Vardar Macedonia. The chaotic, fluid conditions that prevailed in the Balkans following the Axis withdrawal gave impetus to the movement. During the months of final consolidation of CPY power in Vardar Macedonia, Tito endeavored to press his advantage in Bulgarian Macedonia, but for a combination of reasons, he was cautious for a while with regard to intervention in the Greek situation. Relations with the Greek Communists had become tense. In May 1944 what was left of the Axis-oriented Slav gendarmerie in northwestern Greece had jointed Goči's SNOF units. A quarrel ensued between ELAS headquarters and Goči about the disposition of the Gendarmes' weapons. Meanwhile, the CPY had its own agents and small detachments scurrying about northern Greece. The KKE was extremely upset about Yugoslav dalliance with the issue most dangerous to the Greek Communists—the unification of Macedonia. In June 1944 Macedonian partisan headquarters issued new instructions to the political agitators and CPY military units in Greek Macedonia. Warning that unfortunate "mistakes on the question of Macedonia" must not disturb the fraternal relations with ELAS, the instructions nevertheless reminded the agents that "the national freedom and equality acquired [by the Yugoslav Macedonians] is the ideal of the entire Macedonian people . . . also those in Greece and Bulgaria."[1]

In early August Tempo and Radosavljević sent the Greek communists a radiogram urging the creation of a joint commission to control the quarrels between "our bands and the Greek partisans in the Kostur-Larin [Kastoria-Florina] region."[2] The controversy arose, according to the Yugoslavs, because the Greek partisans had begun forced mobilization of the Slavs. It was the CPY contention that the Macedonian minority wanted to fight the Germans, but only in "their own brigade." The Greeks had refused this request and were "repressing" the Slavs. The CPY complaint continued:

> There began a mass extermination of the Macedonians living in these regions and they fled to Bitolj, where men of Vančo Mihailov received them and organized them into military units to fight against the Greeks . . . . Radosavljević made the correct decision to take these emigrants and form them into units to take action in the Bitolj-Larin sector. In carrying out these directives some of our leaders overstepped the line and started propaganda

to the effect that every Macedonian could enter our army, . . . then there began a mass crossing over of Macedonians from Greece into our Army. The Greek partisans reacted with terrible reprisals on the Macedonian population . . . . Furthermore, they are arresting all the Macedonians who are with the Greek partisans . . . and are interning them in southern Greece. All of our propaganda material is proclaimed illegal. In a discussion which Radosavljević had with one member of the CC KKE for Macedonia, "Steve," he was told that it would be better if all Macedonians fled to the Germans, rather than to our military units . . . . We thought that the Greeks should demand the formation of one such [Greek Macedonian] brigade, if not, we ourselves shall start to form one. In that case, we shall inevitably come into controversy with the Greeks. [3]

In October the dispute between the Greek Communists and Goči came to a head. Faced with the deployment of ELAS forces before the positions of his SNOF units, Goči fled across the border into Yugoslavia with 800 men.[4] He and his band were treated with the same suspicion by Tito's men as were any other pro-autonomy Macedonians. The Goči group was put in semi-internment for several months, to be drawn on the following year for CPY inspired operations in Greek Macedonia.[5]

Gradually CPY concern over Greek Macedonia waned. The party-controlled press, apart from a November 1944 attack on Papandreau's government for "terrorizing the Macedonians," and a bitter editorial in *Politika* in late December, did not take the initiative vis-à-vis the Greek imbroglio for several months. A number of factors lay behind the CPY's change of pace. Tito, being in close touch with Moscow, may have concluded that it was more important for the Greek Communists to come to power than that he should win Aegean Macedonia at that time. Also, the only effective Greek Macedonian fighting units were strongly inclined towards autonomy, and Tito was limited somewhat by the existence of the rival government of Ivan Subasić which still had some backing from the western powers. Caution was still in order. Only when these conditions no longer fully applied was the CPY to reactivate its concern over Greek Macedonia.

With the seizure of power in Bulgaria by the Fatherland Front under Kimon Georgiev on September 9, 1944, the Bulgarian Army was ordered to change sides and join with the Yugoslav partisans against the Germans.[6] Not all the Bulgarian units in Macedonia accepted this order. According to the Yugoslavs, some officers of the Fifth Bulgarian Occupation Army, comprising four divisions, refused to have any contact with the partisans. They arrested partisans sent to negotiate the terms of cooperation. Some units surrendered their arms to the Germans. The officers of the 29th Division returned to Bulgaria for a "counterrevolution."[7] On the other hand, Macedonian leaders recruited volunteers in Sofia who marched off to help liberate Macedonia. Meanwhile, the Yugoslavs attempted to gain control of Pirin Macedonia militarily. The Pirin Macedonians apparently gave some support; they seized weapons from a divisional depot and formed a Macedonian brigade, no doubt under the guidance of Yugoslav operatives.[8] The Fatherland Front's communication media continued to ignore the ASNOM decisions of August.

Sometime during the first half of September 1944, Tempo and Koliševski went to Sofia for a CC CPB meeting to exchange opinions about Macedonia. The Yugoslavs claimed the Bulgarians accepted criticism and promised to correct their stand. The Bulgarians agreed to give the Pirin Macedonians administrative as well as cultural autonomy, while the Yugoslavs went along with the proviso that the unification of Pirin with Yugoslav Macedonia would not be taken as an "action slogan" and would be postponed until "conditions were right for it." It was also made clear, according to Tempo and Koliševski, that the question of the unification of Macedonia should not be linked to the question of the formation of "a close union between Yugoslavia and Bulgaria." A provincial National-Liberation Committee for Pirin was to be formed at Gorna Dzhumaya (Blagoevgrad), all "fascists" were to be removed from the Bulgarian Army, and the Yugoslavs were to be allowed to send Macedonian newspapers and other propaganda material into the Pirin region. Koliševski made it clear that these steps were to prepare Pirin Macedonia "for union with the Macedonian democratic federal state of Tito's new Yugoslavia."[9]

The Yugoslavs were later to complain that these "common conclusions" of September 1944 were very quickly "forgotten" by the CC CPB. At a Regional Party Conference for Pirin in Gorna Dzhumaya, the Bulgarian Macedonian Communist Poptomov, who had been on the AVNOJ Council in 1943, was reputed to have given "a serious warning concerning the intention to incorporate Pirin Macedonia" in Yugoslavia. Ljubčo Arsov of the CC CPM, who was present, protested.[10] In a letter to the CC CPM, Arsov and Vera Aceva claimed Poptomov had held that the Macedonian question could be solved only by the strengthening of the progressive forces in all Balkan countries. He said the conditions for uniting Greek Macedonia with the other two parts were not favorable, for there was mass emigration from that region and the "physiognomy of Greece is still not clear." This probably was a delaying tactic, for the CPY-CPB negotiations on Macedonia apparently had not made the resolution of the Pirin problem contingent upon what happened in Aegean Macedonia. Poptomov was also quoted as asking, "Why should the Gorna Dzumaia region unite with Macedonia in Yugoslavia, why not vice versa and have the Tsaribrod and Bosiligrad districts [taken from Bulgaria by the Treaty of Neuilly after World War I] returned to us?" He claimed that the question of Pirin Macedonia's detachment from Bulgaria was not an "actual" one among the people there, that the Bulgarian people were not yet ready for such a move and that the Macedonian question was closely tied to the projected Yugoslav-Bulgarian union. A further insult to the CPY was Poptomov's contention that, while Bulgaria was safely under the influence of the Russians, no one knew who would predominate in Yugoslavia; might it not be the British? [11]

The Yugoslavs were especially sensitive to the barrage of Bulgarian press and radio propaganda giving "undue" prominence to the liberating activities of the Bulgarian units in Macedonia. Actually, the Bulgarian forces were better armed and organized than the Yugoslav Macedonian partisans and some of them were quite successful against the Germans. The CPY claimed the Bulgarians took credit for the "glorious feats" of liberating Skopje and other cities "into which Bulgarian troops did not come or came only after they were liberated by units of the National-Liberation Army of Macedonia." [12] Also the Bulgarians were accused of treating Macedonia as an "independent" state, separate from Yugoslavia. [13] In October, Tempo wrote a sharply worded letter to Kiro Miljovski, the Yugoslav Macedonian representative to the CC CPB, protesting:

> Still another question must be put before the Bulgarian Party, the question of their references to our Army. In their radio propaganda they say: "Our National Army is fighting shoulder to shoulder with the glorious Red Army, the National-Liberation Army of the legendary Marshal Tito and the Macedonian Partisans and Brigades." If they still have not realized that the Macedonian Partisans and Brigades are in the composition of the National-Liberation Army of the legendary Marshal Tito, it is necessary to tell them that again. Furthermore, they should be told that our units are called the *"Macedonian Units of the National-Liberation Army of Yugoslavia."*

The Bulgarian Communists were aware of the post-occupation disillusionment among the Yugoslav Macedonians on the question of union with Bulgaria and also of the prestige of Marshal Tito with the Western Powers and with Stalin for his partisan exploits. The unification of Macedonia under Bulgaria was a futile hope. Hence, they opposed its becoming a part of Yugoslavia and advocated an autonomous Macedonia which could perhaps later be united with Bulgaria.

Following Tempo's blast the CC CPB on November 2 allegedly sent Tito a mollifying letter, signed by the ill-fated Traičo Kostov. The "enormous service" of the Yugoslavs against the "Hitlerite hordes in the Balkans" was acknowledged. "Our people are conscious of the great guilt which they have with regard to the Yugoslavs and especially the Serbian and Macedonian people," apologized Kostov. The Bulgarians' ostensible retreat on the Macedonian issue continued:

> Especially in connection with the creation of a Macedonian free state in the framework of new, federative Yugoslavia, which represents the first decisive step toward the realization of the Macedonian ideal of free, united Macedonia, we give you assurance that our party and our people acclaim the new Macedonian state most warmly. We shall work for its popularization . . . . especially among the inhabitants of the Bulgarian part of Macedonia. We shall help in the work for the awakening of Macedonian national consciousness among this population, utilizing the heroic past and present of the Macedonian people, . . . publishing Macedonian newspapers, etc. . . . We shall develop wide agitation . . . for the most painless realization of the Macedonian ideal of free, united Macedonia in the framework of new Yugoslavia.[15]

Although the BCP officially acknowledged the existence of a Macedonian nationality and declared support for a Macedonia united under Yugoslavia, there was strong opposition, even from some leading Bulgarian party members, to this policy. However, despite approval of the Yugoslav plans for Macedonian unification, the Bulgarians retained firm control of party and government organs in Pirin Macedonia.

Federation of Balkan peoples had long been a goal of socialists and later Communists of the Balkan Peninsula. With Communist dominance in both Bulgaria and Yugoslavia, the time appeared to be propitious for the creation of such a federation. In December 1944 Edvard Kardelj went to Sofia to win Bulgarian approval for the CPY plan for a Bulgarian-Yugoslav federation. Although Tempo and Koliševski stated in their letter from Sofia earlier that fall that the question of Macedonian unification was not to be tied to a Bulgarian-Yugoslav union, once talks on federation were underway the question of Macedonia became enmeshed in the question of federation.

In discussions with Kardelj, the Bulgarians favored a defense pact between the two countries. After the pact had been concluded a joint commission would draw up plans for union. Calling this proposal inadequate, Kardelj proposed immediate movement toward federation, including a meeting of representatives of all the Yugoslav republics with the Bulgarians. The disagreement over the make-up of a commission to draw up plans for federation was the first evidence of the conflicting Bulgarian-Yugoslav views which later hampered federation agreement. The Yugoslav proposal called for Bulgaria to become the seventh republic in the Yugoslav federation. The Bulgarians on the other hand favored a federation between the two countries as equals. A Bulgarian proposal which was sent to the Yugoslavs in January 1945 called for a South Slav Federation with common ministries and a common national assembly. The transition to full federation would be carried out by a temporary executive body composed of equal numbers of Yugoslavs and Bulgarians. The Yugoslav counterproposal called for the formation of a commission composed of representatives of the seven federal units to draw up a constitution. Yugoslav accounts maintain that Stalin favored the Yugoslav proposal to include Bulgaria as one of several republics.[16]

After the failure of Kardelj's mission to Sofia in January 1945, both parties sought to revitalize the stalemated negotiations by appealing to Moscow. Pijade presented the Yugoslav case and Dimitrov, accompanied by other Bulgarian communist leaders, presented the Bulgarian position to the Soviet Leaders. However, Britain at that time had expressed opposition to any federal arrangement and Stalin declared that the time was not propitious for any change in the status quo. The CPY temporarily dropped its efforts to annex Pirin Macedonia and concentrated on consolidating its own position in the MPR.

The Bulgarian government continued to support Yugoslav efforts to create the MPR as the Macedonian national homeland. The old-line Macedonian irredentist organizations were abolished in Bulgaria and a number of vehement Macedonian irredentists were moved to other parts of the country.[17] Dimitrov, according to a Yugoslav account, indicated that the CPB did not have a closed mind on the Pirin question. He was quoted as having told the National Assembly on December 6, 1945, that the solution was "not the division of Macedonia, not a struggle for rule over it, but respect for the will of its people, the largest segment of whom have obtained freedom and equality in the framework of the FPRY."[18] Delegates from the Pirin region to the January Plenum of the CC CPB claimed that seventy percent of the people there had declared themselves to be Macedonian.[19] Vulko Červenkov, however, replied that talk about the unification of Macedonia would damage the Fatherland Front, the non-Communist elements of which were decisively against any move which would result in the loss of Bulgarian territory. They were joined by a number of party leaders from Pirin Macedonia itself, notably Vladimir Poptomov and Dimitar Ganev. The latter expressed his doubts about Yugoslavia's future on the basis of dangers from the CPY's "adventuristic policies on the Trieste question."[20]

On Ilinden (August 2) 1946, Koliševski voiced continued CPY interest in Bulgarian Macedonia. He characterized it as a Yugoslav-Bulgarian, not a great power, problem. In an extra-ordinary statement, he told the First Congress of the People's Front ot Macedonia:

> The strivings of *our* people from Pirin Macedonia for union with the MPR are a clear fact. . . . We are convinced that the responsible factors . . . will make it possible for *our* people in Pirin Macedonia to have those conditions for free national development which the Bulgarian national minority enjoys in Yugoslavia. To raise the question of the union of Macedonia outside the borders of Yugoslavia means common provocation, and is against the independence and interests of the Macedonian people. [21]

The CPB made a quick response. Four days later at its Tenth Plenum it was resolved that work for the unification of the remaining parts of Macedonia should include cultural rapprochement between the Pirin region and the MPR, but that unification must be achieved on the basis of a treaty of alliance, defining the exact borders of Bulgarian Macedonia. The CPB insisted that the population of Pirin should have the right to·opt for Bulgarian citizenship and that there be no customs barrier between Macedonia and Bulgaria. [22] The resolution was not released to the public.

The Bulgarian party was in an awkward position. The Yugoslavs were again insisting upon Macedonian unification. Negotiations for the peace treaties were underway in Paris, and Bulgaria was anxious to have Yugoslav support for its position there. Hence there was a desire to avoid any action which might antagonize Belgrade. At the same time the Bulgarian leaders were facing strong opposition both within and outside the party to surrendering Macedonian territory to Yugoslavia. The BCP CC passed a resolution agreeing to eventual Macedonian unification as desired by the' Yugoslavs, but did not make it public until much later. In the Pirin district itself, the party followed the same kind of policy. Government and party organs were kept firmly under Bulgarian control, but at the same time the Pirin district was being culturally Macedonianized by Yugoslav Macedonians.

Macedonian unification was a major issue at the Bled Conference between Tito and Dimitrov in July 1947. The communique on the meeting indicated that the two government had signed a series of agreements which provided for close economic cooperation, the eventual establishment of a customs union, mutual assistance for action against "frequent frontier provocations of the Greek Monarchist-Fascists." [23] The statement did not mention federation and Dimitrov unequivocally declared that "a federation of South Slavs or a Balkan Federation . . . was not the subject of talks at the conference." [24] However, after the Cominform expelled the CPY, a resolution of the BCP Central Committee and Dimitrov himself clearly stated that the two governments "had agreed on a series of measures regarding the forthcoming establishment of federation."[25]

At the Bled talks, Dimitrov insisted that the unification of Macedonia would only be achieved on the basis of federation. He also indicated that it had been agreed that Bulgaria would be compensated for the loss of the Pirin region:

> Within the framework of such a [South Slav] federation would have been solved correctly, all the old unsolved problems legated by the bourgeois-monarchic regimes regarding the unification of the Macedonians from the Pirin district with the People's Republic of Macedonia, as well as the return to Bulgaria of the purely Bulgarian Western Border Region the Yugoslavia of King Aleksandar had grabbed after World War I.[26]

It has also been suggested that the Bled agreements involved the Greek Communists and that Yugoslavia was to receive Aegean Macedonia in addition to Bulgarian Macedonia. Bulgaria was to be compensated for the loss of the Pirin district by receiving Western Thrace. In return for loss of its territory, the Greek Communists would receive extensive Bulgarian and Yugoslav support in the guerrilla struggle against the Royal Greek government.[27] Although there is no documentary evidence to support this point of view, it is consistent with Yugoslav ambitions at that time. The Greek party in public statements prior to the agreement strongly opposed any such transfer of territory,[28] hence the question remains open. Despite numerous post-1948 revelations about other aspects of Bulgarian-Yugoslav relations during this period, neither Bulgaria nor Yugoslavia has disclosed any detailed information on this aspect of the Bled negotiations.

Although no agreement was reached at Bled on the immediate transfer of Pirin Macedonia, Tito did receive Bulgarian approval for Yugoslav Macedonian cultural workers to enter the Pirin region. The CPY published a newspaper, *Pirinski Vesnik,* for Bulgarian Macedonians. The Bulgarian Assembly passed a law calling for the teaching of the Macedonian language and Macedonian history in the Pirin region's schools. Many teachers from Yugoslav Macedonia were allowed to enter Bulgaria.[29] In November 1947 Tito visited Bulgaria and signed a Bulgarian-Yugoslav treaty pledging consultation, mutual military support, economic cooperation and the creation of a customs union. Despite this apparent agreement at top government-party levels, problems developed between the Yugoslav cultural workers and the party officials and population of the Pirin district.[30]

The BCP insisted upon federation before relinquishing its hold on Pirin Macedonia. No Bulgarian government would give up its part of Macedonia to a foreign country. Unification of Macedonia could take place only within a federation to which Bulgaria belonged. However, the Soviet Union now announced its opposition to the establishment of any South Slav federation. In response to a statement of Dimitrov in Bucharest suggesting customs unions for all countries of the Soviet bloc, *Pravda* editorially denounced federation: "What these countries need is not a problematical and artificial federation, confederation or customs union, but the consolidation and defense of their independence and sovereignty."[31] But as differences between the Yugoslav and Soviet Party leaders became more pronounced, Stalin reversed his opinion and attempted to force a Bulgarian-Yugoslav federation in February 1948 in order to subvert the CPY.[32] The Yugoslavs refused to follow Stalin's instructions. In this confused situation the First Congress of the Bulgarian Fatherland Front in February 1948 avoided the Macedonian question, but a party conference of Pirin Macedonians held at the end of April in Blagoevgrad took a hostile stand toward Yugoslavia's Macedonian initiatives. The Yugoslav break with Moscow came when the CPY was expelled from the Cominform on June 28, 1948.

After the Cominform resolution, the Bulgarian party directed a vicious attack against the Yugoslavs and took immediate steps to eliminate Yugoslav influence in Pirin Macedonia. The Sixteenth Plenum of the BCP CC on July 12, 1948, declared that:

> the federation of South Slavs and the eventual annexation of the Pirin region to the Macedonian People's Republic are possible only on the supposition that Yugoslavia remains faithful to the common front of socialism [i.e., the Cominform].

The Macedonian cultural workers from Yugoslavia were expelled from the Pirin region; "compulsory" instruction in the Macedonian language and "compulsory" subscriptions to Macedonian newspapers were stopped.[33] Though strongly opposing Yugoslav annexation of its portion of Macedonia, the Bulgarian party continued to recognize the Macedonian nationality and advocate the unification of Macedonia. Dimitrov told the Fifth BCP Congress in December 1948, "Our party has always advocated and continues to advocate that Macedonia belongs to the Macedonians." But he added that national unity is possible "only within the framework of a federation of South Slavs."[34] Both countries set up organizations of Macedonian refugees from the opposite country and from Greek Macedonia. There were frequent trials of alleged provocateurs. Bitter polemical editorials were frequent on both sides. Much of the testimony at the Traičo Kostov trial in December 1949 related to his and the other defendants alleged conspiracy to detach Pirin Macedonia from Bulgaria.[35] After the Cominform break the Bulgarians talked vaguely and infrequently about a united Macedonia in a Balken federation. But Sofia propaganda concentrated on one of the sore spots of the Macedonian question, charging that the new Macedonian language and other CPY changes were directed solely towards the Serbiazation of the MPR.

After the Cominform break with Yugoslavia in 1948 Bulgaria and the USSR utilized the Macedonian issue with the intention of weakening Tito. Their hope was that the Yugoslav party would split and that a pro-Cominform group could seize power. With traditionally strong Bulgarian sentiment, the propaganda from Sofia was calculated to encourage pro-Cominform feeling in the MPR. It was the opinion of some pro-Bulgarian emigre observers that many of the Macedonian communists secretly became Cominformists because of renewed anti-Serbism.[36] While this suggestion is a bit strained, there were some defections to the Cominform in Macedonia. Although the top party leadership remained firmly pro-Tito, Remzi Ismail, the Turk heading the Macedonian republic trade union organization, and several of his Macedonian associates in the union organization were removed for pro-Cominform sympathies.[37] In addressing the Sixth Plenum of the CC CPM in July 1952, Organizational Secretary Krste Crvenkovski admitted defections to the Cominform stating that the CPM was strengthened and made monolithic by the expulsion of "scum, who for personal reasons" supported the Cominform resolution.[38] The attraction of the mother Soviet Party to staunch Communists and the still-strong Bulgarian sentiment presented a challenge to the Macedonian party. However, expulsions from the party for Cominform sympathies in Macedonia were the lowest among the Yugoslav republics.[39] The relatively young men and women in the ranks of the CPM were painstakingly selected, trained and tested by the party. The older, pro-Bulgarian leaders had already been excluded from leading positions with the exception of Andrejev, who in the crucial days of the break first sided with Tito but was later purged for Cominformism. Another party element which tended to be Cominformist elsewhere in Yugoslavia—leading partisan warriors who had not been rewarded to their satisfaction—was generally lacking in the Macedonian organization. Also, staunch Bulgarian adherence to the Cominform and to the Soviet type of Communism greatly cooled Macedonian sympathies for Bulgaria.

The Cominform break not only ended all prospect of Pirin annexation, it also effectively halted Yugoslav progress in Aegean Macedonia. Until the Communists had gained full control in Belgrade and were strong enough in Macedonia to deal with autonomist leaning Macedonian units in Greece, the CPY had been cautious in pressing for the annexation of Aegean Macedonia. However, once the CPY was firmly in power, the question of unification of Aegean Macedonia was revived. In mid-1945 Yugoslav articles lamented the "unbearable situation" of the Macedonians in Greece, beset by "the terror of Greek chauvinists" who were said to be preparing "orgies of

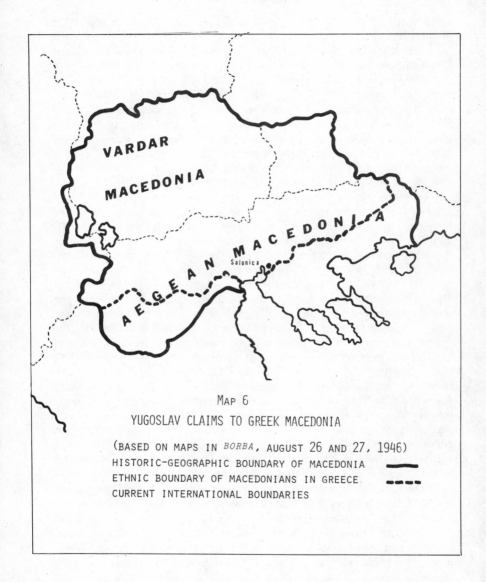

MAP 6

YUGOSLAV CLAIMS TO GREEK MACEDONIA

(BASED ON MAPS IN *BORBA*, AUGUST 26 AND 27, 1946)
HISTORIC-GEOGRAPHIC BOUNDARY OF MACEDONIA   ━━━━
ETHNIC BOUNDARY OF MACEDONIANS IN GREECE   ━━━━
CURRENT INTERNATIONAL BOUNDARIES

extreme fury."[40] Tito, speaking in Skopje in October, averred that Yugoslavia would never deny the right of the Macedonian people to unite.[41] The KKE naturally did its best to play the Macedonian issue down. In the early spring of 1946 Nikos Zahariades, the Party's Secretary General, visited Belgrade and Prague, in preparation for the next phase of the Greek civil war. As the Greek Communists were readying themselves, the CPY contributed to the clarity of its aims by having *Borba* come out with a front page map of Aegean Macedonia, showing an "ethnic boundary" of Macedonia which included Salonika and a sizeable part of Northern Greece. In the accompanying article, the fate of "significantly more than 250,000 Macedonians in Greece" was decried. "Greek reactionary circles had decided to exterminate them." The Greek Macedonians had fought in Greek partisan units for their liberation, the article continued, and they deserved the right to self-determination and to unite with their comrades in the MPR. The article ended with the threat that Yugoslavia "could not remain indifferent towards the annihilation of our inhabitants in Greece."[42]

When the Greek civil war began again, the CPY did not publicly push the Macedonian issue as vigorously in order to avoid complicating the KKE's domestic political position. However, the Yugoslavs continued working quietly to increase their influence among the Slavs in Greek Macedonia. They used a guerrilla training camp established in Yugoslav territory to elicit support among Greek slavs for a union of Greek Macedonia with the MPR.[43] Tito was willing to go all out short of general war to assist the aggressive Greek guerrilla leader Markos Vafiades. Yugoslavia was in a far better position to offer material assistance than were Bulgaria and Albania since the Greek guerrillas were based in the mountainous area contingent to Yugoslavia. Markos became beholden to Tito and apparently gave the CPY the right to send organizers into Greek Macedonia. The SNOF, renamed NOF, swung into action again in early 1947. The NOF professed that its purpose was to secure Macedonian national rights within a communist Greece. However, the strong Yugoslav influence through instructors and "volunteers" from the MPR as well as its propagation of the Macedonian language, establishment of schools, and frequent demands for greater autonomy to the Slavic Macedonians indicate that the NOF was used to further Yugoslav expansionist ambitions.[44]

The expulsion of Yugoslavia from the Cominform ended Yugoslav action aimed at securing Aegean Macedonia. Although the CPY continued to support Markos for over six months after the Cominform break, there was a serious struggle going on inside the KKE between pro-Yugoslav and pro-Cominform factions.[45] The pro-Cominform group finally gained the upper hand. Markos was relieved of his duties and expelled from the party by the Fifth Plenum of the Greek CC in late January 1949. The CC promised the Greek Macedonians "full self-determination" but warned them of the destructive actions which were being developed by "opportunistic and reactionary elements, moved by foreigners, which aim at breaking the units of the Macedonian, Slavo-Macedonian, and Greek people."[46] The reorganized NOF tried a Macedonian policy similar to the one used by Bulgaria and the Cominform calling for the union of Macedonia as an independent equal state in a federation of Balkan peoples. Greek reaction to the statement was so uniformly and strongly adverse that the NOF had to deny putting up its united-Macedonian trial balloon.[47]

Yugoslavia closed its borders to the Greek guerrillas in late July 1949, thereby contributing much to their final defeat. But Koliševski invited the Aegean Macedonians to make the MPR their rallying ground for achieving their national aims.[48] Yugoslav involvement in the Greek revolution had been so extensive that the CPY felt compelled to offer detailed analyses for the revolution's failure. The general conclusion was that the KKE failed because it did not recognize unequivocally the Macedonian nationality and it had been too cautious in military action, particularly after Markos had been removed "under a lying excuse."[49]

The CPY has never renounced its goal of a united Macedonia, although propaganda on the Macedonian question has shifted its emphasis from national self-determination and unification of all Macedonians within the Yugoslav federation to recognition of the Macedonian nationality and granting it minority rights. Yugoslav insistence on recognition of the Macedonians as a separate nationality implies they have not abandoned their ambitions. The Bulgarians, who have refused to recognize the Macedonian nationality since 1956, interpret Yugoslav demands for minority rights for the inhabitants of the Pirin region as a territorial claim by Yugoslavia.

The CPY Policy of recognizing a Macedonian nationality not only aided in establishing Communist dominance of Vardar Macedonia, it also proved to be a most useful tool in the Yugoslav plans for hegemony over all of Macedonia. The failure of the Yugoslavs to secure Pirin and Aegean Macedonia was not due to any lack of effectiveness of their Macedonian policy nor to their vigor in pursuing this aim. The movement which began during the war continued well after the boundaries and the political situation had become relatively stable. The momentum of the Yugoslav drive was only checked by the Cominform resolution which heaped on Belgrade the hostility of the entire Soviet bloc, fragmented the Greek communist movement, and forced Yugoslavia to concentrate on strengthening itself internally in fear of a possible Soviet-led attack.

PART III
MACEDONIAN NATIONALISM UNDER
YUGOSLAV COMMUNISM

CHAPTER 8
POLITICAL AND ECONOMIC IMPACT
OF YUGOSLAV FEDERALISM

The CPY's policy of recognizing a separate Macedonian nationality has profoundly effected the Macedonian question since World War II. The unification of Macedonia within Yugoslavia was not accomplished, but the CPY's policy was not at fault. Recognition of the Macedonian nationality did aid the Yugoslav Communists in their bid for power in Vardar Macedonia. Although neither Greece nor Bulgaria recognizes a separate Macedonian nationality, the Yugoslav Communists still follow essentially that policy which evolved on the Macedonian question during the interwar years and the partisan struggle. This policy has had a significant impact on the internal affairs of the Macedonian republic and upon Yugoslav foreign policy in relations with other Balkan states.

It is often difficult to distinguish between the Macedonian policy which the CPY wanted to apply and that which residual Bulgarophilism and separatism, Cominform pressure, and the Yugoslav nationalities problem in general, have impelled the party to apply. Similarly, it is difficult to discern which elements of opposition to the regimes in Skopje and Belgrade stem largely from Macedonian national dissatisfaction and those which spring from anti-Communism or from difficult living conditions imposed during the period of transition from a subsistence to an industrial economy. The CPY recognition of a distinct Macedonian nationality with a right to its own party organization and its own federal republic has revolutionized the Macedonian question. The actual power exercized by Skopje in vital matters is modest when compared to that wielded by Belgrade, and the Macedonian leadership does not stray from the guidelines set by Belgrade. Nevertheless, Macedonia exists as a political unit.

During the latter phases of the war period most of the leading Communists and many non-Communist people in Yugoslav Macedonia, although wary of accepting CPM promises at face value, tempered their opposition and participated in the Communist campaign. There were no real alternatives to Tito, but the establishment of Macedonian state and party organs on the republic and local levels made it easier to accept a Yugoslav Com-

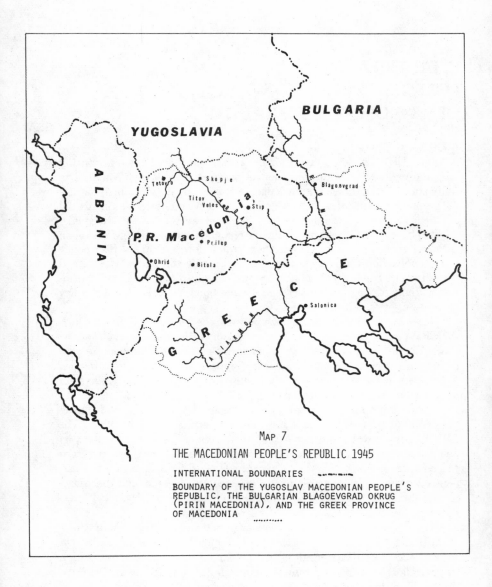

MAP 7

THE MACEDONIAN PEOPLE'S REPUBLIC 1945

INTERNATIONAL BOUNDARIES   ▬ ▬ ▬ ▬
BOUNDARY OF THE YUGOSLAV MACEDONIAN PEOPLE'S
REPUBLIC, THE BULGARIAN BLAGOEVGRAD OKRUG
(PIRIN MACEDONIA), AND THE GREEK PROVINCE
OF MACEDONIA   ·············

munist government. At the end of the war, the CPY was in a position to continue or to reverse the trend of putting into reality the rights of the Macedonians for a distinctive national existence. During the war the party was
forced to give the Macedonians some forms of party and administrative
autonomy in order to acquire the support of a sufficient segment of the population to gain some measure of control, but after the war there was less
necessity for granting further concessions. Hence, Belgrade moved to consolidate its power in Macedonia and limit the autonomy of the republican
government and party in Macedonia.

From the very beginning the CPY made it clear that the creation of
republic party organizations for each nationality did not make the party a
federation. There could be only one unified party. In his address to the founding congress of the CP of Bosnia and Hercegovina in 1948, Moša Pijade
explained the limitations of the republican parties:

> This new organization of our party according to the People's Republics
> corresponds to the needs of our federative organization of the people's state,
> although naturally it does not mean that the CPY has thus received the char-
> acter of some kind of federation of six Communist parties, that it has ceased
> being one united and centralized party. . . .The formation of the CP's of Slo-
> venia, Croatia and Macedonia was an expression of the need that our party
> strengthen the party leadership in those countries . . . that the leadership
> could move with more independence and strength, placing itself at the head
> of the laboring masses and of their nations in their struggle against the
> Great Serbian reactionary regime which was oppressing them socially and
> nationally, and so that the laboring masses . . . would be led away from the
> leadership of the wrong "national" leaders.[1]

The postwar aims of the republic parties, Pijade said further, were quite
different. It was no longer a question of national rights since "the national
question is solved," but "the building of a socialist society" in which process
the republic CP's were to be guided by the principle of democratic centralism.

Thus the CPM was essentially a facade built around the small nucleus
of wartime "pro-Yugoslav" members. However, its leaders were given ad-
vantageous positions and privileges, which they dispensed in such ways as
to attract others to the cause. Macedonian party membership jumped from
400 in 1941 to 27,029 in 1948 and reached 43,595 in 1954.[2] While not
all of these party members can be presumed to adhere absolutely to the CPY
policy on Macedonia, the leadership of the party certainly does. Most party
members soon developed a vested interest in the power structure and, hence,
supported the Belgrade position.

After the war, Belgrade also moved to limit any real autonomy in the sphere of republic governments. In a speech in Zagreb in May 1945, Tito explained the competence of the republics and the meaning of federalism in Yugoslavia:

> Many people still do not understand what Federal Yugoslavia means . . . that [it] does not mean emphasizing the borders between this or that federal unit. . . . The borders of the federal states in federal Yugoslavia are not borders which divide but borders which unite. What do the federal units mean in today's Yugoslavia? We cannot consider them small countries, they have a more administrative character, the freedom to govern oneself. This is the character of the independence of the federal units, full independence in the sense of free cultural and economic development.[3]

The Yugoslav constitution adopted in 1946, like its Soviet model, established a highly centralized state despite its federal form. The constitution confirmed the right first recognized at the AVNOJ Council at Jacje in 1943 of self-determination including succession for each nationality. But this right, as in Soviet practice, was not to be exercised to permit any nationality to withdraw from Yugoslavia.[4] Although the constitution reserved to the republics all powers not granted to the federal government, the powers granted to the federal government were substantial, including the obligation "to defend the security as well as the social and political order of the peoples' republics" [Article 9]. It also specified that the six republics "form a single state and economic area" [Article 45]. The central government was given responsibility for international relations, external and internal trade, defense and internal security, transportation, money and credit, basic industry, mines, construction, and other "enterprises of general significance" [Article 44]. Two types of ministries were provided for: federal ministries for areas in which only the central government had competence and federal-republican ministries for areas in which the republics shared power with the federal government. In this latter category were included finance, internal affairs, justice, industry, mines, trade and supply, agriculture and forestry, labor and construction [Articles 86, 87, 88]. The republican organs were essentially only part of the transmission belt for the implementation of orders from the central government in Belgrade, whose power in the 1946 constitution was in no essential way restricted. The constitution specified the form of government for all republics and declared: "The government of the Republic rules on the basis of the Constitution of the FNRJ, the Constitution of the republic, of federal laws, laws of the republic, and on the basis of the regulations, directives and ordinances of the federal government" [Articles 90, 114].

In the government and party structure created right after the war, there

was no room for real autonomy in Skopje. In order for the ,
properly, the CPY had to fill leading party and governme
men faithful to Belgrade. It proved to be a difficult task
find men loyal to Belgrade but still able to command confid
Macedonian people. It was natural that attempts were made
large the area of Macedonian responsibility. For two years \   ..c after
the war there were frequent purges and trials of Macedonian communists
and non-party people charged with autonomist deviation. In 1946 Metodi
Antonov-Čento, who had been President of the ASNOM, resigned from the
government and was later arrested and convicted of having worked for a
"completely independent Macedonia" as an IMRO member. In the Macedonian assembly he had called for increased self-determination and, shortly
before his arrest, made a speech in the Prilep town square attacking the prevailing official tendencies of orientation towards Belgrade. He expressed
specific disapproval of the projected uprooting of the traits of the Bulgarian
language, and of Skopje's dependence on Serb administrators and experts.
There was much popular resentment about his arrest; reportedly, thirty-
seven people were killed in a protest demonstration at Resen.

The Čento incident probably typified the reaction of many sincere Macedonian nationalists who discovered that the reality of Yugoslav Communist
self-determination fell short of what they had been led to expect. Of course
overt IMRO operatives, such as Džuselov and Čkatrov, were executed. But
many of the other nationalists, including some Communists who had fought
with the partisans, were shocked by the extent of the de-Bulgarization process during the early postwar period. Though they favored an autonomous
Macedonia in a Balkan federation as a first choice, they were willing to see
Macedonia in a federative Yugoslavia, provided the Macedonians were allowed a significant degree of self-rule. The postwar letdown of those who
were already consciously nationalist was prompt and widespread. The Bulgarophiles deeply resented the attacks on the use of their native language.
The sincere autonomists soon realized that, whatever the formal republic-
federation arrangements, the real power gravitated from Belgrade.

The utilization of non-Macedonian Yugoslavs in the Macedonian republic administration aroused immediate suspicion in many quarters. Immediately after the war, a noticeable number of Serbian experts took over
positions of authority and influence. There was a lack of technically trained
and politically reliable Macedonian cadres. Many of the most able middle-
level Macedonian Communists were for a time fully occupied with Agitprop
work in consolidating the CPY's position in Macedonia, and later, with further attempts to bring Bulgarian Macedonia into Yugoslavia. It was essential
for the Macedonians to have assistance in the elementary techniques of

political and economic management if there was not to be chaos. Also, in view of the Macedonians' strong anti-Belgrade bias, the CPY knew it was imperative to give early and rather precise direction at all levels. But the influx of Serbian advisers gave rise to charges of new Great Serbianism and the party had to handle this touchy problem with great care. The pervasiveness of Serbian "instructors" in the immediate post-revolution period can not be calculated by an examination of the names of office holders in various levels of the republican government since advisers and loaned experts were not enumerated. However, some reports claimed manifestations of "Serbianism" which recalled to Macedonian memories the inter-war years, for instance, Serbian settlement on the farms left by emigrating Turks. Most of the key internal security posts in the Macedonian republic were held by Serbs.[5]

The casualty rate of the early second-level republican officials was high. Men like Andrejev who had some popular support were needed for prestige purposes during the period of consolidation of power. Even after the removal of those who had obvious autonomist sympathies, the middle echelons of administration were something less than stable, and cabinet reshuffling was frequent. After the Cominform break a second major purge was necessary. However, by 1948 apparently most Macedonian officials deemed unreliable had been replaced—not by Serbs, but by Macedonians. Given the relatively small number of trained men available, Macedonians received as many republican jobs as any regime except a completely independent Macedonia could have been expected to give them. While some experienced Macedonians were not usefully employed because of doubts about their devotion to the regime, any pattern of great-Serbian domination on the republican and local levels of administration is lacking. The thoroughness with which the Macedonian party and government cadres were purged and filled with officials faithful to Belgrade is one of the reasons for the small rate of defections among the Macedonian party membership at the time of the Cominform dispute with the Soviet Union.

The participation of Macedonians in responsible echelons on the federal government level was limited at first, but gradually they have approached formal proportional equality.[6] At the constituent assembly in 1946, Dimitar Vlahov was one of the six vice-presidents of the presidium; among the twenty-six regular members of that Presidium were two Macedonians—Bane Andrejev and Lazar Koliševski. There has always been at least one Macedonian holding ministerial position of secondary importance. Andrejev, and later Strahil Gigov, served in these positions before the government reorganization program of 1953 replaced the former cabinet and presidium system by the Federal Executive Council. When the reorganization was carried out there were four Macedonians on this federal cabinet level – Gigov, Krste Crvenkovski, Nikola Minčev and Ljubčo Arsov.[7]

Following the elections and government reorganization in the spring of 1958, three Macedonians on the executive council continued in the federal government — Minčev as Secretary of Finance, Crvenkovski as Secretary of Education and Culture, and Arsov as Chairman of the MPR Executive Council continued ex-officio.[8] Following the adoption of the new constitution in 1963, six Macedonians were included in the 38-member Federal Executive Council.[9] Of the 67 members of the Council of the Federation, seven were Macedonians.[10] When the Council of the Federation was expanded to 87 members in 1967, there were nine Macedonians on it.[11] The Federal Executive Council was also expanded in 1967 but the number of Macedonians dropped from six to five members; however, Kiro Gligorov became one of the two vice-presidents of the council. Vidoe Smilevski was also chosen at that time to head the Chamber of Federal Affairs of the Yugoslav National Assembly. The government selected in May 1969 included a Macedonian as one of the two vice-chairmen and three Macedonian representatives. Each republic was granted three members and each autonomous region two members to insure equal nationality representation.[12] Generally, since the late 1950's Macedonian representation in the leading bodies of the Yugoslav government has been about proportional to the Macedonian population.

Immediately after the war there were few Macedonians in the central organs of the CPY. But in the party, as in the government, Macedonian representation at higher levels has increased to about proportional equality. At the Fifth Party Congress in 1948 there were six Macedonians of a total of 63 elected to the Central Committee — Koliševski, Smilevski, Gigov, Vera Ačeva, Temelkovski and Cvetko Uzunovski, all of whom had been loyal to the CPY during the war.[13] Macedonian candidate members of the CC were Andrejev, Arsov, Crvenkovski, Naum Naumovski and Vera Naceva. Vančo Bruzevski and Minčev were selected for the Central Revision Committee, an organ of internal party control.[14] There were no Macedonians on the party politburo or Executive Committee until the Sixth Party Congress in 1952 when Lazar Koliševski became one of the thriteen members of that body. The number of full members of the CC was expanded to 109 at the Sixth Congress but there were no candidate members. Ten were Macedonian.[15] Fourteen of the 135 members of the CC chosen in 1958 were Macedonians, and Koliševski remained the only Macedonian on the Party Executive Committee.[16]

At the Eighth Party Congress in December 1964, there were sixteen Macedonians on the 155 member Central Committee, two representatives on the Party Control Commission, two on the Audit Commission, and two members on the Executive Committee—Crvenkovski in addition to Koliševski. Following the new LCY policy of rotating positions, eight of the 16 Macedonians on the Central Committee were chosen for the first time in 1964 and six members of the CC chosen in 1958 were dropped. For the first time an Albanian from Macedonia (Azem Zulfičari) became a member of the Central Committee.[17] The party was reorganized on the federal level at the Ninth Party Congress in March 1969. A Presidium of 52 members replaced the Central Committee as the supreme body of the party. In a departure from party tradition, each republic party elected seven representatives to the Presidium at the republican party congresses held before the all-Yugoslav congress. Tito surprised the congress by announcing the creation of a party executive committee to be composed of 15 members. The committee, whose purpose is apparently to smooth the transition from Tito to his successor, was constituted along strict nationality lines: in addition to Tito, each republic had two, and each autonomous province one representative.[18]

One factor which limited Macedonian representation in high party councils immediately after the war in addition to lack of experience and the question of loyalty, was the relatively small degree of Macedonian participation in the partisan war. A special camaraderie exists between Tito and those men who were with him throughout his military campaigns. This is one of the reasons why Montenegrins have been so heavily represented in Belgrade. However, since the early postwar years there has been an attempt to insure that at least the major Yugoslav nationalities have approximately proportional representation in the central government and party organs. The 1963 constitution codified this practice on the government level by specifying that the Federal Assembly would take nationality into consideration in the composition of the Federal Executive Council.[19] The Macedonians who have attained high federal or party positions of authority have been staunchly pro-Yugoslav and many have past Serbian connections. For example Apostolski was an officer in the prewar Yugoslav army. Koliševski received a scholarship to Belgrade University in the thirties; he divorced his Macedonian wife and married a Serb. Thus the Macedonian leadership, while numerically proportional, does not necessarily reflect the cross section of the Macedonain population.

The process of the CPY's consolidation of power in Macedonia has involved a continuing campaign to eliminate the stubborn traces of "old-fash-__d" nationalism and to root out anything Bulgarian. The leadership in ____roughly pro-Belgrade and pro-Yugoslav. The most promi-____ssociated with the idea of Macedonian autonomy, Vlahov, was used solely for window dressing. The only two other Macedonian communists with popular followings, Čento and Andrejev, were disposed of because their Bulgarophilism was not in tune with Belgrade's conception of Macedonian nationalism. The government and party forms would seem to permit the Macedonians some degree of autonomy, but in reality the Yugoslav government and party remain essentially centralized.

Despite this tight control by the central Yugoslav organs of power, the Macedonians have shown resistance on occasion to Belgrade. At the time of the Cominform conflict Macedonian officials later admitted there were serious problems among the Macedonian population.[20] In the elections of December 1952 for district and town councils, non-official (non-party) lists of candidates were permitted in an effort to increase voter interest and make the elections seem more democratic. Opposition candidates were elected in two Skopje wards.[21] The following year four party approved nominees were defeated in the elections for the Macedonian Republican Assembly. A *Borba* article partially attributed the "election surprises" to the "use of demagogic methods" by the official candidates. One of those defeated was a member of the CC LCM, Risto Bajalski from Gevgelija.[22] The *Borba* article may not have made full admission of the extent of the election upsets in Macedonia. According to the MPO, the districts of Strumica, Gevgelija, and Kriva Palanka, all in eastern Macedonia near the Bulgarian border, elected a total of twenty-seven opposition delegates to the assembly. Upon arriving in Skopje, they were reportedly denied the privileges of the Parliamentary Club and other fringe benefits such as free railroad travel, and most were disfranchised for various "technical" reasons.

Even though at present the Skopje government's exercise of power is severely limited, no people can play with the forms of government very long without acquiring a desire to make those forms more meaningful. A Macedonian assembly and Macedonian administrative organs exist all the way down to the village level. Thousands of Macedonians are participating in the highly bureaucratized administration of Macedonia and thus have some personal interest in the regime. Koliševski told the Third Congress of the LCM in 1959 that 122,000 citizens in Macedonia, or one-sixth of the population over 14 years of age, were involved in the various committees, councils, and "social" government bodies of the republic.[23]

Yugoslavia since the Cominform conflict has been slowly moving toward greater—though at present still limited—autonomy for the republics. The effect this may have on the further development of Macedonian nationalism will be interesting to observe. The constitutional law of 1953 reflected this new trend in Yugoslav federal philosophy. Yugoslavia was no longer considered a federation of national republics in the traditional sense. The new theory was that the local people's committees were the repository of all rights not specifically granted to the federal and republic governments. The change attempted to play down the national character of the republics and stress the economic character of the communes. Despite the emphasis on local government, the republics gained increased autonomy. The authority of federal officials to intervene in republic affairs was formally limited somewhat, powers granted to the federal government were enumerated more specifically, and republics were permitted some participation in economic planning.[24]

This trend of increasing, but still limited, autonomy for the republics was continued in the Yugoslav constitution promulgated April 7, 1963.[25] The national right of self-determination including succession, which was mentioned in the 1946 constitution but not in the 1953 constitutional law, was reiterated as a basic principle. The rights of the Federation and the republics were more clearly spelled out. New powers given to the republics included permission for republics to cooperate among themselves without federal involvement on problems of common concern [Article 110]. Also republics were given power to legislate in fields of solely federal competence if the federal government failed to legislate in that area [Articles 119-120]. An interesting innovation was the creation of a Constitutional Court empowered, among other things, to "resolve disputes concerning rights and duties between the federation and a republic" [Article 241]. A series of ammendments to the constitution which are clearly calculated to further this trend towards republican autonomy were approved late in 1968.[26]

While constitutions of Communist states are no barrier to action which the central government wishes to take, the Yugoslav constitution reflects more faithfully than any other Communist basic document the powers of the central and republic governments. Despite the growing autonomy of the Yugoslav republics, Yugoslavia is still a highly centralized, hierarchical government. Though republics wield greater power in Yugoslavia than under the Soviet federal system, the Yugoslav republics have far less power than Western federal states.

Although the party has been somewhat slower to grant more powers to the republic party organizations, even here there are indications that greater republic autonomy is developing. The LCY has never been as centralized as the CPSU. Although there are party organizations for each of the Soviet republics and autonomous units, they are absolutely subordinated to the central party apparatus. Party cadres are shuffled from republic to republic in accordance with the party's needs and the necessitites of the internal power struggles. These lateral transfers are without regard to nationality. Thus Brezhnev, a Russian born in the Ukraine, was first secretary

of the Moldavian and later of the Kazakstan party organization. The Yugoslav party organization is more truely federal in nature. Each of the six republics has its own party organization but only at the federal level is the leadership drawn from all republics and nationalities. There is no lateral transfer
of party cadres between republics. While Serbs and Albanians hold positions
in the Macedonian party organs, they are not Serbs from the Serbian republic or Albanians from the Kosmet. The Yugoslav republics have representation from among the nationalities living in the individual republics but do
not exchange cadres across republic lines. Hence Macedonian party members
are not scattered among the other Yugoslav peoples but remain concentrated
in the Macedonian republic.

Changes have been introduced into the party which grant some limited
autonomy to the republican organization. These innovations will probably
have a greater impact than the constitutional changes on republic autonomy.
The Eighth Party Congress of the LCY in December 1964 revised the party
statutes to specify that republican party congresses would henceforth be
held before, rather than after, congresses of the LCY. In addition republic
congresses were given the responsibility to "determine the policy . . . of the
League of Communists of the socialist republic in line with the policy of the
League of Communists of Yugoslavia and [in line] with conditions in the
republic; take the initiative in making proposals to the congresses and central committee of the League of Communists of Yugoslavia on specific questions."[27] In explaining the change it was specified that the party was attempting

> to make the statute more specifically define the independence of the Lea-
> gue of Communists in the socialist republics, taking into consideration the
> national character and economic development of each republic. The em-
> phasis on independence will make it possible for Communists in the repub-
> lics to work creatively, freely and with full responsibility in carrying out
> under specific conditions the League's general policy.[28]

The reorganization of the party central organs following the purge of
Aleksandar Ranković in 1966 has furthered this trend of republic party
autonomy.[29] Discussion of the reorganization indicates that it was intended
that republic parties would gain increased autonomy and power:

> The organizational structure and method of work of the League of
> Communists will have to be adjusted to the new relations and the develop-
> ment of the federal system in our country. Along with the development of
> a unified social-economic system and with the increasing decentralization
> of social and state functions, the League of Communists in the republics will
> gain greater independence in evolving ideological and political attitudes,

especially in operative functions. . . . This decision provides the possibility
for the Central Committees in the republics to develop greater initiative and
independence with regard to their own reorganization.[30]

As this trend toward greater autonomy in the republican parties develops,
the impact on Macedonia may be to stimulate further development of a separate Macedonian consciousness or it may permit Bulgarophilism to reappear. While the trend is clearly toward greater autonomy for the LCM, the
Macedonian party leadership are clearly Belgrade's men. There is little possibility that the leadership will move away from Belgrade of its own accord.
However, as this autonomy advances—particularly on the local level—the
Macedonian leadership will be increasingly subject to pressures from the
Macedonian population which could force the leadership to deviate in some
areas from the Belgrade line. The traditional Bulgarophile sentiment of the
Macedonian people may reappear. Fear of this happening, even under the
conditions of limited independence that now exist, may be an explanation
for the response of the Yugoslav and Macedonian leaderships to recent Bulgarian denials of the Macedonian nationality.

The impact of economic developments on Macedonian nationalism has
been no less profound than the political influences. In Yugoslavia since the
late 1950's the revival of the national question has been closely linked with
questions of economics. With an ideology preaching economic determinism
and a country underdeveloped and unevenly developed, economics became
a prime concern of the Yugoslav Communists. The struggle against German
occupation had not ended before the CPY was drawing up grandiose plans
for the industrialization of all of Yugoslavia.

The task was formidable. Slovenia, Croatia and the Vojvodina (an
autonomous province in the Republic of Serbia located north of the Danube
River) had been under Austrian domination for centuries prior to joining
Yugoslavia in 1918. They were far more advanced economically, technically, and educationally than the southern parts of Yugoslavia. Macedonia,
the Kosmet, Sandžak—the regions which were taken from Turkish domination only in 1913—plus Montenegro and Bosnia-Hercegovina were the
least developed regions in Yugoslavia.[31] Not only was Macedonia one of the
least developed regions economically, it was poor in natural resources and
lacked such basic raw materials as high grade iron ore. The transportation
system was primitive and its land-locked, mountainous position made transportation especially difficult. The population was scattered, uneducated,
lacking skilled labor and engineers. Although the potentialities for hydroelectric power in the western mountains had been recognized by the construction of a small power plant at Treska, Macedonia was notoriously ne-

glected in the field of industrial development by the interwar Yugoslav governments.

The Yugoslav Communist government took immediate steps to promote development of the southern regions. Boris Kidrić, explaining economic plans to the Fifth CPY Congress, told the delegates: "We cannot speak about the complete, final solution of the national question if there exists economic inequality between the republics or if, on the other hand, our Yugoslav economy does not develop in the concept and direction of an indivisible and socialist economic whole."[32] The five year plan that was launched in 1947 declared Macedonia as well as Bosnia-Hercegovina and Montenegro to be underdeveloped regions and launched programs "to insure a faster rate of development in the economically backward republics and to remove the consequences of uneven development." The goal of the plan in Macedonia was to increase the value of industrial production by 1951 to 26.3 times its value in 1939. Macedonia by 1951 was to have an industrial output greater than Croatia did in 1939.[33] With such goals, Macedonian optimism was high. Koliševski, reporting on the five year plan to the First CPM Congress, pledged:

> The development of the national economy in the MPR is progressing with a much faster tempo of development than Yugoslavia as a whole or the other more advanced people's republics. Thus, with the help of all of the advanced, brotherly republics, our people's republic is to be changed, by the end of the Five Year Plan, from an extremely backward region to an industrially developed and electrified country to a great extent, with a consolidated agriculture in which industry will have an important place.[34]

Fulfilling these promises proved to be more difficult than making them. Resources were not adequate to meet the ambitious over-all goals of the plan. After 1948 trade relations were severed with the Soviet Union, from which the Yugoslavs expected to purchase a large portion of the capital equipment required by the plan. In the ensuing economic crisis, investment was concentrated in northern areas which were already relatively advanced. These areas, particularly Slovenia, had raw materials, adequate transportation facilities, skilled labor and marketing opportunities which Macedonia and the southern republics were lacking. With inadequate federal resources to follow the plan, the ministries invested relatively more in the areas where certain productivity could be expected in a reasonably short time rather than in those like Macedonia, where the reaping of purely economic rewards would at best be years away. The fear of a Soviet invasion led to increased investment in defense industries which were constructed in the less acessable areas of Montenegro and Bosnia-Hercegovina. Macedonians were told that when the "conditions of direct danger of war" from the Cominform countries had passed, the goals for economic development would be fulfilled and would "secure a new increase of industrialization in our republic and its transformation into a powerful economic region of the FNRJ." [35]

While most of the development plans for Macedonia went overboard, a few projects were saved. The most spectacular was the Mavrovo scheme, which involved diverting the headwaters of the Radika River into the ancient lake basin of Movrovo from which tunnels and canals carry the water to the Polog basin. The plan involved several hydroelectric power plants. [36] Textile mills were also set up at Tetovo (woolens), Titov Veles (silk) and Štip (cotton). [37] The mills were set up in Macedonia to process the locally grown fibers, to create maximum possible local employment in overpopulated areas, and to encourage peasants in these areas to grow the fibres locally, thus replacing imports of these goods with domestic production. Some investment was made in metal processing industries. However, an integrated steel works for Skopje was not included in the plans until 1953 and its full capacity of 1 million tons of steel per year will not be reached until completion of the third phase, scheduled for 1971. Other than these projects, efforts in Macedonia were concentrated on economic activities which either already existed or which did not involve large capital outlays—light manufacturing and expansion of industries using local agricultural products.

There was bound to be a letdown when the economic progress promised by the Communists did not materialize. The failure to give the Macedonians what they considered their just share of development and construction funds was widely held to be a manifestation of the traditional, wilful discrimination against Macedonia and occasioned many explicit complaints, even on the part of members of the CPM. Macedonian discontent became so open that a plenum of the Macedonian Central Committee in 1952 declared the following to be among its tasks:

> Through the party's ideological struggle, which will cast light upon our achievements in the development of socialism, there should be further strengthening of Yugoslav patriotism and the pride of our masses in their socialist achievements which they are making despite all difficulties. The party organizations should unmask and point out the origin of various chauvinist occurrences and prejudices, such as the theory concerning our "economic backwardness" or the theory concerning neglect of these or those towns or districts in our social plan, in our development and so on. [38]

Party propaganda stressed those Macedonian projects on which construction was not stopped and Macedonians were repeatedly reminded that they were enjoying tremendous benefits from completed investments. Since official figures were given as multiples of the prewar or immediate postwar levels of production, the improvement was made to seem spectacular.

Just as unfulfilled promises of economic development produced dissatisfaction among the educated and working class Macedonians, the attempt at collectivization of agriculture provoked anti-Belgrade sentiment among the peasantry. The government's aims in collectivizing agriculture in Macedonia, as elsewhere, were unrelated to its national program. The economic aim of collectivization in Macedonia was not so much to produce more food as to reduce agricultural overpopulation and thereby make available additional labor for industry and to break down subsistence farming by encouraging the production of agricultural products of use in industry. The collectivization attempt failed throughout Yugoslavia, but the opposition in Macedonia appears to have been stronger than in any other of the country's underdeveloped regions. Resistance was especially strong among peasants whose lowland plots had been passed down to them by preceding generations. In the upland villages where stock and land were traditionally owned in common, collectivization did not so materially alter the way of life, but even there it was not really successful.[39]

By late 1951 there were reputed to be 981 Macedonian peasant working cooperatives (collectives) with 60 percent of the total number of farmsteads and 62 percent of the total area of arable land. The percentage of farmsteads in the most fertile regions was claimed to run as high as 94 percent.[40] However, even the party press admitted peasant opposition. One report confirmed that, as a result of the forceful measures, speculators and enemies of socialism tried to undermine the cooperatives and actually induced many farmers to apply for permission to withdraw. The Macedonian peasants were also accused of retaining the best part of their land for personal use, of keeping up to 80 percent of their pigs and of avoiding work in the cooperatives to which they belonged.[41]

By late 1952 peasant resistance to collectivization throughout Yugoslavia had become so intense and production had fallen so appreciably that the government was forced to call a partial halt to the process. It was decided to eliminate those collectives which were not productive, mostly those in hilly or mountainous areas which were not suitable for agricultural mechanization. Much of Macedonia's terrain fits this category. When a regulation was enacted on March 30, 1953, permitting peasants to withdraw from the collectives, a mass exodus commenced. There was considerable ideological confusion among Communists working in agricultural affairs about interpreting the decree. They were not sure whether they were to allow the peasants to leave freely. In any case, peasants who had contributed good land to the collectives were either given back the same acreage of inferior land elsewhere or were charged for the "improvements" made on their original land by the collective. By December 1953 the number of peasant working cooperatives in Macedonia had fallen to 10.1 percent of the number reported at the end of the previous year.[42] Part of this large decrease in Macedonian cooperatives was due to the unsuitability of the land for collective agriculture. However, some of the decline was also due to the greater resistance of the Macedonian peasantry. In part this resistance was an expression of national opposition to what the peasants considered a new Serbianization process, an opposition which conditions of control made impossible for them to express in a more direct manner.[43]

With an end to the government's policy of forced collectivization, opposition among the peasantry abated somewhat. However, at this same time economic problems in Macedonia became more acute as the gap between promised economic development and actual economic conditions widened.[44] The federal government, no doubt under pressure from Macedonian leaders, recognized the problem, indicated that action would be forthcoming, but asked the Macedonians to be patient:

> In the course of these years we have strongly pushed Bosnia, but Macedonia has lagged behind. A prospective plan is especially necessary to us in order that the disproportions, which can exist in one year, are corrected in the course of the following years. The reason is not any kind of mistake, rather, our natural economic needs have driven us to such an orientation. But in the course of the coming years the orientation will change towards those republics and regions which up to now lagged behind most, and in this way these differences will be diminished over a period of ten years.[45]

The government and party attempted to hammer out general policy guideline for assistance given the underdeveloped regions. However, the divergent interests of the more-developed and less-developed republics as well as the limited Yugoslav resources prevented agreement on general principles.

Despite the fact that no program was agreed upon, investment in Macedonia increased significantly between 1952 and 1958. The Second Five Year Plan for 1957—1961 called for an annual federal investment in Macedonia of 20 billion dinars—four times the level of previous federal investment. Although the amount of investment planned for Macedonia was realized, the disparity between Macedonia and the developed Yugoslav republics actually increased.[46] After extensive investment of federal and republican funds, Macedonia remained an underdeveloped region. Frustration at failure to make real progress was intensified by the hope and optimism generated through party promises. In areas where some progress had been made, the disparity between the rural regions and the more affluent cities only intensified the frustration.

While Macedonia and the other southern republics became increasingly concerned with the growing disparity between themselves and the northern regions, Slovene and Croatian economists became more concerned and vocal about the flow of investment capital from north to south for construction of costly, inefficient, "political" factories. With the decentralization of the Titoist reforms, local empire building became common and economic considerations, particularly in the less developed republics, were not the prime factor in economic planning.[47] Between 1961 and 1965 economic reform was undertaken which emphasized economic rather than political factors in the allocation of investment funds. Opposition from the less developed regions and from the conservative government and party bureaucrats led to uneven progress in implementing the reforms. A special investment fund to aid the poor regions, and thus reduce their resistance to reform, was created in 1965, four years after it was first discussed. The fund grants credits and makes technical assistance available to the less developed regions for projects that will develop into economically efficient operations in time. Although this investment fund has taken the edge off the economic reforms for the less developed regions, the burden for economic growth has begun to shift from the federal government to the local enterprises and republics.

Krste Crvenkovski, head of the LCM from 1962 to 1969, was liberal on economic policy and advocated economic reform. Although beneficial for the Yugoslav economy as a whole, the effect of the reforms in Macedonia would be to reduce funds available for investment and to increase pressure on the numerous uneconomic enterprises. It is not surprising that there was strong opposition within the Macedonian party to the reforms. As in the rest of Yugoslavia, the economic question took on definite nationality aspects. In the summer of 1965 steps were taken to implement the reforms. However, opposition among the conservative, principally Serb-Montenegrin, bureaucracy prevented any real progress. At the Third Plenum of the CC LCY (February 25-26, March 11, 1966), the party leaders were bluntly told to follow the party line. Crvenkovski strongly advocated adherence to party directives. He also implied that the conservative Serbian opposition to the reforms had support in Macedonia:

> At the Eighth Congress and after we stressed Lenin's motto that each needs to fight against nationalism in his own house. We were aware that this was first of all correct in the interest of this nation [Macedonia] whose interests these [Macedonian] communists and this [Macedonian] League of Communists represent. We should fall to the level of the common petty bourgeois if we listen only to what is said about us in the "neighborhood," whether Serb or Macedonian, and do not have the courage to struggle

against everything that harms reciprocal relations and makes it impossible
to develop socialism in this nation.

After denying the claim that Yugoslav Communists were divided into a
"progressive northwest" and a "conservative southeast," Crvenkovski continued:

> If we speak on this problem [of underdevelopment] , we are criticized
> by Macedonian communists in our republic that we make a poor struggle for
> some rights, that we are being led along. . . . The people who maintain these
> theses at the same time do not see the results achieved in their republic, they
> do not sustain these results so they can further develop, but they demand
> new projects in another field. They always make megalomaniac requests and
> in fact hinder what has already been achieved. [48]

A further indication of Macedonian recalcitrance came the following
month when the Fifth Plenum of the Macedonian Party Central Committee
met. Four days before the session, the LCY weekly published an article on
the forthcoming meeting. After several paragraphs citing general difficulties
of implementing the principles of economic reform and the decisions of the
Third LCY CC Plenum, the article concluded:

> We may expect that the forthcoming plenum of the CC LC Macedonia . . .
> will reply more clearly to certain unsettled questions of the internal life and
> ideological-organizational development of the League of Communists. [49]

At the session Tome Buklevski, the main speaker, chided the Macedonian
communists for "didactic repetition" of party slogans instead of "political
struggle and tackling actual problems" in implementing the general political line. Even though Krste Crvenkovski presided over the session, there
was strong opposition expressed and the meeting adjourned without approv-
ing a resolution. [50]

The removal of Aleksandar Ranković from his leading government
and party positions in early July 1966 signaled an intensification of the campaign to push economic reform. Although there was apparently strong anti-
reform sentiment in Macedonia, Crvenkovski and the other leading Macedonian Communists were staunchly pro-Tito and pro-reform in the crucial
central committee sessions. Vladimir Bakarić, head of the Croatian party,
later admitted that the majority coalition which led to Ranković's removal
was made up of Slovenes, Croatians and Macedonians. [51] The purge of Ranković followed by the removal of other leaders of the conservative bureau-
cratic faction broke the log jam and the reform proceeded in earnest. With
the principal opposition eliminated and with increasing pressure from the
Macedonian party leadership, Macedonian opponents of reform reluctantly
followed the party line.

Since the Communist regime has come to power in Yugoslavia, much has been done to further the economic development of Macedonia. Despite this progress, however, there is still discontent with Belgrade over economic issues. The extent of this unrest is not clear, but some of the reasons for it are. First, despite the progress, much more was promised. For example, under the First Five Year Plan (1947-1951), industrial production in Macedonia was scheduled to increase 26.3 times over the 1939 level of production. The Macedonian communists have admitted that Macedonia in 1939 had almost no industrial production—hence the actual output even 26 times greater would still be modest. However, by 1960 production had only reached 8.6 times the 1939 level.[52] Reports on current industrialization and economic growth exaggerate the successes. The man in the factory or in the village is acutely aware of the shortage of housing, the high cost of living, low wages, and irregularities in supply. This gap between promises and reality is one source of discontent.

A second problem is the unemployment which has continually plagued Macedonia. Macedonia has traditionally had a subsistence agricultural economy with surplus population. The shift of population away from agriculture has made the unemployment problem more serious and more visable.[53] The rate of unemployment in Macedonia has consistently been about twice as high as the Yugoslav average. After economic reforms were attempted and as federal investment in Macedonia leveled off after the Second Five Year Plan, unemployment in Macedonia rose to 19.2 percent of the working force. In 1967 Macedonia continued to average one unemployed worker for every five employed, and in some regions the ratio was even greater.[54] At the Fifth LCM Congress, unemployment was still cited as a serious economic problem and a vigorous struggle against it was urged.[55] With the economic reform, emphasis on profitability has hit the less efficient Macedonian plants very hard.

While the gap between promised economic development and real economic performance as well as unemployment and inefficient production are certain to produce discontent, it is difficult to determine the extent to which this has affected or induced national discontent. Throughout Yugoslavia problems of the economic system have quickly become connected with the national question and there is every reason to believe that the same thing has occurred in Macedonia. Crvenkovski told the Fifth LCM Congress that the Macedonian party "actively opposed views and theories which attempted to prove that the economic reform was in the main and above all initiated in the interest of the developed areas."[56] The fact that such views had to be actively opposed indicates their widespread existence. When the developed regions are Slovene, Croatian, and in some cases Serbian, the effect is to emphasize the national aspects of economic questions. Where strong national feelings exist it is convenient to blame Belgrade for the economic difficulties associated with industrialization. The fact that the leadership of the Macedonian party has supported Belgrade at the expense of Macedonian interests on economic issues is sure to have national overtones.

The organization of the Yugoslav League of Communists, the Yugoslav federal system and the economic structure have given the Macedonians limited local control. Although the forms of autonomy exist in all cases and although Macedonians hold the majority of positions in these economic and political organizations, most important decisions are still made by Belgrade. The Macedonian leadership, in order to remain in power, is thoroughly pro-Belgrade even at the expense of Macedonian interests. Belgrade can change the LCM leaders — a popular referendum cannot. Thus there is a gap between the leadership and the Macedonian people, who in seeking satisfaction of their own interests, desire greater independence from Belgrade. While this has put pressure on the Macedonian leadership, it has thus far produced no unresolvable difficulties. Belgrade remains in control.

However, one cannot say with confidence that the pattern will remain the same. There are definite trends towards greater autonomy for leaders on the republic level and towards increasing self-government for local political-economic units. While the autonomy exercized by the local organizations or by the republic party and government remain limited, the trend is clearly toward greater local control. With powerful centrifugal forces pulling at the national republics and with no popular Yugoslav leader on the scene to replace Tito, autonomy may well increase after his death. If the ties binding the federation do weaken, Macedonia may well gain the autonomy which some Macedonians have sought.

CHAPTER 9
THE ENCOURAGEMENT OF
MACEDONIAN CULTURE

The autonomy granted Macedonia in political and economic affairs was severely limited by Belgrade. Thus it has been a limited stimulus to the development of Macedonian nationalism. Any grant of power to Skopje would be at the expense of Belgrade. However, in the cultural sphere Macedonia was allowed much greater national autonomy as long as certain basic limitations were observed—cultural autonomy must strengthen and not weaken Macedonia's links with the rest of Yugoslavia, it must weaken Bulgarian consciousness of the Macedonians, and it must fit the current requirements of Yugoslav socialist realism. With close regulation of education and cultural affairs by the Federal Executive Council, by the party Central Committee's Commission of Agitation and Propaganda, as well as by the pro-Belgrade party leadership in Macedonia, cultural "Macedonianism" has been kept within these bounds. However, cultural development has given greater impetus to Macedonian nationalism than any other aspect of the Communist program to develop a Macedonian consciousness.

Macedonia's postwar cultural development springs partly from indigenous seeds and partly from the almost frantic party cultivation of Macedonian cultural forms calculated to differentiate the Macedonians from the Bulgarians. During the inter-war period when Belgrade followed a policy of Serbianization, the Macedonians refused to be assimilated. As the Bulgarophile sentiment began to wane under Bulgarian occupation during World War II, many Macedonians acknowledged cultural differences from the Bulgarians. Hence, when Macedonians were recognized as a separate nationality with a distinct national language in 1943, the desire to develop a Macedonian culture was given the opportunity to express itself.

The stronger impetus to Macedonian culture, however, came from the Yugoslav Communists. They recognized the existence of a Macedonian nationality to quiet fears of the Macedonian population that a communist Yugoslavia would continue to follow the policy of forced Serbianization. At the same time, the modern conception of the national state implies that a nationality should be a part of a state with its co-nationals. Hence, for the

Yugoslav communists to recognize the inhabitants of Macedonia as Bulgarians would be tantamount to admitting that they should be part of the Bulgarian state. However, by declaring the people to be of the "Macedonian" nationality, the Yugoslav Communists could fully justify keeping the territory in a Yugoslav federation composed of various other Slavic peoples. Cultural "autonomy" was an excellent means to further Yugoslav aims in Macedonia. By using a Macedonian language for newspapers and in schools, opposition to Belgrade was reduced. At the same time, furthering Macedonian culture could be used to root out traces of Bulgarian national consciousness and culture, thus weakening Bulgarian irredentism. The Yugoslav Communists, at first with the approval of the Bulgarian party, went so far as to spread Macedonian culture in Pirin Macedonia. This anti-Bulgarian or de-Bulgarizing aspect of Macedonian culture has been one of the principal forces behind Belgrade's encouragement of culture.

The progress of Macedonian culture has been uneven—at times stimulated by internal pressures, at times forced by Bulgarian irredentism. However, the encouragement and evolution of Macedonian culture has had a far greater and more permanent impact on Macedonian nationalism than has any other aspect of Yugoslav policy. While development of national music, films and the graphic arts has been encouraged in Macedonia, the greatest cultural effect has come from the creation of the Macedonian language and literature, the new Macedonian national interpretation of history, and the establishment of a Macedonian Orthodox Church.

The Macedonian language is considered by most Macedonians to be one of the most positive contributions to their separate status. The question of what language Macedonians actually spoke prior to 1945 has caused disagreements among even the most disinterested linguists. The Macedonian dialects made a gradual transition from Serbian north of Skopje to Bulgarian in Eastern Macedonia. Even those who claim that a separate Macedonian language existed before 1945 admit that all these dialects have a very close affinity to Bulgarian.[1] The elements of distinction between the central Macedonian group of dialects (i.e., the language spoken roughly within the region Prilep-Bitolj-Kičevo-Titov Veles) and western Bulgarian were noticeable but not significant.[2] Bulgarian linguistic influence was strengthened by intense secular and religious propaganda in the past and by the fact that Bulgarian was the language used by the old Macedonian nationalists.

It was natural that the Yugoslav government regarded a distinct Macedonian language as a bulwark against Bulgarian irredentism. At the same time, it was a very real concession to the Macedonians vis-à-vis the Serbs. The First Assembly of the ASNOM in August 1944 passed a resolution declaring Macedonian the republic's official language. A commission was created to determine which features of the spoken dialects were to be incorporated in the written language, and in May 1945 an alphabet was adopted by law.[3]

As the basis for the new literary language the Central Macedonian dialect was chosen. The explanation was that this region was the most populous area and that it was important in Macedonian history. In addition Krste Misirkov, an advocate of the creation of a separate Macedonian language in the early twentieth century, and other Macedonian nationalists used the central dialects.[4] However, this dialect is also the Macedonian dialect most unlike both Serbian and Bulgarian. This was probably a far more important consideration in the government's decision. It has been claimed that, in fact, the north-western Macedonian dialects (those most similar to Serbo-Croatian and most unlike Bulgarian) had been originally chosen as the basis for the new language but had to be abandoned because of popular opposition.[5]

From the very beginning, Macedonian linguists concentrated on showing the Macedonian language to be different from other languages. The first grammar, published in 1946, established nine distinctive traits of the new language and stressed its differences from other Slavic languages.[6] At first the language had many words, especially political, literary, philosophical, and technical terms, which were borrowed from Bulgarian, Serbian and Russian. However, from the beginning an effort was made to purge these foreign elements, particularly those from Bulgarian. The commission which codified the language was guided by the principle:

> The vocabulary of the literary language should be enriched with terms taken from all Macedonian dialects. New words should be created with living inflections of the folk speech. Borrowed words from other languages should be retained only where necessary.[7]

As a result, Bulgarian, Russian (after 1948) and other foreign words were replaced by words existing in one of the local Macedonian dialects or by terms created by combining native elements.

In addition to making the modern Macedonian literary language different from Bulgarian, Yugoslav linguists also have great effort in attempting to show that the old Macedo essentially a separate language. The Macedonian tion of their linguistic development i an ivory tower matter; the campaign i Numerous articles on the alleged hist to the middle ages, are carried by news on this subject, the party expressed con knowledge the separate existence of a di past:

We are meeting with blind acceptance of Great Bulgarian theories with regard to the struggle of our people for its national language. Study of the struggle for a national language is important, because language is one of the four basic elements without which there cannot be talk of a nation. The broad reading public, and even some teachers of national history, know little about the one hundred year struggle of our people for its own national language, or they underestimate it or misunderstand it, and thus they unconsciously become bearers of an anti-historical, unscientific stand with regard to our language. Some lecturers and publicists of our history are bringing to the masses the conception that the Macedonians started in their schools and in their other cultural institutions with the use of the Bulgarian language as their literary language and that this language was used during the whole 19th and 20th centuries until the thirties, when progressive Macedonian publicists took as their literary language one of the Macedonian dialects. Thus it is made to seem that the Macedonian literary language appeared as a shot out of the dark, because with such a conception the struggle for a national language, which started in the middle of the 19th century, is ignored. [8]

This pamphlet then cites several of the historical examples of the use of a Macedonian language, including that "little masterpiece of political agitation," a manifesto made in the name of the ill-fated Kruševo Republic of 1903. The Macedonian Communists do not deny that the language of Goce Delčev and most other national heroes was Bulgarian, or that Bulgarian was the written Macedonian language generally until the Second World War. But Macedonian linguists explain that the Macedonian and Bulgarian peoples were facing essentially the same conditions in their struggle for national liberation against Turkey therefore; they coordinated their efforts. Since the Bulgarian bourgeoisie was more advanced than the Macedonian bourgeoisie, the Bulgarian literary language was further developed; hence, it was used by the Macedonians. The bulk of Macedonian linguistic history is aimed at magnifying the few historical instances of the written use of Macedonian dialects. [9]

Much was done from the beginning to secure wide usage of the new language. The first grammar was published in 1946, an orthography in 1951. An 80,000 word dictionary was published in three volumes between 1961 and 1966. Two journals were started to encourage the use of the Macedonian language—*Makedonski jazik* (1950) and *Literaturen zbov* 954). The new literary language was employed from the very beginning he mass media of the republic. However, in the early years there were difficulties in securing wide usage of the still-changing Macedonian e. Writings of the old Macedonian revolutionaries and often even nd articles by party leaders had to be translated or adjusted before being used. The lack of adequate language standards and of experience in using the norms that had evolved resulted in linguistic hodgepodges in composition and speech. The vast majority of the population spoke the Macedonian dialects of their regions and the new Macedonian literary language only gradually penetrated the natural speech habits of a population just beginning to pull itself out of the depths of illiteracy and isolation.

A decade after the war, special institutes had to be held for Macedonian language instructors. Commenting on the use of the new Macedonian in literature in 1952, Lunt wrote:

> Many Macedonians have not yet learned to use their native Macedonian on all stylistic levels. . . . It is only the small group of intellectuals daily concerned with the written word who now write easily, without frequent Serbisms of Bulgarisms. . . . The writers were burdened by their education in Serbian or Bulgarian; they had learned in the long hard years of school Macedonian was only for intimate friends and the most familiar ideas and feelings, but in broader spheres Serbian (or Bulgarian) must be used. This means that even today many Macedonians unconsciously slip into Serbian when discussing political, philosophical or artistic matters. [10]

The standardization of the new literary language has been a continuing process. But with its constant use in schools, the press, radio, books and theater, Macedonians have gradually come to understand and use the new language. The major non-Macedonian cultural pull, because of party pressure, has been to Serbo-Croatian rather than Bulgarian. Serbo-Croatian is the second language in Macedonian schools. As the output of original Macedonian literary works and even translations of standard Communist works into Macedonian was modest in the beginning, Serbo-Croatian was widely read. In time the supply of Macedonian textbooks, manuals and propaganda pamphlets has improved. Bulgarian books were discouraged before 1948 and prohibited for a time after the Cominform break. [11] Although at times when Bulgarian-Yugoslav relations have been good, Bulgarian works have been available throughout Yugoslavia, their accessibility in Macedonia has always been more limited.

It is not surprising that the output of Macedonian literature has been limited both in quantity and quality. This is natural in view of the relative newness of the Macedonian language, the availability of Serbo-Croatian literature, and the fact that secondary linguistic problems are only now being solved. The early postwar literary efforts were limited primarily to poetry and a few short stories. As the language has become more firmly established and as writers have become accustomed to using it, literary works have increased both in volume and quality. Of those literary figures who have appeared, none can be said to be towering.[12]

It is doubtful if the impact of Macedonian literature as such on the development of nationalism will prove as powerful as the use of the new language in the mass media and increasingly in everyday speech. In addition to the difficulty of developing a separate literature for a group of one million people in the shadow of the well-established Serbian and Croatian literatures, the literary themes called for are not always such as will encourage a "nationalist" literature. Immediately after the war the main themes were the partisan struggle with emphasis on the brotherly struggle of all Yugoslav peoples as a precondition for Macedonian liberation. Although since 1948 there has been a shift away from the sterile black-and-white Soviet style of "socialist realism," *Nova Makedonija* and the Macedonian party leadership have continued to exhort writers to deal with "progressive" subjects. A campaign in the early 1950's opposed literary concentration on folklore and encouraged treatment of universal Marxist motives. Works based on Macedonian national characteristics are frowned upon, but still produced.

Reports on Macedonian acceptance of the language have varied greatly. Some emigres claimed that the efforts to de-Bulgarize the language led to the inclusion of so many foreign elements that almost all Macedonians instinctively reject it. One Serbian specialist in Macedonia in the early 1950's reported that the new Macedonian was used mostly by government employees loyal to Belgrade. However, one British expert on Macedonia held the language to be "immensely popular,"[13] and another expressed uncritical enthusiasm about the "happy" acceptance of it and the other new Macedonian cultural forms.[14] A more realistic assessment comes from a Skopje schoolteacher who emigrated from Yugoslavia:

> Among the wide masses of the urban population and the intelligentsia, the Macedonian language is accepted as the most important, and often the only good, aspect of the present day Yugoslavia. The children are learning it in the schools and their parents are very satisfied that this is the case. There are places in the country-side where people were reluctant to send their children to school in the days of old Yugoslavia, but now they do so willingly, for they want their children to learn the Macedonian language. . . .
> The new literature and poetry in the national language has aroused great interest, for through it is created and formed the new national spirit and language. This new literature, as well as the printing of prewar literature and poetry by Macedonians in the national language, has resulted in much reading.

Having been taught in schools and used extensively throughout the SRM for over twenty-five years, the Macedonian language is accepted by most Macedonians.

The concern of the Macedonian and Yugoslav Communist leaders whenever the existence of the Macedonian language is questioned reflects their feeling that the language is one of the principal elements of a separate Macedonian national consciousness. In 1958 several Bulgarian statements declared that the Slavic inhabitants of Macedonia spoke Bulgarian, not the "semi-Serbian literary language which is fabricated in Skopje." Lazar Koliševski, defensively answering the Bulgarian claims, denied the "alleged 'Serbianization'" of the Macedonian language but justified the frequent use of Serbian expressions:

> The Macedonian language cannot be isolated from the mutual influence of the languages spoken by the Yugoslav peoples. Our common socio-economic development and socialist practice have created and are creating a number of new general expressions and terms accepted by all Yugoslav peoples. . . . The development of the languages of nations which have appeared late on the stage of history provides numerous examples showing that they are subjected to the influence of more developed languages and richer national cultures of related and neighboring peoples. [15]

Denial of the existence of the Macedonian language is considered so serious a challenge to the Macedonian nationality that Belgrade has not hestiated to condemn the Bulgarians regardless of the state of relations with Sofia. Vigorous and vehement denunciations of Bulgarian academicians have been published by leading Yugoslav newspapers even during periods of good relations with Bulgaria. The Yugoslav leaders thus acknowledge that the wide, if imperfect, usage of the Macedonian language is one of the most vital contributions to Macedonian nationalism.

The treatment of Macedonian history has the same primary goal as the creation of the Macedonian language—to de-Bulgarize the Macedonians and create a separate national consciousness. Since Marx claimed to have discovered the immutable laws of history, Communists have considered the "correct" interpretation of history as the foundation of all social science and a key element of nationality. In the Balkans, history is a primary ingredient in the development of national consciousness which possesses a current relevance that extends beyond mere academic interest. Hence, the Yugoslav Communists were most anxious to mold Macedonian history to fit their conception of Macedonian consciousness.

In setting the tone for the new interpretation of history, Communist experts found past Macedonian history to suffer from two defects. First, "bourgeois historians, although they may have certain merits for the elaboration of the material facts of history, suffer from the weakness of their idealistic theoretic basis."[16] Hence, new historical works must be based on a correct Marxist-Leninist interpretation of history. Second, and perhaps more important, Macedonian history had to sever the umbilical cord to Bulgaria. It was advanced as a principle of Macedonian historiography that key aspects of Macedonian culture had origins separate from Bulgaria, that Macedonian history was distinctively different from Bulgarian history.

Lazar Koliševski gave the initial clues as to the correct interpretation of Macedonian history in his report to the First Congress of the CPM in 1948. The resolution adopted by the First Congress stressed the importance of ideological conformity and emphasized the use of history to re-educate the Macedonian masses:

> Great interest should be created [in history] and there should be a systematic approach, with a materialistic elucidation of the historical past of our people in general, and special elaboration of the socialist movement in our country. The history of the people's liberation struggle should be particularly elaborated. A struggle should be carried out for systematic studies of our past among the broad masses as well as among party members. This is a necessary condition for the ideological uplift of party cadres and for the education of the masses in the spirit of socialism. [17]

Macedonian historians, however, apparently had some difficulty in adjusting to the new guidelines for Macedonian history—particularly in distinguishing Macedonian from Bulgarian history. In an article in *Komunist* in January 1950, Vidoe Smilevski gave a summary of the correct interpretation of Macedonian history.[18] Another article by Kiro Miljovski appeared about the same time but went farther, specifically criticizing Macedonian historians and setting out in more detail the party guidelines for interpreting history. Miljovski was particularly critical of the failure to eliminate Bulgarian influences:

> Some of our people fail to understand correctly Kuzman Šapkarov's cultural activity in the struggle for the Macedonian language, and they are suspicious about the national character of our entire early national movement simply because Šapkarov or others in the movement were not clearly, explicitly and to the very end nationally inclined, because some of them felt "now a Macedonian, now a Bulgarian." In the same way, some people fall into uncertainty about the Macedonian character of the national liberation movement in Delčev's time simply because Goce Delčev wrote in Bulgarian, because he did not say definitely that Macedonia is one nation and that Bulgaria is another. [19]

To avoid future uncertainty, Miljovski listed a number of expressions (most of them frequently used in Bulgarian historical writing) which were to be banned from Macedonian history.

Although Macedonian historical works began to appear, historians found that research on Macedonia was "complex and difficult" because existing literature "is still permeated with Great Bulgarian spirit, with omissions, distortions and falsifications of many historical facts."[20] The Scientific Institute for National History of the Macedonian Nation was established "to eliminate the influence" of the Macedonian Scientific Institute in Sofia which during the interwar period "published most of the documentary and propaganda materials about Macedonia."[21] The Institute, which had indeed published a great deal of material on Macedonia (including its periodical *Makedonski pregled*), was the principal scholarly advocate during the interwar period of the thesis that the Macedonian Slavs are Bulgarians.

The question of Bulgarian influence on Macedonian history was the thorniest problem of the new historiography. Obviously it was impossible for the Yugoslav Communists to deny completely the role of Bulgaria in the Macedonian revolutionary movement. One of the early attempts to cope with Bulgarian influence utilized the device of "contradictions." According to this explanation Macedonia's national revival developed as "Macedonian in its inner content and Bulgarian in its outer forms," although late in the process some Macedonian national forms were used along with the Bulgarian forms. The "contradiction" between content and forms extended throughout the entire historical process of the Macedonian revival; it was because of this conflict that Macedonian forms took shape, and it was through the development of these forms that Macedonia "categorically proved its individual national character."[22]

Reconciling progressive Marxist historiography with Macedonian national history has proved to be especially difficult. The Macedonian revolutionaries were generally not socialists and the Balkan socialists did not recognize the Macedonian nationality. To walk such a tightrope required great historical agility and the party was frequently called upon to restore balance for historians who went too far in one direction. A *Nova Makedonija* article for example, counseled historians to avoid errors of the epoch of bourgeois idealization, as there is "no reason for interpreting past events with a romantic pathos." The article explained that in approaching the past, all positive traditions should be included as the inheritance of the proletariat, but conservative tendencies should be rejected. The approach toward historical personalities was criticized as being idealized. For example, although Delčev was a forerunner of Marx in Macedonia, it would be mistaken to call him and others like him real Marxists.[23] In dealing with the Balkan socialist movement, writers had to exercise caution:

> Our socialists did not have a clear idea of the national belonging of the Mace-
> donian people, nor of the need to establish it as a separate unit, and they
> adopted the stand that the population in Macedonia was composed of mem-
> bers of the Bulgarian, Serbian, and Greek nations and of the minorities.[24]

Although the socialists were wrong on the Macedonian question, they were
socialists—hence, progressive and instrumental in the eventual triumph of
socialism in Macedonia. The socialist movement was an approved topic for
history, but its treatment required delicate handling.

In order to conform to the standards of Yugoslav Marxist historiography and at the same time degrade Bulgarian influence and affirm the
Macedonian nationality, Macedonian historical writing has stressed certain
themes. In order to create a continuous record of Macedonia as a nation,
there is constant re-analysis and rediscovery of probable and improbable
historical fragments. The medieval empire of Samuelo with its capital at
Ohrid has been designated as a "Macedonian" empire (despite the fact that
the empire was destroyed by Basil II who earned the title "Bulgar-slayer"
for his campaigns against Samuelo). The "Slavic" missionaries Cyril and
Methodius are treated with greatest respect and emphasis is placed on their
Macedonian birthplace (Salonika) and on their use of a "Macedonian" dialect
as the first Slavic literary language. Macedonian revolutionary heroes are
carefully treated. In addition to appropriating the historical legacies of the
key founders of the original IMRO—Goce Delčev, Damian Gruev and Pere
Tošev—Macedonian historians play up lesser figures who might have given
the slightest indication of "socialist" inclination or who were not openly
Bulgarophiles. Thus there is glorification of men like Jane Sandansky, Dimo
Hadži-Dimov, Petar Peparsev and Nikola Karev, who, because they defected
from the IMRO or lost out in internecine organizational fights, have long
been forgotten by chroniclers of the IMRO. The more recent IMRO leaders
—Aleksandrov, Protogerov and Mihailov—are excluded from the ranks
of the progressive for having been tools of Sofia. Besides, they are symbols
which are too dangerous and too recent to attempt to manipulate. Pre-World
War II Macedonian history orients events of the past towards the final successful climax of the liberation struggle during the war. However, it is emphasized that victory was possible only because of the fraternal assistance
of the other Yugoslav nationalities under guidance of the Communist party.

Despite the difficulties of dealing with the national history, in the beginning Macedonian writers enjoyed a relatively larger degree of permissive
action with regard to the employment of nationalist symbols than historians
of the other Yugoslav republics. In Macedonian history, the main concentration is on genuine national heroes like Delčev and on their nationalistic

character, regardless of their attitudes toward the Serbs and socialism. The accepted heroes of other Yugoslav national groups are portrayed almost exclusively from the point of view of their progressive, anti-religious or anti-Hapsburg attitudes. In the case of Croatia and Slovenia, the heroes selected by the Communists are those who favored union with Serbia. However, Belgrade permitted Macedonia to treat the role of the Serbs rather negatively, usually as Serbian imperialism. But, to balance these concessions, Macedonian historians are required to give special emphasis to the role of the CPY in their liberation from Bulgarians and Serbs. The struggle in the twenties and thirties for the correct party line on the nationality question is often stressed. The Party's efforts to liberate the Macedonians from the Bulgarian occupiers are combined in historical treatises with attacks against old Great Serbism.[25]

Although the party had some difficulty in establishing a historiography to suit its political needs, numerous works on Macedonian history were published by the Scientific Institute for the National History of the Macedonian People (since shortened to the Institute for National History). The early institute publications include a large number of document collections and writings of early Macedonian revolutionaries. Though some monographs were published they were usually limited in scope.[26] In addition to publications of scholarly interest frequent historical articles and programs are carried in the newspapers and mass media of the Macedonian republic. In the campaign of inspiring a Macedonian consciousness among the population, the Communist approved interpretation of history was used as one of the primary tools.

The first serious challenge to the new Macedonian historiography came in 1958. Yugoslavia and the Soviet Union, which had re-established close ties after 1955, had a second era of unfriendly relations beginning in Fall 1957 and Spring 1958. As part of the anti-Yugoslav program of the bloc, Bulgaria launched a vigorous campaign to deny the Macedonian language, culture, and nationality and to reassert Bulgarian claims to Macedonia. The Macedonian Communist leadership countered by emphasizing more forcefully the elements of Macedonian culture. Evidencing concern with Macedonian history, Lazar Koliševski delivered a long speech on Macedonian history at Titov Veles in November 1958. He explained at the beginning that his purpose in dealing with the Macedonian past was "to contribute to the forming of trends towards a correct, scientific understanding of historical events and their underlying social processes," because "we are still faced with many major tasks in the field of clarification of our national history."[27]

The thrust of Koliševski's treatment of history was two-fold—first, to reduce even further the significance of Bulgaria in Macedonian history, and second, to stress positive treatment of Serb-Macedonian relations. Although earlier Macedonian historians had explained Bulgarian influence by means of a contradiction with Macedonian inner forms and Bulgarian external forms, Koliševski degraded Bulgarian influence even further. He argued

> the Macedonian nation did not emerge as a result of political manipulations in the twentieth century, but it emerged from the general struggle, resistance and awareness of the people, which began early in the 19th century.

Koliševski went on to explain that from the very beginning of the 19th century Macedonian national consciousness grew independently and distinctively from Bulgarian consciousness. But with the development of Macedonian consciousness, the Bulgarians developed imperialist ambitions towards Macedonia. The last part of his speech was particularly critical of the most recent Bulgarian denial of the Macedonian nationality.

The role of the Serbs in Macedonian history, however, he treated much more favorably than Macedonian historians had been doing up to that time. Though admitting that the Serbian bourgeoisie intended to establish its hegemony over Macedonia, Koliševski quoted extensively from Serbian diplomatic correspondence to show that some Serbs acknowledged a Macedonian nationality and opposed the negation of Macedonian consciousness by Bulgaria. The Serbian bourgeoisie came to deny the Macedonian nationality, Koliševski claimed, when they entered into a tacit agreement with the Bulgarian and Greek bourgeoisie that only Serbs, Greeks and Bulgarians lived in Macedonia "with their respective number to depend on the manner in which Macedonia was carved up." He asserted that nations can only be created by powerful forces at work among the people and never by the actions of politicians.

Although Koliševski's speech placed new emphasis on the anti-Bulgarian aspects and softened the anti-Serbian aspects of Macedonian history, it did not represent a real departure for Macedonian historiography. The same ideological line adopted after the Communist consolidation in Macedonia is still the historical guideline. In recent years the quality and volume of Macedonian historical writing has increased, but the themes and their treatment, although more sophisticated, are much the same as before. The national-liberation struggle, the socialist movement in Yugoslavia and the Balkans, and the Macedonian revolutionary tradition dominate historical works. There is still some reticence to treat Macedonian relations with Yugoslavia and Serbia between the wars, but there is greater emphasis on Serb-Macedonian relations during earlier periods.[28]

The goals of the national history are unchanged—to reduce the Bul-

garian role in Macedonian history and to stress Macedonian national development at the same time emphasizing the importance of close ties with
other Yugoslav peoples. However, Macedonian national history has not
developed in a vacuum and external problems have affected its course. Since
1956 Bulgaria has not recognized the Macedonian nationality and her historians have been permitted to reassert Bulgarian historical claims to the
Macedonian territory and population. Even in periods when Bulgarian-Yugoslav relations have been very good, academic historical controversies have
continued, frequently developing political repercussions. The Macedonian
historians have thus been forced to defend their dubious historical claims,
with the result that their history has become even more polemical and political. The rising nationalism of the Yugoslav peoples has also had its effect
in Macedonia. Although increased nationalism first reappeared as the result
of economic problems in the late 1950's, it has since spread throughout
Yugoslavia's cultural life. The problem reached the point that Tito denounced "nationalistic manifestations" in the field of history at the Eighth
Party Congress.[29] The problem was as much present in Macedonia as the
other republics. Crvenkovski, at the Fourth Congress of the LCM, just before the Eighth all-party congress, criticized "the still present phenomenon
of national romanticism [i.e., over-glorification] in uncovering our national
past." Although acknowledging the difficulties of dealing with Macedonian
history, Crvenkovski called on historians to adopt the approach which would
"contribute to the national consciousness of our people freeing itself of
nationalist deviations [pro-Bulgarian and anti-Serb sentiments], to building
respect for everything that is positive and common in the struggle of our
neighbors [i.e., Serbs and other Yugoslav peoples] and which is a component
part of our own national history."[30]

    One of the most interesting aspects of Macedonian cultural life was the
struggle for the creation of an independent Macedonian Orthodox Church.
In the Balkan countries, one's religion is a key element of nationality. The
concept that nationality is determined by religion is a remnant of the era
of Turkish domination (which in the case of Macedonia goes back less than
sixty years). Under Ottoman rule, all subjects of the Sultan who were not
of the Muslim ruling class were of the Rayah class. Each religious group
of this class was organized into an internally autonomous community called
a *millet* which was allowed to maintain its traditional laws and internal administration under direction of its religious leaders. In the Balkans generally,
religion is characterized by a sense of loyalty that is meant to be perpetual.
Hence, to the Balkan subjects of the Sultan, religion was the key element
of ethnic and social identity.[31] The establishment of the Bulgarian Exarchate

in 1870—which included all of Yugoslav Macedonia—was the first recognition of the Bulgarian nationality and the real beginning of Bulgarian nationalism.

When Vardar Macedonia became part of Serbia and later of Yugoslavia, the Serbian Orthodox Church reached agreement with the Patriarch in Constantinople that the Orthodox churches of Macedonia should be under domination of the Serbian church. The policy followed by the Serbian hierarchy toward the Macedonians complemented the "Serbianizing" policy of the government. Vardar Macedonia was called "South Serbia," its inhabitants were called Serbs, and government and church officials were imported from Old Serbia. It was only natural that one of the first demands of the Macedonians after being acknowledged by the Yugoslav Communists as a distinct nationality was the creation of an independent church.

In October 1943 a meeting of clerics in the western part of Macedonia which was under Partisan control demanded creation of a Macedonian church. After the liberation in March 1945, the first national church convention was held at which the Macedonian clergy took the initiative in petitioning the Serbian Patriarchate for independent ecclesiastical status. Although the Serbian Synod refused the petition, an Initiative Committee for the Establishment of the Macedonian Orthodox Church was created by the convention. The Macedonian church remained by organization and in name a part of the Serbian Orthodox Church, although in practice it enjoyed a measure of autonomy. The Macedonian priests had their own republican clerical association as part of the government-sponsored Federation of the Association of the Orthodox Clergy of Yugoslavia. Significantly, *Vesnik,* the official organ of the Orthodox Federation, was published in both Serbian and Macedonian editions.

The Yugoslav Communist government was at first tempted to authorize the establishment of an independent Macedonian church in order to weaken the Serbian church which was a potential opposition threat. The party openly "considered" the proposal for Macedonian church autonomy.[32] However, by going no further, the Communists were able to elicit some support from the Macedonians who hoped for acceptance, and from the Serb hierarchy, who hoped to be able to prevent it. This threat was employed in 1947 to persuade the Patriarch Gavrilo to return from his self-continued exile in the United States and to declare in favor of the new regime, thereby further splitting Serbian national opposition to the Communists. The threat was further used to secure Serbian Orthodox cooperation in skirmishes with the recalcitrant Roman Catholics. In addition, the government needed to be on moderately good terms with at least one of the major Yugoslav churches, out of consideration for foreign opinion as well as for the maintenance of domestic balance. There was also concern among some of the Yugoslav Communists that a Macedonian church would encourage Macedonian nationalism to the point that it might be difficult to regulate effectively. It does not appear that the Macedonian Communists were particularly eager to push the question of church autonomy at that time, although the issue aroused intense interest among the general Macedonian public, as well as among the clergy. The early establishment of a national church, whose leaders would acquire much prestige, could have impaired the somewhat fragile public standing of the local party luminaries.

At the Second Annual Session of the Association of Macedonian Orthodox Clergy in 1951, the delegates, having subscribed over two million dinars to the Second Public Loan and contributed one hundred thousand dinars to hydroelectric schemes, "suggested that a Macedonian national Orthodox Church should be founded."[33] Some months later, Vikentije, the new Patriarch of the Serbian church following Gavrilo's death, declared that the Holy Synod would examine the problem of the Macedonian Orthodox Church but that there was "no question of any changes to be made in the Church constitution."[34] In June 1952, the Serbian Archiepiscopal Synod was given the task of endeavoring "to set normal religious conditions in the People's Republic of Macedonia."[35] Late in 1953 a Serbian bishop was sent by the Patriarch to work for the futher organizational integration of the Macedonian churches into the Serbian church, but there was such a storm of objections that he was forced to leave. Even those priests in Macedonia who had received their seminary training in Serbia reportedly joined the protest.

At the Congress of the Orthodox Priests Federation in February 1955, a representative of the Initiative Committee for the Establishment of the Macedonian Orthodox Church renewed the demand that the Macedonians "be granted a certain national distinction on the condition that they fully recognize canonical unity and jurisdiction of the Serbian Orthodox Church."[36] The resolution of the Congress pronounced the Macedonian demands justified, declaring, "Church organizations in Macedonia should not go under the name 'Serbian.'"[37] The Serbian hierarchy was much more reluctant than the priest's association to grant the demands, and a compromise agreement was not worked out until spring 1957. The Serbian church would permit use of the Macedonian language for church administration and preaching, but Old Church Slavonic was to be used for the Divine Liturgy, church seals were to have "People's Republic of Macedonia" and the name of the diocese in the Macedonian alphabet around the Church coat of arms, and bishops and church officials appointed for Macedonia were to be native Macedonians.[38] The accommodation was worked out with Yugoslav government assistance, despite its claims of non-interference in religious affairs. At a reception for the Serbian bishops given by the Federal Executive Council a month after the compromise was agreed upon, Patriarch Vikentije thanked the government for its help in church affairs:

> I cannot help mentioning and expressing my special gratitude to the Federal Executive Council for the assistance extended in consolidating the Church in the People's Republic of Macedonia.

He concluded with "long live" the Yugoslav state and its President Marshal Tito.[39]

The accommodation proved to be short-lived, however. In May 1958 the Serbian church leaders insisted upon appointing Serbian bishops for the Macedonian dioceses, which aroused considerable resentment in Macedonia. This time the Macedonian party leadership strongly supported the organization of a separate Macedonian church. A national church convention of clergy and laymen was called for October 4-6, 1958, at Ohrid, the seat of an ancient Orthodox Archbishopric. The involvement of the Macedonian party and government leadership was obvious throughout the conference. Several sessions were held at a trade union rest home, and government officials were present for most of the meetings. The first speaker at the conference was Strahil Gigov, Vice-Chairman of the MPR Executive Council and Chairman of its religious affairs commission. Gigov told the convention that "the Commission for Religious Affairs of the Executive Council has positively evaluated the decision of the steering committee in calling the national church convention."[40] A letter was also read to the convention from Dobrivoje Radosavljević, who played an important role in Macedonia during the war and who was then serving as chairman of the Commission for Religious Affairs of the Federal Executive Council.

The conference declared the re-establishment of the Archbishopric of Ohrid and the establishment of the Macedonian Orthodox Church. Elected head of the Macedonian Church — with the title Archbishop of Ohrid and Skopje and Metropolitan of Macedonia—was Dositej, a Macedonian bishop who had served as Vicar-General to Patriarch Vikentije. Although the Macedonians had created their own church, the links with the Serbian church were not completely severed. In a move to placate Serbian opposition, the Macedonian church declared that it would "remain in canonic unity with the Serbian Orthodox Church through her head, his Holiness Patriarch of the Serbian Orthodox Church,"[41]—i.e., the Serbian Patriarch would be patriarch of both the Serbian and Macedonian churches.

Although the Macedonian and Yugoslav leaderships had opposed creation of the Macedonian church for thirteen years, new conditions brought about a change of attitude. First, by 1958 the Macedonian party leadership had a firm grip on Macedonia. An independent church hierarchy would pose little threat to its power or prestige. Since the party and government were instrumental in setting up the new church and would have to continue to support it for it to survive, there was little possibility that the church would be awkward to control. Second, the Serb heirarchy was temporarily immobilized by the death of Patriarch Vikentije on July 5, 1958. He had been on good terms with the government and was a strong opponent of Macedonian church autonomy. The new Patriarch, German, was chosen September 13 and was still consolidating his position within the church and with the political leadership of Yugoslavia when the Macedonian church declared its independence. It was probably more than just a coincidence that Patriarch German was first received by President Tito on the very same day that Lazar Koliševski, head of state of the MPR, received the newly elected Archbishop Dositej. [42]

Probably the most crucial element in bringing about the establishment of a separate church at this time was the Bulgarian denial of the existence of the Macedonian nationality. As relations between Yugoslavia and the Soviet Union declined before April 1958, the Bulgarian government launched a strong attack against Belgrade, publishing articles and speeches to show that Macedonians are Bulgarians. The Bulgarian campaign provoked vigorous countermeasures in Yugoslavia and Koliševski's speech in Titov Veles which gave a new slant to Macedonian history. Macedonian national holidays on August 2 (Ilinden) and October 11 (the anniversary of the first Macedonian partisan operations in 1941) were used as major occasions to reaffirm the Macedonian nationality. The conference to create the Macedonian church came just two weeks after Dimitur Ganev made the most anti-Yugoslav irredentist speech of any postwar Bulgarian leader up to that time. When the existence of the Macedonian nationality was being more seriously challenged than at any previous time, [43] the creation of the Macedonian Orthodox Church was a powerful way for the Yugoslavs to reaffirm its separate existence.

The Serbian hierarchy was forced to acquiesce in the creation of the church. In 1959 a Serbian council declared that its constitution no longer applied to the dioceses and parishes of Macedonia. However, despite the reluctant formal approval, the Serbian church failed to accept the Macedonian church fully. The Macedonians complained that the Serbian church "did not fulfill her obligation to introduce the independent Macedonian church to other autocephalous Orthodox Churches." The patriarch was accused of using the title "Patriarch of Serbia" rather than his full title "Patriarch of Serbia and Macedonia." Serbian church officials on visits to Macedonia were accused of calling the area "South Serbia" and referring to the Macedonian faithful as "Serbian brothers and sisters." Apparently the crowning indignity to the Macedonians was the Serbian church decision of May 1966 , which prohibited a national church convention from changing the constitution of the Macedonian Orthodox Church without previous approval of the Holy Synod of the Serbian church. [44]

Discontent with the Serbian hierarchy's attempts to retain control and encouraged by the purge of Aleksandar Ranković in July 1966, the Macedonian church Synod met with the Serbian Synod on November 18, 1966, and requested autocephalous status.[45] The request had the full approval of the Macedonian government. Metropolitan Dositej told the churchmen:

> We have agreed to seek independence from the Serbian Orthodox Church. This decision was presented to the Executive Council of Macedonia, which devoted a whole session to the question and notified us that we were not mistaken in seeking independence for our church.[46]

Although at the November meeting the Serbian representatives would not approve autocephalous status for the Macedonian church, a formal request was addressed to the Holy Synod of the Serbian Orthodox Church in December 1966. The request threatened that if the Synod failed to act favorably the Macedonian church would take up the problem at a National Church Convention.

The Synod did not consider the Macedonian request until the following May, but in March the Macedonian church authorities announced that a church convention would be held in July. Patriarch German immediately visited Petar Stambolić, the Serb who was president of the Federal Executive Council, and denounced the prospective Macedonian action as "unlawful" and "uncanonical." When the Serbian Holy Synod considered the Macedonian proposal in May, it declared that the Macedonian church had too few priests and bishops, no theological school, and had dealt with the question in violation of church canons. The request was denied. The Synod's decision concluded:

> But if the Macedonian Church, contrary to the canons, declares her independence at her metropolitan National Church Convention, she will be considered both by the Serbian Orthodox Church and by other autocephalous Orthodox Churches as a dissident religious organization and as such she will be separated from them. [47]

The Macedonian Church, nevertheless, held its national convention at Ohrid July 17-19, 1967, "rectified historical injustice" by declaring itself to be autocephalous, and elected Dositej as head of the church with the title Archbishop of Ohrid and Macedonia. The full support of the government was again in evidence. The chairman of the Federal Commission for

Religious Affairs, Milo Jovićević (a Montenegrin), was present as were two members of the Executive Council of Macedonia and other local Macedonian officials. After the church was declared autocephalous and Dositej chosen to head it, a decree of President Tito was read to the convention awarding Dositej the Order of the Yugoslav Banner with Sash. Following the decision telegrams were sent congratulating Dositej and the conference by Mito Hadživasilev, Chairman of the SRM Assembly, and by Krste Crvenkovski, chairman of the LCM.[48]

It is significant that the Macedonian church declared itself independent only after the removal of Aleksandar Ranković and the break-up of the conservative Serb faction which he headed in the federal Yugoslav government and party bureaucracy. As a representative of Serbian interests, Ranković undoubtedly supported the conservative Serbian hierarchy in its differences with the Macedonian clerics. Krste Crvenkovski commented on the Macedonian church in a meeting of the Macedonian Party *activ* with Tito present:

> It is well known that for twenty years Ranković had personally insisted and had done everything possible to ensure that this [church] question would not be settled in the spirit of our social and federal system and freedom . . . . Therefore it was on the other [Serbian] side that politics had been deeply involved in this question. If this had only been a religious question, it is probable that it would have been solved as long ago as 1945. . . . Certain comrads in Serbia emphasize with good reason that these [links between the Serbian and Macedonian church] were the last remnants of Greater Serbian hegemony in Macedonia.[49]

The timing of the Macedonian demands for independence would support Crvenkovski's claim that Ranković was a major obstacle. The first demand for autonomy was submitted in November 1966—Ranković was removed from his party and government positions in July and expelled from the party in October 1966. While the purge of Ranković removed the chief roadblock, there were also positive benefits to the Macedonian leadership to be gained from granting full independence to the church at this time. Eliminating one of the most obvious remnants of Serbian hegemony was a useful concession to Macedonian national feeling. Granting autonomy to the church was a safety valve for national discontent at a time when unemployment and economic difficulties resulting from the economic reforms were having their most serious effect in Macedonia. By creating a fully independent national church, the political leaders hoped to uncouple national dissatisfaction from economic problems by supporting a popular issue.[50]

The Serbian hierarchy did not accept the Macedonian action passively. Patriarch German visited Milka Spiljak, new Croatian president of the Federal Executive Council, to protest the action, then gathered his forces by calling upon the President of the Serbian Executive Council[51] and visiting Montenegro. The Patriarchate also published the reasons for its decision of May 1967 in refusing to grant the Macedonian church autonomy, and called a special session of the Holy Synod to consider the action of the Macedonians. The leadership of the government-sponsored Association of Orthodox Priests counseled the Synod to pass a "wise, mild and moderate decision" or the "very good relations between the Serbian church and the state could be disturbed and even deteriorate for a long period of time."[52] The special session of the Holy Synod, however, accused the Macedonian clergy of "forming a dissident religious organization" and announced "canonical and liturgical communications with that hierarchy have been broken off and the Holy Synod of the Serbian Orthodox Church has been asked to take proceedings against the perpetrators of this breech."[53]

In Belgrade, newspaper editorials enjoined caution and understanding on both sides. In Macedonia the Serbian Synod's decision created considerable excitement. *Nova Makedonija* declared the decision an "anachronism" and published a lengthy history of the struggle of the Macedonian Church for independence. Macedonian political leaders called the decision an attempt by Serbs to retain a remnant of their hegemony over Macedonia. The Macedonian church announced that it had decided to form its own school of theology and classes began the following month. A synod of the Macedonian church rejected the Serbian decision but "voiced the belief that common sense would prevail and that the leaders of the Serbian Orthodox Church would in the end resume contacts with the autocephalous Macedonian Orthodox Church."[54]

The declaration of independence by the Macedonian church has had far reaching ramifications because of the Balkan concept of identity between church and nationality. Although the conservative Serbs were forced by law to admit the existence of the Macedonian nationality, they refused to go the last step and grant the Macedonians the right to a separate church. But they were not alone in refusing to acknowledge the Macedonian church. Patriarch German sent a letter to the Greek Orthodox Church explaining the Serbian church action against the Macedonian church hierarchy. The Greek organization denounced the Macedonians and resolved to sever all links with the Macedonian church. Athenagoras, the Ecumenical Patriarch of all Orthodox Churches, visited Belgrade in mid-October 1967 and conferred with German. The communique on their visit stated that complete agreement was reached on all church questions, which would imply Athenagoras' support of the Serbian position against the Macedonian church. The Macedonian church took steps to improve its international standing by sending envoys to Constantinople to confer with Athenagoras and also by sending representatives to visit the patriarchs of Rumania, Bulgaria and Russia. Although the Greek Church was the only foreign Orthodox church to take a stand immediately and publicly against the Macedonian church, there are reasons for the other churches failing to recognize the Macedonian church. The Orthodox churches of Greece and Bulgaria would have political problems if they were to recognize the Skopje archbishopric because the government of neither country acknowledges the existence of a Macedonian nationality. Recognition of the Macedonian church would put the Russian Orthodox Church in an awkward position vis-à-vis its Ukrainian faithful who also would like to be recognized as an independent church.

Party assistance in bringing about the full autonomy of the Macedonian church hardly represents a change in party policy towards religion. The party ideology is still atheistic; party leaders officially denounce the effects of religion, oppose religious instruction for children, and take administrative measures to limit the church's influence and ability to carry out its responsibilities. However, the party also recognized the significance of religion as a means of affirming national existence and stimulating national consciousness. Hence, the Macedonian Communists used the church, whose existence they are seeking to undermine, to affirm a policy they are trying to carry out. By supporting the church's independence the Macedonian party and government leaders were also able to secure support and cooperation of the clergy and reduce the hostility of the faithful. While the Orthodox Macedonians may not appear to be very pious, the church touches the consciousness of most Macedonians. The creation of a fully independent Macedonian church, while long delayed and accomplished piecemeal for political purposes, may well be one of the most significant aspects of the new Macedonian culture.

Because of the Bulgarian consciousness of a large part of the Macedonian population, culture in Macedonia has been allowed somewhat greater latitude than in other republics of Yugoslavia. The cultural field has also contributed more to the development of a Macedonian national consciousness than any other area. After twenty-five years the major questions of Macedonian culture have been resolved. The Macedonian literary language has achieved a standard form generally accepted by the Macedonian population; the premises and outline of the Macedonian national interpretation of history have been worked out (although detail is yet to be supplied in many areas); the Macedonian Orthodox Church has been established fully independent of the Serbian church; graphic and performing arts have utilized nationalistic themes, though their direct contribution to Macedonian consciousness has been more limited. The ability of the Macedonian Communists to withstand the very vigorous Bulgarian challenges to the Macedonian national existence since 1958 indicates the success of the new cultural forms. But the serious concern evident in both Skopje and Belgrade whenever Bulgarian scholars criticize the Macedonian language, history or culture indicates that the new culture has not been completely successful in eradicating Bulgarian consciousness.

CHAPTER 10
THE MACEDONIAN REPUBLIC
AND ITS MINORITIES

From a situation in which they were not recognized as a separate nationality or even as a minority but only as poor relations of the dominant Serbs who spoke "South Serbian" dialects, the Macedonians were elevated to the status of one of the "Yugoslav nationalities"[1] and became the dominant nationality in their own republic. Although ninty-six percent of all Macedonians living in Yugoslavia are inhabitants of their own republic, they make up just over two-thirds of the republic's population. There is a large Albanian minority numbering about 200,000 and a Turkish population of over 130,000 as of the 1961 census. Smaller Serbian and Vlah (or Rumanian) minorities also live in the republic. The Turkish population is scattered through the Vardar River Valley where Turkish and Macedonian villages are interspersed. The Albanian population is more compact and is concentrated in the areas of western and northwestern Macedonia bordering Albania and the Kosmet.

The Turks, who are the descendants of the Ottoman conquerors, have inhabited their villages for generations and chose not to go to Turkey after Macedonia was partitioned between Greece, Bulgaria and Serbia. The Albanians, who are ethnic remnants of the original Illyrian tribes, began moving east into the territory of Macedonia by displacing the local Slavs early in the nineteenth century. During World War II western Macedonia as well as most of Kosmet was absorbed by the Italian protectorate of Albania. Following the war the Albanian population opposed its reincorporation into Yugoslavia. Although most Albanians living in Yugoslavia were included in the Autonomous Province of Kosmet, the Albanian areas of western and northwestern Macedonia were not added to the autonomous region. The Macedonians would have objected to this loss of "traditional" Macedonian territory,[2] there was some feeling that the Albanians might be more effectively controlled if they were administratively separated, and the Šar Mountains make communications between Kosmet and western Macedonia difficult.

At the close of the war with the creation of the Macedonian republic, there was a potential for serious difficulty between Macedonians and the

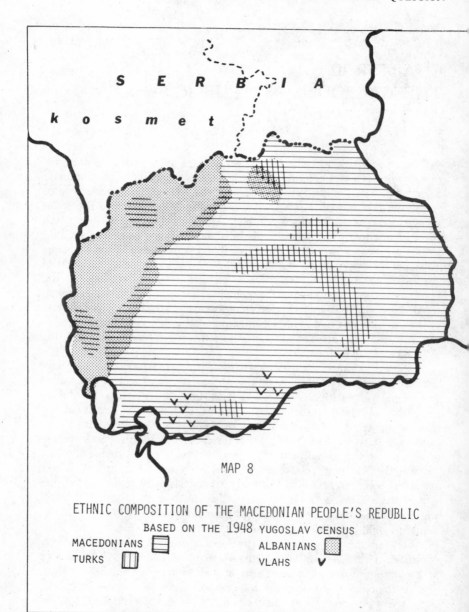

MAP 8

ETHNIC COMPOSITION OF THE MACEDONIAN PEOPLE'S REPUBLIC
BASED ON THE 1948 YUGOSLAV CENSUS

MACEDONIANS   ALBANIANS
TURKS   VLAHS

republic's minorities. Almost all offices of the government and party were held by Macedonians. Although Serbian advisors and centralized party control limited any independent exercise of power, there was a feeling that Macedonians werè governing their own republic. To the Turkish and Albanian minorities, the new government was another alien regime imposed upon them, promising discrimination. The Albanian minority, having lived for a few years under Italian-Albanian adminstration, was particularly reluctant to re-submit to Yugoslav hegemony. The Yugoslav partisans had great difficulty in re-establishing control in the Albanian minority areas.

The Macedonians, frequently maltreated during the Ottoman period by the ruling Turkish and Albanian minorities, had been subject to Serbian and Bulgarian chauvinism for over forty years. After the war with a measure of local control, there was a real danger that the new Macedonian officials would resort to chauvinism. While there were some serious difficulties, the Communist party succeeded in establishing control over the minorities and preventing excesses of Macedonian nationalism.

Although Macedonian chauvinism was not permitted to develop, the policy of the Communist party resulted in discrimination. The campaign against Muslim religious tradition was seen by Turks and Albanians as being directed against specific nationalities since they are Muslim while the predominant Slavs are Othodox. The campaign to prohibit women from wearing the veil, attacks aimed at specific Muslim religious leaders and "abuses" of religious practices were seen by the minorities as directed against them because of their nationality. Before 1950, the Turks as a group were suspect because the government of Turkey was friendly toward the West. The 1948 trial of seventeen Turks for participation in an anti-government conspiracy was widely publicized to intimidate the minority. After the Cominform resolution of June 1948, the Albanian minority, too, fell under a cloud of suspicion. The Albanian government and party began a campaign to encourage the Albanians of Kosmet and Macedonia to oppose Yugoslav rule, promising unification with Albania. The Yugoslavs countered with severe punishment for Albanians guilty of anti-Yugoslav activities and a propaganda campaign to show that the "free" Albanians in Yugoslavia were much better off than their compatriots in Albania. As Yugoslav relations with Turkey improved in the early 1950's, the pressure against the Turks was relaxed but harsh treatment of the Albanians continued. Krste Crvenkovski remarked that many Macedonian Communists felt that the Albanians could be dealt with "only by force."

The dissatisfaction of the Turkish and Albanian minorities in Macedonia became apparent after the Balkan pact was signed. The Yugoslav and Turkish governments reached agreement to permit Turks in Yugoslavia to emigrate to Turkey. In 1954 Koliševski said "a certain number" of Turks had requested permission to emigrate but they did so for "personal reasons. "[4] The exact number who emigrated is difficult to determine since both governments have played down the agreement. However, during the 1950's as many as one-hundred thousand Turks left Yugoslavia for Turkey. An indication of the dissatisfaction with Macedonian treatment of its Albanian minority is indicated by the fact that some Albanians attempted to emigrate as Turks. The 1948 Yugoslav census showed 179,389 Albanians in Macedonia (17.1 percent of the republic's population) and 95,940 Turks (8.3 percent of the population). In the 1953 census, after the agreement for emigration of Turks had been reached, the Albanian population *fell* to 162,524 (12.4 percent of the population) while the Turkish population more than doubled to 203,938 (15.6 percent of the republic's population). Of these "Turks" in Macedonia in 1953, 27,086 gave Albanian and 32,393 gave Macedonian as their native language. At least some of these Albanians were successful in going to Turkey.[5]

Despite action taken against the minorities, the party emphasized its efforts on the question of national equality—particularly the education of the Turks and Albanians.[6] Although schools for the minorities came after schools for the Macedonians, real progress has been made in education of the minorities at the lower levels. However, in the gymnasia and more advanced schools the proportion of Albanians and Turks falls off significantly.[7] In 1959 the teacher's training schools were the only secondary school where instruction was offered in the Albanian language. While this encouraged the preparation of Albanian language teachers for primary schools, it did little towards the accomplishment of the Party's "policy to produce highly-educated people among the ranks of the national minorities." The Third Congress of the LCM in 1959 dealt extensively with the problem of education of the national minorities. Koliševski pinpointed the language barrier as the major problem. For the Albanians and Turks to wait for instruction to be offered in their own languages would require considerable delay and expense for construction of facilities and training of Albanian speaking teachers. He advocated that the minorities learn the Macedonian and Serbo-Croatian languages for instruction in advanced fields:

> Every nationality in the course of its development transcends the exclusiveness of its own language because that presents an obstacle to its further development and its ability to master the modern achievements of science and culture.[8]

To avoid accusations of chauvinism, Koliševski declared that Macedonians living in minority areas should learn Albanian and Turkish. All Yugoslav minority nationalities are required to learn the language of the republic

where they reside. However, use of the minority language in
and opposition, particularly among older persons, to using th
the dominant nationality prevents students from developing r
secondary language. The Macedonian government was also slow to encourage reciprocal language learning. The first Macedonian-Albanian and Mace-
donian-Turkish dictionaries were not published until 1968, after bi-lingual
dictionaries for Macedonian and Serbo-Croatian, Russian, English, French,
Italian and even Bulgarian had been published.[9] Although some progress
has been made in education, much more will be required in order for the
minorities to reach the level of the Macedonian people.

Economically Macedonia is faced with minority areas which are less
developed than some Macedonian populated regions of the republic. With
limited investment resources there has been a tendency to slight these minority areas. Although some projects have been constructed in minority
areas, they have generally been those which utilize nearby natural resources.
In regions with mixed populations there is a concern by the party for employment of members of the minorities in the economic enterprises. At the Third
Congress Koliševski cited figures of Macedonians and Albanians employed
in industry for the Tetovo district, adding approvingly, "This is quite in
proportion to the numbers of the Macedonian and Škiptar [Albanian]
population in the district."[10] The difficulties, however, of integrating the
minorities into the developing Macedonian economy are great. The minorities are not skilled workers and the language barrier makes their training
more costly and less efficient. For the party to prevent managers of enterprises from discrimination both in hiring and promotion policies is even
more difficult. Thus proportionately fewer Albanians are employed in industry and those who do hold jobs perform the more menial tasks.

The Macedonian party organization has long been aware of its failure
to grant proportional representation in positions of political power to the
minorities. In 1952 in an interview before elections, Vice-Chairman of the
Macedonian Executive Council, Nikola Minčev, observed that it was "difficult to develop among the members of national minorities the feeling and
conception that the democratic principles in the nomination and election of
people's committees are their sacred rights." Minčev admitted that the minorities were not represented "in the agencies of popular authority in proportion to their numbers."[11] Despite this early awareness and the concern
expressed at the Third LCM Congress in 1959, little was done to increase
minority representation in the leading bodies of either party or government.
Until 1965 the Macedonian party executive committee included only Macedonians; the central committee before 1965 never included more than one
Albanian and two Turks, though its total membership was as high as 99 at

times. The Macedonian Republican Executive Council included an Albanian or a Turk and occasionally both, but never more than one from each nationality.[12] The nationality composition of the membership of the Macedonian party also reflected discrimination against the minorities. In 1959 almost 85 percent of party members were Macedonian although that nationality made up less than 70 percent of the republic's population. Only 6.28 percent of party members were Albanians, 2.29 percent Turks and 6.80 percent other nationalities. These figures represented little change from the party's nationality composition in 1954.[13]

The party governing bodies selected in 1965 at the Fourth LCM Congress marked the beginning of a trend towards greater representation for the minorities. For the first time, a non-Macedonian, Hadžet Ramadani, was elected to the party Executive Committee. Of the 87 members elected to the Central Committee, eight were Albanian and two were Turks.[14] While this was not full proportional representation, it did represent a significant step forward. The party has also acted to improve representation of the minorities in the local party and government organs. A special session of the Central Committee in March 1968 was devoted to the national minorities. One of the principal subjects was the representation of minorities in local political and economic organizations and there seemed to be at least numerical progress. At the Fifth LCM Congress in November 1968 the decisions and resolutions of the March Central Committee session were included in the materials of the congress and the 52 member Central Committee which was selected included 10 non-Macedonians.

Belated recognition by the Macedonian party of minority rights for the Albanians and Turks was precipitated by concern in Belgrade that the Macedonian republic was not giving its minorities sufficient attention. Even the Serbian republic gave greater numerical representation to its Albanian and Hungarian minorities in the leading party and government organs than Macedonia gave to its Albanian and Turkish minorities, although the two minorities in Serbia were a much smaller proportion of the population. In both Serbia and Macedonia, the representatives of the national minorities were cooperative communists with pro-Belgrade leanings. Since the appearance of minority cadres was an important element of Belgrade's nationality policy, some pressure was put on the Macedonians to comply with the Yugoslav national program. There was also pressure from the Albanian and Turkish population for recognition by the Macedonian authorities. Crvenkovski admitted at the March Central Committee session that there were incidents of unrest among the Albanian minority. Some Albanians in Bitolj were accused of spying for the Albanian intelligence service and of "forming a group with the task of working against the integrity of the people and state and for the annexation of one part of western Macedonia to Albania."[15] These incidents were indicators which the party leaders found unwise to ignore.

Rising discontent among the nationalities impelled the Macedonian leadership to rectify some of the errors of its nationality policy, but crisis developed before this policy could be fully implemented. On November 27, 1968—the eve of the Day of the Albanian Flag (the date on which the Albanian Republic was proclaimed in 1919) and one month after the Albanians won the right to fly the Albanian flag alongside the Yugoslav flag—serious riots broke out among the Albanian minority in Priština and other cities of the Kosmet Autonomous Province. The unrest continued for over a week and was only suppressed by troops and tanks after several police and demonstrators had been seriously injured. One of the principal demands was that the Kosmet be granted republic status and be separated from the Serbian Republic. There was apparently no desire expressed to be annexed to Albania. During this outburst the Albanian minority in Macedonia remained relatively quiet but two weeks later a major outbreak occurred in Tetovo, a city in northwest Macedonia with a mixed Albanian-Macedonian population.

The riot in Tetovo, which began on the evening of December 22 and continued through the following night, was touched off when the Macedonian owner of a photography shop attempted to remove an Albanian flag from the shop of an Albanian tailor. The photo shop as well as several other shops, buildings, and vehicles were demolished; the demonstrators flew the Albanian flag in Marshal Tito Square and from every Muslim minaret in Tetovo; they also put Albanian flags in the windows of the local office of the League of Communists. The demonstrators shouted nationalist slogans, including "Tito-Fadilj." Fadilj Hodža (in Serbian or "Hoxha" in Albanian) is the ranking official of the Autonomous Province of Kosmet and an Albanian. This slogan was symbolic of the program of the rioters to join the Albanian areas of Macedonia with Kosmet in an independent Yugoslav republic. There was no indication of a desire to join the Albania of Envir Hoxha.[16]

Once order was restored, the actions taken against those responsible were immediate. Protest meetings were held throughout the Tetovo district and in other parts of Macedonia with much publicity given the denunciations of the rioters by Albanians and Turks. A special session of the Tetovo local council of the Socialist Alliance was held with the ranking Albanian Communist leaders of Macedonia present. Among the leaders of the demonstration were doctors, school teachers, two delegates on the local *opština* government council, as well as numerous students. Criminal proceedings were begun against the twenty most prominent Albanians involved, all scholar-

ships and school assistance was denied to any Albanian students who could
be proved to have participated, numerous Albanians involved in the demonstrations were dismissed from their jobs, and by January 4, 1969, some
79 people had been sentenced for up to thirty days imprisionment. In addition to swift harsh punishment for demonstrators, the party called for
"maximum engagement of the organizations of the League of Communists
in realizing the policy on the national question." Azem Zulfičari, the Albanian member of the LCY Central Committee from Macedonia and President of the Macedonian branch of the Socialist Alliance, counseled his Albanian brothers that they

> should not seek their interests and their rights outside the S.R. Macedonia
> but within it in active participation and efforts for strengthening the ma-
> terial basis and developing socialist, democratic and self-management
> relations.[17]

The party succeeded in restoring outward calm and utilized the uprising as
an object lesson for the minorities should they upset the balance again.

Although the rioting in Tetovo may not have been initiated by the local
Albanians (the party claims agitators from the outside incited the Tetovo
demonstrations), it did indicate minority dissatisfaction. Regardless of where
the spark came from, the tinder was ready to burn. The fact that the slogans
of the Albanians in Tetovo favored union with a Kosmet Republic indicates
that their expectations of equal treatment were not being satisfied in Macedonia. In part the party produced the crisis with its own policies. Through
educating an Albanian intelligentsia and talking of equal rights for minorities,
but not producing that equality in employment, political participation, and
cultural-religious autonomy, the Macedonian Communists contributed to
the conditions which led to the Tetovo uprising. If the Macedonians continue to educate and train the Albanians, they must be willing to share with
them the responsibilities and perquisites of power.

The existence of minority populations as well as uprisings like the one
in Tetovo have had a significant effect upon the development of Macedonian
nationalism. A non-Macedonian people living in the same area as the Macedonians creates an awareness of the differences between "we" and "they."
The effect is to produce a greater consciousness of one's own distinct national identity. Beyond this, however, the rising discontent of the minorities,
and particularly the Tetovo demonstrations, has produced a feeling that the
Macedonian position in its own republic is threatened. This further encour-
ages national identification. The desire expressed by the Albanians to become part of the Kosmet has increased this sense of threat. The Macedonian
party leadership expressed concern after the uprising that the conception
was developing, "Macedonians unite, the Albanians have begun to expel

us."[18] Despite party injunctions to counter this sentiment, its exists and has heightened national consciousness. The historic Muslim-Christian conflict is still very much alive; the Muslim Albanians and Turks are seen by the Christian Macedonians as a danger to the integrity of their republic. This revival of the conditions under which Balkan nationalism first developed in the nineteenth century can only have the effect of intensifying Macedonian consciousness.

CHAPTER 11
THE MACEDONIAN QUESTION AND
YUGOSLAV FOREIGN POLICY

Macedonia was a major issue in nineteenth century diplomacy because it was located at the convergence of great power spheres of influence. Russia, expanding southward toward the Straits, Austria, seeking dominance over Balkan provinces of the crumbling Turkish Empire, and Britain, anxious to forestall any challenge to her control of the eastern Mediterranean, found their interests converging in Macedonia. The result was that Serb, Greek, and Bulgarian aspirations for Macedonia were thwarted or advanced by various great powers in the pursuit of their own hegemony. Krste Crvenkovski claims that Macedonia today remains a keystone in international politics because it is still at the convergence of great power spheres — Bulgaria backed by the Soviet Union and the communist bloc, Greece allied to the United States and Western Europe through NATO, and Albania supported by Communist China all have footholds in the Balkans, and Macedonia lies in their midst. Crvenkovski further placed the Balkan Peninsula at one of the crucial crossroads of world affairs — midway between recently invaded Czechoslovakia and the constantly smouldering Arab-Israeli conflict.[1] Although the Macedonian leader was perhaps overstating the importance of Macedonia, there is no doubt that the Macedonian question is still alive, that it continues to be a key foreign policy issue of the Balkan Peninsula, and that its repercussions reverberate beyond Southeast Europe.

The Yugoslav recognition (or creation) of a distinct Macedonian nationality, however, has altered the nature of the conflict. At the same time the international significance of the Macedonian question and its effect on Bulgarian-Serbian-Greek foreign relations has had a profound impact on the development of a Macedonian national consciousness. Macedonia (Aegean and Pirin as well as Vardar) is so closely linked by history and a half-century of struggle against Turkish domination that, although the area is now divided by national boundaries, what happens in any part has an impact on the whole. Family relationships, associations and friendships bind the Slavic Macedonians despite frontiers. Hence, the Yugoslav communist recognition of a Macedonian nationality in its own portion of Macedonia implies that the slavic inhabitants of Greek and Bulgarian Macedonia are of the same "Macedonian" nationality. The Yugoslavs, to support their claim that the Slavs of Vardar Macedonia are of the Macedonian nationality, must likewise claim that Slavs in Bulgaria and Greece are of the Macedonian nationality. As *Nova Makedonija* observed editorially:

> [We] could not divide the Macedonian nation just because . . . a section of the Macedonians happened to live within the frontiers of Bulgaria and the second one within the frontiers of Greece.[2]

The existence of Macedonians beyond the Yugoslav borders of course has required Belgrade to follow a policy of seeking recognition of this minority and granting it minority rights:

> The anxiety over the Macedonian minorities in the neighboring countries is a permanent task of this section of our nation, which has made great efforts to help their countrymen [in Bulgaria and Greece] attain the status of national minority.[3]

Since modern nationalism implies congruence between nation and state, the Yugoslavs in claiming a Macedonian nationality exists in Bulgaria and Greece are arguing for Macedonian unification under auspices of Belgrade.

The Bulgarians, who for generations have considered the inhabitants of Macedonia to be their Bulgarian brothers, have been reluctant to admit a Macedonian nationality. Although the Bulgarian Communist Party officially recognized and encouraged the Macedonian nationality in 1944, there was serious opposition from the Bulgarian people as well as within the party to this policy. In 1956 the CPB abandoned unequivocally this unpopular position and has continued since that time to claim that there is no Macedonian minority, that Macedonians are Bulgarians. During the height of the 1958 polemics, an unsigned article in an official Bulgarian party publication set forth the Bulgarian national position.

> There is no reason for granting the status of national minority to the population of the [Pirin] region. Such separation would be artificial. It would amount to creation of differences that do not exist . . . .
>
> To grant the status of national minority to the population of the Pirin region would be tantamount to an artificial creation of national differences. . . . Between the population of the Pirin region and the Bulgarians there are not differences in language, culture, economy; there are no legal or national differences. To transplant the semi-Serbian literary language which is fabricated in Skopje to the Pirin region would be tantamount to pressure on the inhabitants of that region.[4]

At the same time Greece is unwilling to permit Yugoslavia or Bulgaria to annex its portion of Macedonia; hence the existence of any Macedonian nationality is denied. During polemics with the Yugoslavs in 1962, an Athens newspaper set forth the Greek position in a front page editorial:

> The basic fact is that there is not any [Macedonian] minority in Greece. The exchange of populations took place 40 years ago with Bulgaria. And 13 years ago there escaped to Yugoslavia and Bulgaria those who during the rebel war did not feel themselves Greeks. As a result there live today in the border areas under discussion only people who are purely Greek.
>
> Nobody denies the fact that in Greece (not only northern Greece but even here in Attica) there are Greeks who speak a second language in addition to Greek. But they are pure Greeks with a Greek national consciousness . . . .
>
> If Yugoslavia is afraid of Bulgarian claims to a people who were once Bulgarians, or if Yugoslavia has claims to people in Bulgaria, that is its own affair. . . . If Yugoslavia wants to follow a policy of calling for the establishment of a "Macedonian minority," it cannot consider in this connection Greek territory and Greek people whom it arbitrarily calls non-Greek.[5]

The Yugoslavs on one side and the Bulgarians and Greeks on the other are locked into contradictory positions—the Yugoslavs must recognize and must encourage others to recognize a Macedonian nationality, while the Greeks and Bulgarians must oppose recognition of a separate nationality for Macedonians.

The desire to increase their hegemony led the Yugoslav Communists to attempt to annex both Pirin and Aegean Macedonia during the fluid conditions prevailing after World War II. Although the Cominform Resolution and the collapse of the Greek guerrilla movement after 1948 prevented fulfillment of that desire, the expansionist ambitions could be revived. After 1948 the Yugoslavs were forced to cease actively pursuing annexation and to follow a policy recognizing the current frontiers. The policy of encouraging recognition of the Macedonian nationality was ideally suited to Yugoslav expansionist desires at a time when borders could not be changed by direct means. The Yugoslavs have carried on propaganda campaigns and sought through diplomatic negotiations to secure Bulgarian and Greek recognition of Macedonian national minorities entitled to minority rights— use of their "own" language in schools and in public affairs, recognition of their right to cultural autonomy, and of course permission for closer links with their co-nationals in Yugoslav Macedonia.

The Yugoslav campaign has had little success in winning Bulgarian or Greek approval. Its intent is too obvious. By granting national recognition and minority rights, Greece and Bulgaria would encourage identification of their Slavo-Macedonians with the more numerous, more culturally advanced Yugoslav Macedonians. This is particularly true on the question of the use of language. The Yugoslavs seek recognition of the minority's right to use the Macedonian literary language which is far different from the Slavic dialects which the peasants use. The spread of Macedonian culture through granting minority rights would not only increase Yugoslav influence among the people, it would also weaken the links of the Slavo-Macedonians with the Bulgarians and Greeks. In Bulgaria it would probably be necessary for the government to "encourage" the Macefonians to acknowledge their separate non-Bulgarian nationality. The distinction between the history, language, and culture of Pirin Macedonia and that of Bulgaria is insignificant. In addition there is political and economic advantage in being of the majority nationality. In Greece the government is following a policy of encouraging assimilation of the Slavs there. Although differences between Greek and Macedonian are much greater than between Bulgarian and Macedonian, the economic incentives, teaching of Greek in schools and religious control by the Greek Orthodox Church are all having an effect in weakening the Slavic consciousness particularly among the younger generation. The Yugoslav campaign to secure recognition of the Macedonian nationality with minority rights is calculated to strengthen cultural ties with Skopje and weaken links with Athens or Sofia until international conditions permit political action to resume on another level.

Macedonian nationalism is not merely an instrument used by Belgrade to further its hegemony in the Balkans. Although the major effect has been on internal affairs of the Macedonian republic, the international aspects of the question have had an impact upon Macedonian consciousness. Greece since 1945 and Bulgaria since 1956 have denied the existence of a Macedonian nationality. Hence, the Yugoslavs have been forced to continually prove the existence of a separate nation. This has led to constant emphasis on the distinctive characteristics of the nationality. While among the other peoples of Yugoslavia the peculiarities of their national traits have been played down with emphasis on rapproachement between nationalities, in Macedonia the emphasis has been on the unique characteristics of Macedonians. Hence they have been permitted greater latitude in emphasizing their nationalism. The campaign of Bulgarian historians to show that Macedonians are Bulgarians has forced the Yugoslavs to clarify a number of questions of history. Current Macedonian historiography owes much to Bulgarian pressure. Bulgarian linquists and critics have forced the Yugoslavs to devote energy and effort to clarify linguistic and literary questions that otherwise might have been ignored. Sofia's denial of the Macedonian

nationality was the major factor in bringing about the establishment of the
Macedonian Orthodox Church in 1958. Other characteristic attributes of
nationality which have been granted the Macedonians would likely have
been withheld if Bulgarian and Greek opposition had not forced the Yugoslavs to reaffirm Macedonian consciousness.

The concern of Macedonia with Yugoslav policy toward Bulgaria and
Greece gives the republic a greater role to play in Yugoslav Balkan policy.
Particularly in recent years, the federation has paid greater deference to the
individual republics on foreign policy questions which concern them. After
the Fifth LCM Congress in 1968, *Komunist* observed with approval:

> The principal characteristics of the Fifth Congress of the League of Com-
> munists of Macedonia are linked, above all, with its geo-political position.
> The contribution of this Congress to the task of formulating long-term views
> of the League of Communists of Yugoslavia on problems of relations and
> cooperation among Balkan nations is unquestionable.[6]

This greater role in formulating foreign policy is certainly a factor heighten-
ing the self-esteem of the Macedonians.

The opposition of Athens and Sofia to the Macedonian nationality has
not only forced Belgrade to give increased accoutrements of nationality to
the Macedonians, it has also given Belgrade the opportunity to emphasize
that only within the Yugoslav federation do the Macedonians receive recognition of their national rights. Although somewhat greater latitude is permitted the Macedonians in matters of nationality, there is no question that
Macedonia must remain a part of Yugoslavia. After 1956 when the Bulgarian party and government denied the existence of the Macedonian nationality, Lazar Koliševski explained that past plans for an autonomous
Macedonia had been achieved in the Yugoslav federation:

> In their struggle for a free life our people sought a way of solving this ques-
> tion [unification of the Macedonian people] . . . . Their ideas about au-
> tonomy, that is to say, about a South Slav, Balkan or other federation were
> formed on that basis. All these ideas in fact were part of the national essence
> of the Macedonian question. *The federation acquired concrete form on the
> territory of the Yugoslav peoples,* with the distinction that the struggle
> of the peoples — closely linked with the struggle of the other [Yugoslav]
> peoples — moved beyond autonomy and in the direction of the establishment
> of a free state and completely unimpeded national development.[7]

Membership in the Yugoslav federation is made to look as beneficial to
Macedonia as possible. During Bulgaria's most recent anti-Yugoslav campaign which began early in 1968, a newspaper article was published in Za-

greb denouncing Bulgaria's assault on the Macedonian nationality and criticizing scholars of the non-Macedonian republics for failing to aid Macedonian academicians in the struggle against the "hegemonistic theses" of some Bulgarians.[8] To demonstrate solidarity with their sister republic and reaffirm Macedonia's place in the Yugoslav federation, scholarly articles and newspaper commentary appeared in all of the republics.

Although Macedonia is a key factor it is not the only one influencing the relations of Yugoslavia with Bulgaria and Greece. In certain instances the Yugoslav government has been willing to play down—though never abandon entirely—differences over Macedonia in the interest of improving relations with its neighbors. Thus in the early 1950's the Macedonian question was not allowed to interfere with the signing of the Balkan Pact and the establishment of good relations with Greece. During the period between 1962 and 1967 friendly Bulgarian-Yugoslav relations were not upset even though Marshal Tito and Bulgarian party leader, Todor Zhivkov, were unable to reach mutual agreement on the Macedonian question. Occasional outbursts on Macedonia were not allowed to disturb the otherwise friendly relations. At other times vicious propaganda campaigns centering on the Macedonian question have been carried on by Yugoslavia with Bulgaria and Greece, pushing relations between the governments to new lows.

The crucial question in Yugoslav policy toward Bulgaria and Greece is to what extent is Macedonia the *cause* and to what extent is it a *symptom* of bad relations. The question is in no way a simple one. For over one hundred years Macedonia has been the cause of friction between the three nations which now possess parts of it. Every war that has affected the Balkans has produced changes, at least temporarily, in the status of Macedonia. Between the two world wars, the Macedonian question was the principal cause for the unfriendly relations of Bulgaria with Yugoslavia and Greece and was a major factor in the creation of the Balkan Entente which was directed against Bulgaria. The recognition of the Macedonian nationality by the Yugoslav communists has added a new element. Yugoslavia has used the new nationality as a justification for retaining its part of Macedonia and as a means to extend its influence over all of Macedonia. The Bulgarian Communist government, which for a time advocated the establishment of an "autonomous" Macedonia (which the Bulgarians intended would be closely linked with Bulgaria), has not given up its claim to all of Macedonia. Although Greece has not claimed a greater share of Macedonia, the Bulgarian and Yugoslav aspirations still provide ample tinder for a conflagration. However, the fact that Communist governments came to power in both Sofia and Belgrade has changed the nature of the conflict to a great extent. The influence of the Soviet Union upon Bulgarian policy has been at times a restraining influence upon Sofia. The emphasis in both Yugoslavia and Bulgaria on economic development and social transformation as well as on the international solidarity claimed by the Communist movement (when Yugoslavia is considered a part of that movement) have added new elements which have tempered the conflict. While clear distinction between causes and symptoms is impossible, Macedonia has been more a symptom of bad relations between Yugoslavia and Bulgaria since the war, while it more often has been a cause of bad Yugoslav relations with Greece. In neither case, however, is the Macedonian question exclusively either cause or symptom.

Although Macedonia remains an emotional, unresolved, and potentially disruptive issue, the chief determinant of Bulgarian-Yugoslav relations has been *Soviet*-Yugoslav relations. When Belgrade and Moscow are on good terms, Sofia is on good terms with Belgrade, and differences over Macedonia are not permitted to disturb the relations. However, when Belgrade-Moscow relations are strained, relations between Bulgaria and Yugoslavia deteriorate and polemics on Macedonia become vigorous and vitriolic. Although Moscow calls the plays, Sofia at times has been reluctant to follow the signals. Thus, the Macedonian question exerts independent pressure on Bulgarian policy which at times runs counter to Moscow's decisions.

After the Communist-led *coup d'état* in Bulgaria on September 9, 1944, the Bulgarian government and party, following the Soviet lead, pursued a policy of friendship and collaboration with Tito. Bulgaria recognized the Macedonian nationality and advocated Macedonian unification within a federation to include Bulgarians and Yugoslavs. Resistence within the Bulgarian party to this line is indicated by frequent high-level party criticism of "nationalist and chauvinist" deviations on the Macedonian question. Although the party favored unification of all of the separate parts into a whole "autonomous" Macedonia, the Bulgarians clearly intended this Macedonia to have a special relationship with Bulgaria. Despite strong pressure from the Yugoslavs to annex the Pirin district to its own Vardar Macedonia, Bulgaria refused to permit party and government organs in the Pirin region to slip beyond its control. When the Cominform Resolution condemning Yugoslavia was approved in June 1948, the Bulgarian party central committee declared that "the population of the Pirin district [would] be given the possibility of itself deciding about its nationality."[9] Although verbally admitting the continued existence of a Macedonian nation entitled to autonomy within a pro-Cominform (and therefore Bulgarian-dominated) federation, the Bulgarians began to play down Macedonian consciousness. The party declared that use of the Bulgarian language was not an obstacle to the development of Macedonian consciousness; hence use of the Macedonian language was discontinued.[10] The quick decisive action of the party in severing relations with Yugoslavia and in discouraging the use of the Macedonian language indicate the strength of the Bulgarian feeling on the question. This traditional Bulgarian nationalism on the Macedonian question could only be expressed after the Soviet Union pronounced the Yugoslavs schizmatic and signalled a campaign against them.

The next shift in Yugoslav-Bulgarian relations came after the death of Stalin in 1953. Soviet initiative to improve relations culminated in the Khrushchev-Bulganin visit to Belgrade in 1955. Throughout this period the Bulgarians, while following the Soviet lead, were somewhat reluctant to change their policy. Border incidents along the Yugoslav-Bulgarian border continued into 1954, after they had ceased along Yugoslavia's borders with other Communist states. Trade relations between the two countries, which had been severed in 1948, were not re-established until 1954 after trade with the Soviet Union and other Communist states had resumed. However, by 1955 Bulgarian policy was in full accord with the Soviet initiatives.

The Bulgarian party's decision to reverse its stand and to acknowledge the existence of a separate Macedonian nationality was apparently taken at the April 1956 plenum of the CPB CC.[11] However, the Bulgarian census taken in December 1956 showed that 63.6 percent of the population of the Pirin Region was enumerated as "Macedonian."[12] The party's reversion to the position that Macedonians are Bulgarians did not become apparent until Soviet-Yugoslav relations again grew worse in early 1958.[13] One month before Moscow made known its intention to boycott the Seventh Yugoslav Party Congress, a Bulgarian party leader made the first overt denial of the Macedonian nationality in a speech at the celebration of the Eightieth Anniversary of the Treaty of San Stefano. The escalation of polemics over Macedonia throughout the rest of 1958 coincided with a serious decline in Yugoslav-Soviet and Yugoslav-Bulgarian relations. Increasingly explicit Bulgarian denials of the Macedonian nationality were accompanied by denunciation of ideological revisionism in Yugoslavia. Although polemics over Macedonia became somewhat less bitter after 1958, they continued until relations with Moscow again improved.

In 1961 a new Soviet-Yugoslav rapprochement began,[14] but Bulgarian relations with Yugoslavia were slower to respond. Historic attacks against the Macedonian nationality continued in the Bulgarian press. The Bulgarian party succeeded in shifting its policy to satisfy the Soviet line only after its Eighth Party Congress in December 1962, when Todor Zhivkov, with considerable Soviet assistance, succeeded in removing his chief rivals from power. One of those purged was Anton Yugov, who was head of the Bulgarian government and a Macedonian born in what is now Greek Macedonia. The Yugoslav leaders met with Zhivkov in January 1963 and were told by him that "the Bulgarian leadership and party will pursue and develop Dimitrov's course with respect to the Macedonian national question."[15] To the Yugoslavs this implied recognition of the Macedonian nationality since Dimitrov was the Bulgarian party leader who first followed that course.

Although the polemics over Macedonia were reduced in intensity, they did not stop altogether. Despite otherwise friendly relations of Yugoslavia with both the Soviet Union and Bulgaria, the Macedonian question was still a source of irritation. In September 1965 Tito made a state visit to Bulgaria, taking as the second-ranking member of his official party Vidoe Smilevski, Chairman of the Macedonian Republican Assembly. Although no agreement was reached on the Macedonian question, both sides did agree to exercise greater restraint in dealing with Macedonia. In the polemics which accompanied the deterioration of Bulgarian-Yugoslav relations after January 1968 the content of these 1965 talks was made public:

> Todor Zhivkov stated at his meetings with Tito, Crvenkovski and our leaders that the Bulgarian party would return to Dimitrov's principles on Pirin Macedonia and the entire Macedonian question. Although no agreement on these questions as a whole was reached, Zhivkov nevertheless gave assurances that they would not be treated polemically in the press but that they would leave them for expert discussions among scientists. For a certain period the Bulgarians, in fact, promoted cooperation between Bulgaria and Macedonia . . . .[16]

Tito optimistically told a Yugoslav audience on his return to Yugoslavia, "As a result of talks which we conducted, all that made it impossible to maintain good relations earlier [i.e., the Macedonian question] . . . is overcome."[17] The polemics on Macedonia, however, continued. Krste Crvenkovski, the leading party official in Macedonia, visited Sofia at Zhivkov's invitation in the spring of 1967. His account of the talks with Bulgarian leaders indicated the irreconcilable stand of the two parties:

> . . . even when we had considerable differences of opinion, the talks were not only frank but even friendly, inspired by the feeling of responsibility for one's own people and their interest. Such was also the character of the talks which I myself conducted with Tedor Zhivkov and other Bulgarian functionaries in May 1967. Despite the expressed wish for the further development of all relations, the differences in the views on the problem, the treatment and the rights of the Macedonians in Pirin Macedonia and Bulgaria, and the differences in attitude of a great part of the Bulgarian historiographers toward the past of the Macedonian people also found their clear expression during these talks, just as in many previous ones. [18]

Macedonia remained the principal irritant in Bulgarian-Yugoslav relations during the period while relations were good.

Even prior to the most recent deterioration of Yugoslav-Soviet relations, the Macedonian question precipitated a worsening of Bulgarian-Yugoslav relations. The Bulgarian leadership had undertaken a campaign to encourage patriotism among the Bulgarian youth. This campaign sought to reduce western influence among the youth by emphasizing things Bulgarian and to increase the party's standing among the Bulgarian people.[19] Articles commemorating the Treaty of San Stefano (which appeared three months prior to the 90th anniversary of the treaty) caused a serious outburst of new Bulgarian-Yugoslav polemics over Macedonia. Although the level of invective was somewhat reduced by March, in April Soviet-Yugoslav relations began to decline over differences about the liberalization in Czechoslovakia. After the Soviet-led invasion of that country in August 1968, relations between Yugoslavia and the invading countires plummeted to a new low. Throughout the period the intensity of polemics over Macedonia rose in inverse proportion to the decline in Yugoslav-Soviet relations. Although polemics have since passed through cycles of intensely bitter propaganda followed by periods of relative quiet on the issue, as long as Soviet-Yugoslav relations remain bad, Bulgarian-Yugoslav disagreement on the Macedonian question continues to be a major issue in their relations.

Thus, the principal element influencing Bulgarian-Yugoslav relations is the state of Soviet-Yugoslav relations; Bulgaria must subordinate any local disagreements (i.e., Macedonia) to Soviet interests. However, it is also apparent that the Macedonian question does have a significant, generally negative, effect on the relations between Belgrade and Sofia. Bulgaria has been reluctant to silence its claims to Macedonia when Soviet policy calls for this line and overeager to revive the Macedonian question in anticipation of any change of Soviet policy. There can be little doubt that without the dominating influence of the Soviet Union on Bulgarian foreign policy, the question of Macedonia would play a more significant and independent role in Bulgarian-Yugoslav relations. There are some indications that Bulgaria may assume some small measure of greater independence. If Soviet influence over Bulgarian foreign policy is reduced, Macedonia may well become a source of even more bitter controversy.

The Macedonian question is also a symptom of the state of Greek-Yugoslav relations. If relations are bad, no matter what the cause, Macedonia becomes the subject of propaganda campaigns on both sides. However, there is a significant difference between Greek-Yugoslav relations and Bulgarian-Yugoslav relations. Both Bulgaria and Yugoslavia seek hegemony over all of Macedonia. Bulgaria aspires to control all of Macedonia because of its (as

Sofia claims) Bulgarian population and Yugoslavia aspires to control the area because of its (as Belgrade claims) Macedonian population. Greece has made no persistent ethnic claims to the Pirin and Vardar regions. Athens, perhaps because Greece received the largest part of Macedonia in 1913 (about fifty percent of the Macedonian territory), seeks only to retain its portion of Macedonia. Thus in Greek-Yugoslav relations it is Belgrade that determines whether Macedonia will disturb relations. Frequently other considerations have been important enough to require Yugoslav silence on Macedonia in the interest of good relations. Since the Greek government is under no external restraint as is Bulgaria in its foreign policies, the Macedonian question plays a more active role in determining the state of Greek-Yugoslav relations than is the case in Yugoslav relations with Bulgaria.

Yugoslav claims on Aegean Macedonia and support for the Greek Communist guerrillas operating in that area were the principal reason for very unfriendly relations between Greece and Yugoslavia before 1949. After the Cominform break, the threat of invasion by the Soviet bloc nations led Yugoslavia to seek an improvement in its relations with the non-Communist nations on its borders.[20] When the Yugoslav border was closed to the Greek Communist guerrillas in 1949, the way was opened for improved relations. Although Belgrade and Athens both moved slowly, by August 1954 the Balkan Pact was signed by Yugoslavia, Greece, and Turkey. The three countries agreed: to consider an attack on one party to the treaty as aggression against all signatories, to consultations among their general staffs, and to consulation among their political leaders in case of crisis. Although pursuing a policy of improved relations with Greece, the Yugoslav government could not remain silent on the Macedonian issue. Belgrade could not completely abandon the popular Macedonian aspiration for national unification without internal difficulty, and the Hellenization of the Slavs in Aegean Macedonia was a barrier to future claims upon the area. Hence, the Yugoslavs followed a dual policy of friendship with Greece but at the same time tacitly approved barbed references which kept the Macedonian issue alive.

Thus, despite improved relations with Greece, the Macedonian press declared that the Yugoslavs refused to be "blackmailed" into giving "some sort of promise . . . that we shall renounce our claim to defend the interests of the people of Aegean Macedonia."[21] Just weeks before signing the Balkan pact, a book by the prominent Yugoslav Macedonian, Lazar Mojsov, claimed that enemies of Greek-Yugoslav cooperation were fostering chauvinism by encouraging Greeks to look at "Macedonians and the 'Macedonian question' in the old-fashioned way, creating among the Greek people nervousness and intolerance, unleashing occasional calumniatory campaigns against our country."[22] He pointed out that cooperation with Greece was possible only if the rights of the Macedonian minority in Greece were recognized. Since Mojsov at that time was Secretary of the Yugoslav Assembly's Foreign Affairs Committee, Greek reaction was swift and severe. But when foreign correspondents asked the Yugoslav Foreign Ministry if the government wished to dissociate itself from this attack on its ally, a government spokesman replied, "The Secretary for Foreign Affairs has not had the opportunity to study the book. I cannot, therefore, give any comment." [23] Although the Yugoslavs continued to follow the policy calling for minority rights to Slavs in Aegean Macedonia, the campaign was never allowed to escalate to the point of endangering relations with Greece.

The improvement of Yugoslav relations with the Communist bloc in 1955 made the original purpose of good relations with Greece less important; however, the Yugoslavs continued friendly relations with Greece and encouraged Turkey and Greece to resolve their differences over Cyprus to permit improving relations under the Balkan Pact. Periodic outbursts kept the Macedonian issue alive, but were not allowed to lead to a serious worsening of relations. In the early 1960's Macedonia became the cause of a decline in Yugoslav-Greek relations. Intensified by the Bulgarian campaign after 1958 to deny the existence of a Macedonian nation and heightened by a general upsurge of nationalism in Yugoslavia about that time, Macedonian nationalism developed an increased concern for the Slavs of Aegean Macedonia and forced the Yugoslav government to go farther with the campaign than it would have gone otherwise. The polemics between the two countries over Macedonia became quite bitter.

Some Greek leaders, including George Papandreau, felt the Macedonian issue was being used by Belgrade to worsen relations with Greece, a NATO ally of the United States, in order to improve Yugoslav standing with the Soviet Union. However, the difficulties over Macedonia began in 1960, before Yugoslavia had begun the rapproachement with Moscow. Also, Belgrade was interested in keeping good relations. An article in the official party weekly declared that Yugoslavia wanted no confusion in its relations with Greece, which had been "a good example of coexistence." [24] When the Greek government suspended the joint border agreement in March 1962, the Yugoslav government continued to allow border traffic under terms of the agreement. It appears that the Macedonians were forcing Belgrade's hand in the dispute with Greece. The principal Skopje newspaper published a long unsigned article denouncing a Bulgarian diplomat who reportedly told a Greek political leader that Bulgaria supported the Greek position on the nonexistence of the Macedonian nation. [25] However, the Belgrade newspapers and the Yugoslav government ignored the claims of the Skopje articles. In the midst of the campaign, a Greek correspondent in Belgrade reported that the Yugoslav ambassador to Athens was instructed by Tito personally that Yugoslavia desired good relations with Greece.[26]

Although relations with Greece remained strained for some time, they gradually began to improve. In November 1964 a new agreement on border traffic was signed replacing the old agreement suspended two years previously. In February 1965 Premier Papandreau paid an official visit to Belgrade. Macedonia was the only discordant note of his Yugoslav trip. After talks between Papandreau and the Yugoslav leaders, a spokesman for the Yugoslav foreign ministry told newsmen, "We put forward our well-known position" on the Macedonian minority in Greece, but Greece

> thinks the problem does not exist, but she cannot solve it by ignoring it. However, we will bypass this now because we agree on so many other things and wait until the Greeks have another point of view.[27]

Later when newsmen queried Papandreau about this statement, he told them angrily, "For Greece this problem does not exist—therefore it was not discussed!"

After the military seized control of the Greek government in the *coup d'état* of April 1967, relations between Yugoslavia and Greece declined. Although Macedonia was not the cause of bad relations, the more nationalistic stand of the military junta and the Yugoslav government's dislike for the new conservative policies in Athens led to a revival of friction over the Macedonian question. Small border traffic between the two countries under terms of the 1964 agreement was suspended by Athens in the Fall of 1967. The military government not only refused to acknowledge the existence of a Macedonian minority in Greece—which all Greek governments prior to that time had refused to do—some of its leaders made irredentist claims against Yugoslav Macedonia. General Patakos sent a message to a meeting of Macedonian emigrants in Salonika declaring:

> The territory of Macedonia, the entire geographic area of Macedonia, has been and remains Greek. All others are conquerors or oppressors, old or potential.[28]

A further sharp decline of Greek-Yugoslav relations which such a statement would normally have produced was pre-empted by the invasion of Czechoslovakia and an escalation of already bitter polemics with Bulgaria. A real fear that Warsaw Pact troops might invade Yugoslavia led Belgrade to play down its differences with Greece over Macedonia despite sufficient provocation for a vigorous anti-Greek campaign.

The impact of Macedonia on foreign relations in the Balkans has changed in nature because of the Yugoslav decision to recognize a Macedonian nationality and grant it the status of a constituent republic in the Yugoslav federation. However, the significance of the Macedonian question is as great as ever. Between the two world wars Bulgaria was the only state that promised the Macedonians unification, an end to Serbianization or Hellenization, and use of their Bulgarian language and culture. (Almost all Slavo-Macedonians at that time considered themselves to be Bulgarian.) Hence, Bulgaria was the power threatening both Greece and Yugoslavia with loss of territory. The result was the Balkan Entente which was directed against Bulgarian revisionism. However, after World War II the Yugoslavs permitted the Macedonians to have formal government autonomy, to use their own non-Serb language, to develop their culture, and they encouraged a campaign for national unification under Yugoslav egis. Thus, Yugoslavia became the principal threat to the status quo in the Balkans. After Yugoslavia's break with the Cominform in 1948, Bulgaria was allied with the Soviet Union and Greece through NATO with the United States. No change, through force or subversion, of boundaries was possible. Encouraging recognition of the Macedonian minorities in Bulgaria and Greece represents pursuit of the policy of Macedonian unification as far as is possible under present circumstances. Belgrade's role as the chief advocate of unification has been a factor in pacifying its own Macedonian population. However, this has brought Yugoslavia into conflict with both Greece, which wants the retention of the status quo, and Bulgaria, which would like to see Macedonia united under its own sponsorship.

The difference which the Macedonian issue has played in Yugoslav relations with Bulgaria and Greece is largely a function of their internal political systems. In Bulgaria, the key to political power now is the support of the Soviet Union, as Zhivkov has so frequently demonstrated. Hence, Bulgarian policy on Macedonia must be subordinated to Soviet interests. However, the Macedonian question has been one issue on which Sofia shows some independence from Moscow. The Greek government, until the last few years, depended upon national popular support. The Yugoslav claims to Macedonia imply loss of historic, conquered territory and provoke national patriotic feelings that a popularly elected Greek government cannot ignore and remain in power. Hence, Macedonian claims have a direct effect on Greek-Yugoslav relations, and disagreement over Macedonia is more frequently a cause, rather than merely a symptom, of bad relations. The military government has been more nationalistic than most Greek governments, and the Macedonian question plays at least as important a role as earlier in upsetting relations with Yugoslavia.

United States links with Greece and Soviet support of Bulgaria have prevented any serious outbreaks of violence. However, if the two superpowers were not involved it is not unlikely that differences over Macedonia could errupt in violence. Balkan nationalism has produced a number of local wars, touched off the First World War, and was thoroughly enmeshed with the politics of the Second World War. Balkan nationalism, remains intense, volatile, and has by no means abated. Continued non-violent conflict over Macedonia remains a certainty; violent conflict, a possibility.

CONCLUSION

The crucial element of the CPY policy on Macedonia was its decision to recognize the existence of a Macedonian nationality. But did it adopt this policy because such a nationality really existed, or because it was a useful tactic at the time? An answer to this question requires documents from archives and accounts from participants which are not now available and will likely never be available. There were ample political reasons for the CPY decision to declare the existence of a Macedonian nationality whether one existed or not. During the Second World War, there were pressing reasons for implementing this policy. The political goals of the CPY in Macedonia were furthered by recognizing a separate nationality.

First, it was crucial for the CPY to gain control of the area. After the Axis occupation of Yugoslavia and the commencement of the partisan struggle, the Macedonian policy was implemented because the CPY was unable without it to gain control of the Vardar region. Recognition of a separate Macedonian nationality was a crucial element in the success of the CPY in Macedonia during the Second World War.

Second, the policy was useful to justify the retention of Vardar Macedonia within the Yugoslav federation. An area inhabited by a population seventy percent of which was Bulgarian should justifiably belong to Bulgaria. Since the inhabitants of Macedonia strongly opposed being called Serbs, it was not possible after the war to use this method of legalizing their retention as a part of Yugoslavia. However, a non-Bulgarian, non-Serbian population of Slavs could belong to a federation of Slavic peoples as one of the fraternal nations. The decisions of the Jacje Conference carried out this policy by granting Macedonia the status of a national republic and placing it on the same level as Serbia, Croatia, Slovenia and Montenegro.

A third reason for recognizing the Macedonian nationality was to eliminate the Bulgarian consciousness of the vast majority of Vardar Macedonians. Thus, the party has not only recognized the nationality, but also has taken and still undertakes vigorous steps to encourage its culture to differentiate Macedonian from Bulgarian. Republican political and economic "autonomy," the Macedonian language, reinterpretation of history, the Macedonian church, and all other attributes of a distinct nationality have played a major role in de-Bulgarizing the Macedonian population.

The fourth aim of the CPY's policy was to extend Yugoslav hegemony to all of Macedonia. Here, as we have seen, the Yugoslav Communists met failure, not because of their policy but because of external factors over which the Yugoslavs had little control. Although the expansionist corollary of the Yugoslav policy continues to disturb relations with Bulgaria and Greece, its lack of success thus far has not been considered necessarily permanent by any of the states involved in the Macedonian question.

These political reasons in and of themselves justified to the CPY its stand on the Macedonian question. The evidence of timing and the way concessions were granted to Macedonian nationalism—for example, the circumstances around the founding of the Macedonian Orthodox Church in 1958 —indicate that the party has manipulated its policy on the Macedonian question to accomplish its political goals.

However, merely acknowledging that the party adopted an expedient and largely efficacious policy on the Macedonian question does not determine if, in fact, a Macedonian nationality exists. Before World War II there is little doubt that the vast majority of the Slavo-Macedonians considered themselves to be Bulgarian. Even after the disillusionment produced by the Bulgarian occupation during World War II, most Macedonians either still considered themselves Bulgarians or could have been led to consider themselves as such with little difficulty. This is not to deny that there were differences between the Bulgarians and the Yugoslav Macedonians. Some differences, of course, did exist even before the partition of Macedonia in 1913. These differences had grown in Vardar Macedonia under a quarter century of Serbian rule. But it is doubtful that the Macedonians in either Yugoslavia or Greece were sufficiently different that they considered themselves to be a nationality separate from the Bulgarians.

Whether a Macedonian nationality exists today in Vardar Macedonia is a far more complex question. No Macedonian in Yugoslavia would admit openly that he considers himself Bulgarian—it is neither wise nor safe to do so. Macedonian nationalism has been encouraged by the Yugoslav Communists for over twenty-five years, and this surely has had some impact on the consciousness of the Macedonians. The extent to which Communist supervised Macedonian nationalism has enlarged Macedonian national consciousness varies more according to age groups than to social strata, although there appear to be significant differences in the degree of acceptance. For instance, the peasants have been less responsive than the intelligentsia in accepting the party's Macedonian policy. The present adult generation's mode of thinking and feeling about Macedonia was shaped by a milieu radically different from that in which the younger generation is being raised. Among the adults there are many who find the realities of Yugoslav Macedonia to be far from their dreams. This is particularly true in the case of the age group which experienced the worst period of Serbian terror, shortly before and after World War I. They would be wary of any kind of Belgrade-directed government. The dissatisfaction with the forms of autonomy and their centralist content seems to increase in direct proportion to age. Among those whose memories go back only to the late twenties or thirties, the communist efforts seem to have made more progress. Undoubtedly some anti-government sentiment is transmitted to children and youth by their parents, but the Communists with their control over communication media and education have formidable weapons in the struggle for the next adult generation.

Yugoslav Communist policy on Macedonia is at least passively accepted by the population of the SRM. Widespread active resistance and hostility to Belgrade—which was the rule during the interwar period—has been the exception in postwar Macedonia. Although part of the explanation lies in the greater efficiency of the Communists to pinpoint and eliminate opposition, the Macedonian policy has been instrumental in reducing the discontent. There is no alternative to Tito's Yugoslavia. Rule by Athens is desired by virtually none. Macedonians have become disenchanted with Bulgaria, despite occasional irredentist outbursts, because of its Stanlinist internal policy and its subservience to Moscow. An autonomous Macedonia is strongly opposed by Greece, Bulgaria, and Yugoslavia. For Bulgarophils, being Macedonian is a good second best to being Bulgarian. They are not being Serbianized, they can use their own almost-Bulgarian language, they are somewhat independent in running their own affairs. The concept of a separate nationality has secured the acquiescence if not the enthusiastic acceptance of the Macedonians.

With its future linked with the Yugoslav federation, much of the further development of the Macedonian question will depend on the evolution of the Yugoslav nationalities. Party officials maintain that the federal system has "solved" the Yugoslav national question, and some even talk of the future merging of nationalities into a common "Yugoslav" culture. Although the communist theoretical position on the national question postulates the merging of nationalities,[1] the Yugoslavs have extended their revisionism into the sphere of national theory as well as to economics and politics. Lazar Koliševski was one of the vocal advocates of the continuation of separate nationalities. He criticized Stalin for failing to see

> that the essence of the national question has changed, because the working class in a socialist system, by developing socialist social relations, must of necessity become the champion of positive national interests and national progress [2]

Other—particularly non-Serb—Yugoslav communist leaders have declared their opposition to the concept of merging nations. Mika Tripalo, a Croatian Communist leader, told a gathering of the Macedonain party *activ:*

> Comrades, it is perfectly clear to all of us that Yugoslavism as a nationality does not exist, because all of this is based on the illusion that under conditions of socialist development . . . life will develop in the direction of small nations growing into great nations, and that thus also a general Yugoslav nation will grow out of the individual nations in Yugoslavia. This is an illusion, that is quite clear, and we are of course opposing such views. [3]

Although the Macedonian nationality has been acknowledged by the Yugoslav Communists and the right of the Yugoslav nations to continue as separate nationalities has been acknowledged, the Macedonian question is far from settled.

Within Yugoslavia, the Macedonian question remains a potential source of difficulty. Macedonian nationalism is much newer, hence more volatile than the older nationalisms. As the trend for republican party and government autonomy increases, Macedonia may well play a key role in the Yugoslav federation. With Serbs and Croats traditionally hostile and on opposite sides on most major issues, Macedonia may become a crucial balancing factor with greater significance than its numbers or position would warrant. Though Macedonians are traditionally anti-Serb and are certain to oppose any Serbian attempts to re-establish hegemony in Macedonia, this will not prevent Macedonia from aligning with Serbia if its interests require it. There was a strong movement in Macedonia to align with the Serb bureaucracy in opposition to economic reform. The economically under-developed, religiously Orthodox, and culturally Byzantine Macedonians have much in common with Serbs and Montenegrins. The effect of Macedonian national aspirations on the decisions of the SRM will be a key factor in the future course of Yugoslavia.

Although armed hostilities over Macedonia have almost ceased since 1949, the Macedonian question is far from settled in the international sphere. The frequent Bulgarian-Yugoslav polemics and the negative effect on Greek-Yugoslav relations attest to the continued significance of Macedonia. However, the Yugoslav Communist recognition of a Macedonian nationality has transformed the character of the question. In Yugoslavia the Macedonian population is not actively opposing its situation; there is little discontent for Bulgaria to exploit. The unattractiveness of the Sofia regime and its links with the Soviet Union limit the Bulgarian appeal. At the same time the Yugoslav policy has given Belgrade the opportunity and means to advocate Macedonian unification. Yugoslavia—possessing the largest Slavo-Macedonian population, advocating recognition of Macedonian cultural rights by Greece and Bulgaria, and following its own course independent of the Soviet Union and the United States—has become credible as the power most likely to unite Macedonia. Although world conditions do not permit a change in Balkan boundaries, the Yugoslav Communist policy on Macedonia has at present given the Yugoslavs the initiative.

However, the Balkans are not noted for stability. Although at present the Yugoslavs do have the initiative, it might pass to others. The Yugoslav federation will face its most serious internal challenge since the Second World War when aging Marshal Tito dies. Any significant post-Tito instability would likely focus Yugoslav energies on its internal problems and the Macedonian Question would become less important to Belgrade. At the same time, Bulgaria could develop into a more attractive alternative than it now is. The attempted *coup d'état* of April 1965 and the Zhivkov-inspired campaign to foster Bulgarian patriotism and emphasize national history indicate the strength of Bulgarian nationalism. Sharing no frontier with the Soviet Union and separated from the USSR by an increasingly independent Rumania, Bulgaria has the potential to achieve much greater independence vis-à-vis Moscow. Any move for independence from the Soviet Union or the coming to power of a more nationalist regime in Sofia would make Bulgaria a much more attractive alternative. Although Yugoslav Communist policy has been the key to the Macedonian Question for over twenty-five years, the future may produce a different situation. Within Yugoslavia, Macedonian nationalism is probably acquiring a dynamic of its own and this injects still another element of uncertainty into the Balkan equation. Without doubt, Macedonia will continue to be a complex focal point of conflict in Balkan politics and a crucial factor in Yugoslav internal affairs.

BIBLIOGRAPHY

The works listed below have been selected on the basis of their contribution to the study. They do not constitute a complete bibliography on the Macedonian Question, nor do they include all of the materials employed by the writers for background information.

I. YUGOSLAV COMMUNIST SOURCES

A. Congresses and Plenums

V kongres Komunističke Partije Jugoslavije, isveštiji i referati. Belgrade, 1948.

VI kongres Komunističke Partije Jugoslavije (Saveza Komunista Jugoslavije): Borba Komunista Jugoslavija za socijalističku demokratije. Belgrade: Kultura, 1952.

VII kongres na Sojuzot na Komunistite na Jugoslavija. Skopje: Kultura, 1958.

Osmi kongres Saveza Komunista Jugoslavije. Belgrade: Kultura, 1964.

Treči plenum CK SKJ: Aktuelni problemi borbe Saveza Komunista Jugoslavije za sprovodjenje reforme. Belgrade: Komunist, 1966.

I kongres na Komunističkata Partija na Makedonija: isveštai i rezolucii. Skopje: Kultura, 1949.

III kongres na Sojuzot na Komunistite na Makedonija. Skopje: Kultura, 1959.

Četvrti kongres na Sojuzot na Komunistite na Makedonija. Skopje: Kultura, 1965.

XIV Sednica na centralniot komitet na SK na Makedonija: Narodnostite vo samoupravnoto opštestvo. [Skopje]: Komunist, 1968.

II kongres Komunističke Partije Srbije. Belgrade, 1949.

Četvrti kongres SKOJ-a. Zagreb: Centralni komitet narodne omaldine Hrvatske, 1950.

Osnivački kongres Komunističke Partije Bosne i Hercegovine. Sarajevo, 1950.

B. Other Yugoslav Communist Works

Andonovski, Hristo. *Egejska Makedonija.* Skopje, [1951].

Apostolski, Mihajlo. *Završnite operacii na N.O.B. za osloboduvanjeto na Makedonija.* Skopje: Koco Racin, 1953.

Bebler, Aleš. *Peace and Greece.* New York: Permanent Delegation of the Federal People's Republic of Yugoslavia to the United Nations, 1949.

The Constitution of the Federal People's Republic of Yugoslavia [Constitutional Law of 1953]. Belgrade: Union of Jurist's Associations of Yugoslavia, 1960.

Crvenkovski, Krste. "Treba se upornije i sistematskije borbiti za sprovodjenje pisma CK SKJ u delo," *Komunist,* 7:9 (September, 1953), pp. 653-659.

Dedijer, Vladimir. *Dvenik, drugi deo.* Belgrade: Drzavni izdavački zavod Jugoslavije, 1946.

—*Jagoslovensko-Albanski odnosi, 1939-1948.* Zagreb: Borba, 1949.

—*Tito.* New York: Simon and Schuster, 1953.

Dimevski, Slavko. *Crkovna istorija na Makedonskiot narod.* Skopje: Makedonskata pravoslavna crkva, 1965 .

Drugovac, Miodrag. *Biographia Litteraria: 55 kritički impresii.* Skopje: Misla, 1968.

Džambazovski, Kliment. *Kulturno-opštestvenite vrski na Makedoncite co srbija vo tekot na XIX vek.* Skopje: Institut za nacionalna istorija, 1960.

Federativna Narodna Republika Jugoslavije. Savezni Zavod za Statistiku. *Konačni rezultati popisa stanovništva od 15 marta 1948 godine.* Belgrade, 1954.

—*Popis stanovništva 1953.* Belgrade, 1959.

—*Statistički godišnjak Jugoslavije.* Belgrade, 1954—.

Hristov, Aleksandar T. *KPJ vo rešavanjeto na Makedonskoto prašanje (1937-1944).* Skopje: Kultura, 1962.

Industrijata vo N.R. Makedonija. Skopje: Ekonomski institut, 1961.

Institute za Nacionalna Istorija-Skopje. *Istorija na Makedonskiot Narod.* Skopje: Nova Makedonija, 1969. 3 vols.

Istorijsko odeljenje Centranog komiteta KPJ. *Istorijski arhiv Komunističke Partije Jugoslavije,* Vol. II: *Kongresi i zemaljske konferencije KPJ 1919-1937.* Belgrade: Kultura, 1950.

—*Istorijski arhiv Komunističke Partije Jugoslavije.* Vol. VII: *Makedonija u narodnoo-slobodilačkom ratu i narodnoj revoluciji 1941-1944.* Belgrade: Kultura, 1951.

Jagić, Vatroslav. *Kiril i Metodi i nivnite učanitsi.* Trans. by H. Polsanković. Skopje, 1954.

Kepeski, Krume. *Makedonska gramatika.* Skopje: Državno knigoizdatelstvo na Make-donija, 1946.

—*Makedonska gramatika.* Skopje: Državno knigoizdatelstvo na N.R. Makedonija, 1950.

Ko je ko u Jugoslaviji: Biografski podaci o jugoslovenskim savremenicima. 1st ed. Bel-grade: Sedme sile, 1957.

Koliševski, Lazar. *Aspekti na makedonskoto prašanje.* Skopje: Kultura, 1962.

—*Govori na Drugarot vo Skopje i Ohrida.* Skopje, 1950.

Komunistička ta Partija na Makedonija KPJ i makedonskoto nacionalno prašanje. Skopje, 1949.

Koneski, Blaže. *Gramatika na makedonskiot literaturen jazik.* Skopje: Prosvetno delo, 1966.

—*Kon makedonskata prerodba: makedonskite učebnici od 19 vek.* 2nd ed. Skopje: Institut za nacionalna istorija, 1959.

—*Za makedonskata literatura.* Izbrani dela vo sedum knigi, IV. Skopje: Kultura, 1967.

—, ed. *Makedonska književnost.* Srpska književna zadruga, 368. Belgrade: Kultura, 1961.

The Law on the Five Year Plan for the Development of the National Economy of the Feder-ative People's Republic of Yugoslavia in the Period from 1947 to 1951. Belgrade: Of-fice of Information, 1947.

Martulkov, Alekso. *Moeto učestvo vo revolucionernite borbi na Makedonija.* Skopje: In-stitut za nacionalna istorija, 1954.

Miljovski, Kiril. *Makedonskoto prašanje vo nacionalnata programa na KPJ (1919-1937).* Skopje: Kultura, 1962.

Miljovski, Kiro. *Za nekon prašanja od rabotata nad našata nacionalna istorija.* Skopje: Kultura, 1950.

Ministry of Foreign Affairs of the Federal People's Republic of Yugoslavia. *White Book on Aggressive Activities by the Governments of the USSR, Poland, Czechoslovakia, Hungary, Rumania, Bulgaria and Albania towards Yugoslavia.* Belgrade, 1951.

Mitrev, Dimitar. *Pirinska Makedonija vo borba za nacionalno osloboduvanje.* Skopje: Glavinot odbor na Narodniot front na Makedonija, 1950.

Mojsov, Lazar. *Bulgarska Radnička Partija (komunista) i makedonsko nacionalno pitanje.* Belgrade: Borba, 1948.

—*Okolu prasanjeto na makedonskoto nacionalno maltsinstvo vo Grcija.* Skopje, 1954.

Nikolov, Kiril. *Za Makedonskata nacija.* Skopje: Zemski odbor na Nariodniot front na Makedonija, 1948.

Popovski, Blagoj. *Spiuni vo odbrana na linijata na Informbiroto i na BKP.* Skopje, 1949.

—*Sudskata provokacija vo Sofija.* Skopje, 1950.

Smilevski, Vidoe. "Osvrt na razvoj makedonskog nacionalnog pitanja," *Komunist,* 4:1 (January, 1950), pp. 81-118.

Spomeni na Gorče Petrov. Materijali za makedonskata nacionalrevoluciona istorija, 1. Skopje: Naučen institut za nacionalna istorija na makedonskiot narod, 1950.

Tito, Josip Broz. *Isgradnja nove Jugoslavije.* Vol. I. Belgrade, 1948.

Tošev, Krum. "Die mazedonische Schriftsprache," *Südost-Forschungen,* 15 (1956), pp. 491-503.

Ustav Federativne Narodne Republike Jugoslavije. Belgrade: Službeni List, 1950.

Ustav na makedonskata pravoslavna crkva. Skopje, 1958.

Ustav Socijalističke Federativne Republike Jugoslavije sa ustavima socijalističkih republika i statutima autonomnih pokrajina. Belgrade: Službeni list, 1963.

La Vérité sur la Grèce Monarcho-fascist. Belgrade, 1947.

Vlahov, Dimitar. *Govori i statii, 1945-1947.* Skopje, 1950.

—*Makedonija: momenti od istorijata na makedonskiot narod.* Skopje: Državno knigoizdatelstvo na N.R. Makedonija, 1950.

Vukmanović-Tempo, Svetozar. *How and Why the People's Liberation Struggle in Greece Met with Defeat.* London, 1950.

Zbornik na dokumenti od Antifašističkoto Sobranie na Narodnoto Osloboduvanje na Makedonija (ASNOM) 1944-1946. Skopje: Institut za nacionalna istorija, 1964.

Zografski, Dančo. *Jugoslovenskite socijalisti za makedonskoto prašanje.* Skopje: Kultura, 1962.

—*Za rabotničkoto dviženje vo Makedonija do balkanskata vojna.* Skopje: Institut za nacionalna istorija na Makedonskiot narod, 1950.

—and others. *Egejska Makedonija vo našata nacionalna istorija.* Skopje: Institut za nacionalna istorija na Makedonskiot narod, 1951.

II. OTHER WORKS

Anastasoff, Christ. *The Tragic Peninsula: A History of the Macedonian Movement for Independence Since 1878.* St. Louis: Blackwell Wielandy, 1938.

—, ed. *The Case for an Autonomous Macedonia.* Indianapolis: Central Committee of the Macedonian Political Organization of the United States and Canada, 1945.

Ancel, Jacques. *La Macédonie.* Paris, 1929.

—*Peuples et Nations des Balkans.* Paris, 1930.

Armstrong, Hamilton Fish. *The New Balkans.* New York: Harper and Brothers, 1926.

—*Tito and Goliath.* New York: Macmillan, 1951.

Avakumovic, Ivan. *History of the Communist Party of Yugoslavia.* Vol. I. Aberdeen: Aberdeen University Press, 1964.

Barker, Elizabeth. *Macedonia: Its Place in Balkan Power Politics.* London: Royal Institute for International Affairs, 1950.

—*Truce in the Balkans.* London: P. Marshall, 1948.

Beard, Charles A. and George Radin. *The Balkan Pivot: Yugoslavia, a Study in Government and Administration.* New York: Macmillan, 1929.

Belić, Aleksandar. *La Macédoine: Etudes ethnographiques et politiques.* Paris: Barcelone, Bloud and Gay, 1919.

Brailsford, H.N. *Macedonia: Its Races and their Future.* London: Methuen, 1906.

Bulgaria. Ministry of Foreign Affairs. *The Bulgarian Question and the Balkan States.* Sofia: State Printing Press, 1919.

Bulgarian Academy of Sciences, Institute of History. *The Macedonian Problem: Historical-Political Aspects.* Translated by Radio Free Europe, Bulgarian Press Survey, No. 694 (February 17, 1969).

Bulgarian Autrocities in Greek Macedonia and Thrace, 1941-1944: A Report of Professors of the Universities of Athens and Salonika. Athens, 1945.

Burks, R.V. *Dynamics of Communism in Eastern Europe.* Princeton, N.J.: Princeton University Press, 1961.

Carnegie Endowment for International Peace. *Report of the International Commission to Inquire into the Causes and Conduct of the Balkan Wars.* Washington, 1914.

Christides, Christopher J. *The Macedonian Camouflage in the Light of Facts and Figures.* Athens: Hellenic Publishing House, 1949.

Christopoulos, George. *Bulgaria's Record.* Chicago, 1944.

Christowe, Stoyan. *Heroes and Assassins.* New York: R.M. McBride, 1935.

Ciliga, Anton. *La Yougoslavie sous la ménace intérieure et extérieure.* Paris: Les Iles d'or, 1951.

Clissold, Stephen. *Whirlwind: An Account of Marshal Tito's Rise to Power.* London: Crescent, 1949.

Colocotronis, V. *La Macédoine et l'Hellénisme: Etude historique et ethnologique.* Paris: Berger-Leurault, 1919.

Cvijić, Jovan. *Balkansko poluostrovo i jugoslovenski zemlje.* Belgrade: Državna štamparija, 1922.

Dakin, Douglas. *The Greek Struggle in Macedonia, 1897-1913.* Salonika: Institute for Balkan Studies, 1966.

Dami, Aldo. *Fatalités Bulgares.* Geneva: Editions de la Voix des peuples, 1946.

deBray, R.G.A. *Guide to the Slavonic Languages.* London: J.M. Dent and Sons, 1951.

Dellin, L.A.D. "The 1924 Blueprint for the Solution of the Macedonian Question Within a Balkan Federation," *Bulgarische Jahrbücher,* I (1968), pp. 225-238.

Dimitrov, Georgi. *Govori, članci, i izjave.* Zagreb, 1947.

—*Political Report: V Congress of the Bulgarian Communist Party.* Sofia: Press Department of the Ministry of Foreign Affairs, 1949.

Djilas, Milovan. *Conversations with Stalin.* New York: Harcourt, Brace and World, 1962.

Djordjivić,Tihomir. *Macedonia.* London: Allen and Unwin, 1918.

Documents on International Affairs, 1947-1948. London: Royal Institute for International Affairs, 1952.

Durham, Mary Edith. *Twenty Years of Balkan Tangle.* London: Allen and Unwin, 1920.

Fisher, Jack C. *Yugoslavia—a Multi-national State: Regional Difference and Administrative Response.* San Francisco: Chandler, 1966.

Frankel, Joseph. "Communism and the National Question in Yugoslavia," *Journal of Central European Affairs,* 15:1 (April, 1955), pp. 49-65.

—"Federalism in Yugoslavia," *American Political Science Review*, 49:2 (June, 1955), pp. 416-430.

Genov, Georgi P. *Bulgaria and the Treaty of Neuilly*. Sofia: H.G. Danov, 1935.

Geshkoff, Theodore Ivanoff. *Balkan Union: A Road to Peace in Southeastern Europe*. New York: Columbia University Press, 1940.

Gewehr, Wesley M. *The Rise of Nationalism in the Balkans, 1800-1930*. Hamden: Archon Books, 1967.

Gyorgy, Andrew. *Governments of Danubian Europe*. New York: Rinehart, 1949.

Halperin, Ernst. *The Triumphant Heretic: Tito's Struggle Against Stalin*. London: Heinemann, 1958.

Hamilton, F.E. Ian. *Yugoslavia: Patterns of Economic Activity*. New York: Praeger, 1968.

Hoffman, George W., and Fred Warner Neal. *Yugoslavia and the New Communism*. New York: Twentieth Century Fund, 1962.

Hoptner, J.B. *Yugoslavia in Crisis, 1934-1941*. New York: Columbia University Press, 1962.

Ivanoff, Iordan. *Les Bulgares devant le Congrès de la Paix: documents historiques, ethnographiques et diplomatiques*. Bern: P. Haupt, 1919.

—*La Question Macédonienne au point de vue historique, ethnographique et statistique*. Paris: J. Gamber, 1920.

Jelavich, Charles and Barbara Jelavic, eds. *The Balkans in Transition: Essays on the Development of Balkan Life and Politics since the End of the Eighteenth Century*. Berkeley and Los Angeles: University of California Press, 1963.

Kaladizhiev, Hristo. *Federalna Makedoniia i velikobugarskiiat shovinizum*. Sofia, 1945.

Kanchev, Vasil. *Makedoniia: Ethnografiia i statistika*. Sofia, 1900.

Keramopoulos, Antonios D. *Origin of the Macedonians*. Trans. by John Tozis. Detroit: Pan-Michigan Hellenic Association, 1946.

Kerner, Robert J., ed. *Yugoslavia*. Berkeley: University of California Press, 1949.

Kofos, Evangelos. *Nationalism and Communism in Macedonia*. Salonika: Institute for Balkan Studies, 1964.

Kolarz, Walter. *Myths and Realities in Eastern Europe*. London: L. Drummond, 1946.

Korbel, J. *Tito's Communism*. Denver: University of Denver Press, 1951.

Kousoulas, Dimitrios. *Revolution and Defeat: The Story of the Greek Communist Party.* London: Oxford University Press, 1965.

Krainikovski, Asen Ivanov. *La Question de Macédoine et la Diplomatic Europeanne.* Paris: M. Riviere and cie, 1938.

Ladas, S.R. *The Exchange of Minorities: Bulgaria, Greece and Turkey.* New York: Macmillan, 1932.

Londres, Albert. *Terror in the Balkans.* London: Constable, 1935.

Lukacs, John A. *The Great Powers in Eastern Europe.* New York: American Book Company, 1953.

Lunt, Horace G. *Grammar of the Macedonian Literary Language.* Skopje, 1952.

—"A Survey of Macedonian Literature," *Harvard Slavic Studies,* I (1953), pp. 363-396.

Lybyer, A.H. *The Balkan Policy of the Paris Peace Conference.* Indianapolis, 1945.

La Macédoine Hellénique en 1928. Athens, 1928.

Maclean, Fitzroy. *Escape to Adventure.* Boston: Little, Brown, and Company, 1950.

—*The Heretic: the Life and Times of Josip Broz-Tito.* New York: Harper, 1957.

Markert, Werner, ed. *Osteuropa Handbuch: Jugoslawien.* Cologne and Graz: Bohlau Verlag, 1954.

Markham, Reuben H. *Tito's Imperial Communism.* Chapel Hill: University of North Carolina Press, 1947.

Marriott, J.A.R. *The Eastern Question.* 4th ed. Oxford: Clarendon Press, 1940.

McNeill, William Hardy. *The Greek Dilemma.* Philadelphia: J.B. Lippincott, 1947.

Mihailov, Ivan. *Macedonia: Switzerland of the Balkans.* St. Louis: Pearlstone Publishing, 1950.

—*Macedonia's Rise for Freedom, 1903: The Great Insurrection.* Indianapolis, 1953.

—["Macedonicus"]. *Stalin and the Macedonian Question.* St. Louis: Pearlstone Publishing, 1948.

Miller, William. *The Ottoman Empire and its Successors, 1801-1927.* Cambridge: University Press, 1936.

Mosley, Philip. *The Kremlin and World Politics.* New York: Vintage, 1960.

Mylonas, George E. *The Balkan States: An Introduction to their History.* St. Louis: Eden Publishing House, 1946.

Neal, Fred Warner. *Titoism in Action: The Reforms in Yugoslavia after 1948.* Berkeley and Los Angeles: University of California Press, 1958.

Newbegin, M.I. *Geographical Aspects of Balkan Problems in their Relation to the Great European War.* London: Constable, 1915.

Newman, Bernard. *Balkan Background.* New York: Macmillan, 1945.

— *Tito's Yugoslavia.* London: Hale, 1952.

Ostović, D.O. *The Truth About Yugoslavia.* New York: Roy Publishers, 1952.

Owings, William A. *The Communist Party of Yugoslavia: Its History and Organization, 1919-1941.* Unpublished Master's Thesis. Indiana University, 1952.

Panaiotov, Ivan. *Greeks and Bulgarians.* Sofia: H.G. Danov, 1946.

Pirinski, George. *For a Free Macedonia.* New York: United Committee of South Slavic Americans, 1945.

Possony, Stefan T. *A Century of Conflict: Communist Techniques of World Revolution.* Chicago, 1953.

Pozzi, Henri. *Black Hand Over Europe.* London: Francis Mott, 1935.

Radev, Simion. *La Macédoine et la renaissance bulgaré au XIX siècle.* Sofia: Impr. de la Cour royale, 1910.

Radulović, Monty. *Tito's Republic.* London: Cold Harbour Press, 1948.

Rappaport, A. *Au Pays des Martyrs.* Paris, 1927.

Reiss, Rudolphe. *The Comitadji Question in Southern Serbia.* London: Hazell, Watson and Viney, 1924.

Rizoff, D. *Les Bulgares dans leurs frontières historiques, ethnographiques, et politiques.* Berlin, 1917.

Ronai, Andrew. *Atlas of Central Europe.* Unpublished Doctor's Thesis. Budapest, 1945.

Rothschild, Joseph. *The Communist Party of Bulgaria: Origins and Development, 1883-1936.* New York: Columbia University Press, 1959.

Roucek, Joseph S. "Geopolitical Aspects of the Macedonian Problem," *World Affairs Interpreter,* 21 (April, 1950).

Rubenstein, Alvin Z. "Reforms, Nonalignment, and Pluralism," *Problems of Communism,* 17:2 (March-April, 1968), pp. 31-41.

Schevill, Ferdinand. *The Balkan Problem*. Chicago, 1931.

Seton-Watson, Hugh. *Eastern Europe Between the Wars, 1918-1941*. Hamden: Archon Books, 1962.

— *The East European Revolution*. 3rd ed. New York: Praeger, 1956.

Shoup, Paul. *Communism and the Yugoslav National Question*. New York: Columbia University Press, 1968.

Slavonic Nations in the Fight Against Fascism. Moscow, 1941.

Slijepčević, Boko. *Pitanje makedonske pravoslavne crkve u Jugoslaviji*. Biblioteka Svečanik, 27. Munich: Biblioteka Svečanik, 1959.

Slijepčević, Djoko. *The Macedonian Question: The Struggle for South Serbia*. Chicago: American Institute for Balkan Affairs, 1956.

Soteriadis, George. *An Ethnological Map Illustrating Hellenism in the Balkan Peninsula and Asia Minor*. London: E. Stanford, 1918.

Stalin, Joseph. *Marxism and the National Question: Selected Writings and Speeches*. New York: International Publishers, 1942.

Struggle of the Bulgarian People Against Fascism. Sofia, 1946.

Strupp, Karl. *La Situation Juridique des Macédoniens en Yougoslavie*. Paris: Les Presses Universitaires de France, 1929.

Swire, Joseph. *Bulgarian Conspiracy*. London: Robert Hale, 1939.

Temperley, H.W.V. *A History of Serbia*. London: G. Bell and Sons, 1917.

Todorov, Kosta. *Balkan Firebrand*. Chicago: Ziff-Davis, 1943.

Tomasić, D.A. "Nationality Problems and Partisan Yugoslavia," *Journal of Central European Affairs*, 6:2 (July, 1946), pp. 111-125.

The Trial of Traicho Kostov and His Group. Sofia: Press Department, 1949.

Trouten, Ruth. *Peasant Renaissance in Yugoslavia, 1900-1950*. London, 1952.

Truhelka, Ćiro. *Studije o podrijetlu; etnološka razmatranja iz Bosne i Hercegovine*. Izvanredno izdanje suvremene knjižnice Matice hrvatske, 6. Zagreb, 1941.

Ulam, Adam B. *Titoism and the Cominform*. Cambridge, Mass.: Harvard University Press, 1952.

United Nations Security Council. *Report by the Commission of Investigation Concerning Greek Frontier Incidents*. New York, 1947.

Villari, Luigi. *The Balkan Question: The Present Condition of the Balkans and of European Responsibilities.* London: John Murray, 1905.

Vucinich, Wayne S. *Serbia Between East and West: The Events of 1903-1908.* Stanford: Stanford University Press, 1954.

West, Rebecca. *Black Lamb and Grey Falcon.* New York: Viking, 1941.

Wilkinson, H.R. "Jugoslav Macedonia in Transition," *The Geographical Journal,* 118:4 (December, 1952), pp. 389-405.

—*Maps and Politics: A Review of the Ethnographic Cartography of Macedonia.* Liverpool: University Press, 1951.

Wolff, Robert Lee. *The Balkans in Our Time.* Cambridge, Mass.: Harvard University Press, 1956.

Woodhouse, C.M. *Apple of Discord.* London: Hutchinson, 1948.

Zotiades, George B. *The Macedonian Controversy.* 2nd ed. Salonika: Institute for Balkan Studies, 1961.

NOTES

INTRODUCTION

[1] H.R. Wilkinson's *Maps and Politics: A Review of the Ethnographic Cartography of Macedonia* is an excellent expose of such political use of maps in the Macedonian question. World War I, Wilson's Fourteen Points, and League of Nations idealism encouraged a flurry of works on the ethnography of Macedonia. Standard Bulgarian points of view are found in Iordan Ivanov, *La Question macédonienne,* and D. Rizoff, *Les Bulgares dans leur frontieres historiques, ethnographiques et politiques.* The classic Serbian statements are contained in Aleksandar Belić, *La Macédoine: études ethnographiques et politiques,* and Tihomir Djordjević, *La Macédoine.* The Greek view is represented in such works as I.V. Colocotronis, *La Macédoine: étude historique et ethnologique.* On the IMRO side there is Christ Anastassoff, *The Tragic Peninsula.* After World War II, IMRO chief Ivan Mihailov for the first time published his views under his own name: *Macedonia: Switzerland of the Balkans* and *Macedonia's Rise for Freedom, 1903.*

[2] Classic works on these and later Balkan migrations and infiltrations are Jovan Cvijić, *Balkansko poluostrvo* and Ćiro Truhelka, *Studije o porijetlu.*

[3] Horace G. Lunt gives examples of such proscription in his "A Survey of Macedonian Literature," *Harvard Slavic Studies,* I (1953), pp. 363-396.

[4] For a perceptive analysis of the development and danger of Balkan nationalist creeds, see Walter Kolarz, *Myths and Realities in Eastern Europe.*

[5] When Macedonia is mentioned hereafter, Yugoslav or Vardar Macedonia is meant unless the connotation clearly denotes "greater" Macedonia.

[6] One of the best accounts of the period is Hugh Seton-Watson, *Eastern Europe Between the Wars.*

[7] By the time of the 1965 Bulgarian census, the party and government no longer recognized a separate Macedonian nationality and the inhabitants of the Pirin region were not encouraged to call themselves Macedonians. As a result, only 8,750 "Macedonians" were reported in Bulgaria.

CHAPTER 1

[1] Josip Broz Tito, *V Kongress, Komunističke Partije Jugoslavije: Izveštije i Referati* (Belgrade, 1948), p. 14. Cited hereafter as *V Kongres.* A good account of the party's treat-

ment of the national question as a whole is found in Paul Shoup, *Communism and the Yugoslav National Question*. A good history of the party in the interwar years is Ivan Avakumovic, *History of the Communist Party of Yugoslavia*, Vol. I.

2 Lazar Koliševski, Political Report to the First Congress of the Communist Party of Macedonia, *I Kongres na KPM*, p. 34. Koliševski was head of the Macedonian party organization from the end of the war until 1962 when he gave up his position in Macedonia to devote full-time to party affairs in Belgrade. He became a member of the Yugoslav party Executive Committee (later the Presidium) in 1953 and is still a member of that body.

3 There were interesting parallels between the Green Cadre controversy and the CPY's subsequent handling of the question of working with the IMRO.

4 Tito, *V Kongres*, p. 21.

5 Koliševski, *I Kongres na KPM*, p. 34.

6 *Ibid.*, p. 35.

7 June 20-25, 1920.

8 Tito, *V Kongres*, p. 22.

9 Koliševski, *I Kongres na KPM*, p. 36.

10 *Ibid.*, p. 36.

11 The *comitadjis* were Bulgarian or pro-Bulgarian irregulars, usually organized by the IMRO, who made frequent, disruptive raids into Yugoslav Macedonia from the end of World War I until 1934.

12 *I Kongres na KPM*, p. 38.

1ͻ Conversation with leaders of the Macedonian Patriotic (formerly Political) Organization of the U.S. and Canada, Indianapolis, Indiana, hereafter cited as MPO. They confirmed many of the claims made by Koliševski and other Communist sources with regard to Macedonian reaction to the Serbian "annexation" policy.

14 Data on the elections are found in *Ustavotvorne skupštine, statistički pogled izbora narodnih poslanika* (Belgrade, 1921). For a discussion of the meaning of the elections in Macedonia, see R.V. Burks, *The Dynamics of Communism in Eastern Europe.*, pp. 78-80.

15 The text of the *Obznana*, except for four articles relating to the right to keep explosives, was reprinted in "Repression in the Yugoslav State", *The Nation*, No. 113, October 12, 1921. Article 18 outlawed the Communist Party.

16 "K proletaratu balkano-dunaiskikh stran, k kommunisticheskim partiiam Bolgarii, Ruminii, Serbii i Turtsii ot Kommunisticheskogo Internatsionala," *Kommunisticheskii Internatsional*, No. 9, N.S. (March, 1920), pp. 1405-1410.

17 Barker, *Macedonia*, p. 47.

18 Belgrade made much of Radić's "negotiations" with the Soviet leaders. According to the standard Croatian version of his trip, Radić quickly cooled to the idea of accepting

Soviet "cooperation". Upon his informing Chicherin that collaboration was impossible, Radić was put under house arrest. To secure his release, he sent a telegram to his Party's acting secretary, Maček, asking the Party ostensibly to support the Soviet proposals. When Radić returned to the Kingdom the Croatian Peasant Party reneged on the agreement. Belgrade, however, took the opportunity to jail Radić.

[19] Tito, *V Kongres*, p. 36.

[20] Koliševski, *I Kongres na KPM*, p. 42.

CHAPTER 2

[1] After Stamboliski was killed in 1923, Bulgarian Macedonians largely dominated the Sofia Government. In their fanatic efforts to regain Yugoslav Macedonia, the revisionist extremists pushed Sofia into situations wherein Bulgaria was a dangerous threat to the peace of the Balkans. The Treaty of Neuilly prohibited Bulgaria from having a strong army by which moderate Bulgarian elements might have controlled the impetuous Macedonians.

[2] A 1923 Congress of the Balkan Communist Federation had sharply condemned the rightists, and the Communist press in the USSR and Vienna supported the CPY left wing.

[3] *Istorijski Arhiv KPJ*, Vol. II, *Kongresi i zemaljske konferencije KPJ 1919-1937*, hereinafter cited as *IA, II*, (Belgrade, 1950). The summarizations of and quotations from the Third Conference Resolutions are from pages 67-77.

[4] A Serbian name for Albanians.

[5] The Thracian question was somewhat similar to the Macedonian in that Western Thrace had been a part of Bulgaria from 1913 until it was ceded to Greece by the Treaty of Neuilly (1920). Many Bulgarians had fled or had been expelled when Greece took over, and Thracian emigre groups in Bulgaria were exerting pressure for revision of the boundary.

[6] The italics and those which follow are those of the *Arhiv*.

[7] Koliševski, *I Kongres na KPM*, p. 42.

[8] Tito, *V Kongres*, p. 37.

[9] Vidoe Smilevski, "Osvrt na razvoj makedonskog nacionalnog pitanja," *Komunist*, January, 1950, p. 97. Smilevski has held leading party and government positions in the Macedonian republic and in federal organizations since the end of the war. In 1966 he was one of the four Macedonians elected to membership on the 35-member Party Presidium.

[10] Stoyan Christowe, *Heroes and Assassins* (New York, 1935), p. 168. Christowe is pro-IMRO and, now at least, pro-Communist. The opposite bias is held by Kosta Todorov, *Balkan Firebrand* (Chicago, 1943). Joseph Swire, *Bulgarian Conspiracy* (London, 1939) is more balanced. For a succinct resumé of inter-war IMRO machinations see Barker,

Macedonia (London, 1950), pp. 36-77. Barker's section on the IMRO has been criticized, with some justification, for minimizing IMRO's strength among the Macedonians.

[11] No attempt is made here to review in detail the activities of the IMRO in the interwar period. Rather, those IMRO-Communist relations which are pertinent to the development of the CPY's nationality policy are examined.

[12] The line dividing the two groups was exceedingly hazy and there was some switching of sides. Later, for instance, Aleksandrov and Protogerov stood for much more of an "autonomous" concept than did the extreme faction which succeeded them. Chaoulev later became a Communist.

[13] Barker, *Macedonia*, p. 40.

[14] Christowe, *Heroes and Assassins*, p. 176.

[15] Todorov, *Balkan Firebrand*, p. 212.

[16] The Federation's March program was published in *International Press Correspondence* (A publication of the Communist International), 4:24 (April 10, 1924), pp. 224-226.

[17] *Fédération Balcanique* (a communist periodical put out by Dimitar Vlahov and the Bulgarian Nikola Harlakov), July 13, 1924, parts are reproduced in Barker, *Macedonia*, pp. 55-57.

[18] *International Press Correspondence*, 4:64 (September 5, 1924), p. 683.

[19] *International Press Correspondence*, 4:54 (August 4, 1924), p. 572.

[20] Christowe claimed Aleksandrov was dispatched as the result of a conspiracy between Atanasov and Aleksandar Vasilev (alias Aleko Pasha), the IMRO chief in the Petrich Department. A standard IMRO version is that Protogerov was responsible for Aleksandrov's death; hence the ten-year vendetta between the Protogerovists and Mihailovists.

[21] Koliševski, *I Kongres na KPM*, p. 42-43.

[22] What relation this had with the positive aspects of the foundation of IMRO (United) seventeen years before, Koliševski failed to explain.

[23] Koliševski, *I Kongres KPM*, p. 43.

[24] J. Stalin, *Marxism and the National and Colonial Question*, (London, 1936), p. 204.

[25] Stalin's Sverdlov address also provided a useful backstop for Tito's Macedonian policy during World War II.

[26] Stalin, *Marxism*, p. 228. During the Second World War, Tito was to take precisely this "constitutional" approach in his jurisdictional dispute with the Bulgarian Communists over Macedonia.

[27] Pecanac was the Vojvoda (Supreme Leader) of the government-sponsored paramilitary Serbian Četniks, who engaged in terroristic activities against Croatians and Macedonians.

[28] *I.A.*, II, p. 98.

[29] *Ibid.*, p. 112.

[30] A leader of the "anti-factionalists" was Josip Broz Tito. *Ibid.*, p. 145.

[31] *Ibid.*, p. 465. Togliatti's speech is reproduced in its entirety, pp. 460-468.

[32] *Ibid.*, p. 153. Italics supplied.

[33] *Ibid.*, p. 155. This is probably the only instance on record of an official CPY admission that the Macedonians might not wish to be included in Yugoslavia.

[34] *Ibid.*, pp. 182-192.

CHAPTER 3

[1] Tito, *V Kongres*, p. 44.

[2] According to one observer in position to know, the Comintern's specific charge against Gorkić was his poor handling of the transport of Yugoslav volunteers being sent to Spain to fight in the Civil War alongside the Loyalists. In November 1936 a contingent of about 350 was apprehended by police while waiting in boats to go aboard a ship off the Dalmation coast. Gorkić's excuses for the fiasco were not deemed satisfactory.

[3] *International Press Correspondence*, 9:21 (May 10, 1929), p. 493.

[4] Pavelić had defended some IMRO revolutionists at a trial in Skopje in 1927 and had asked the IMRO to instruct his Ustaša agents in the Macedonians' assassination techniques.

[5] See Ulam, *Titoism*, pp. 14-18.

[6] *I.A.* II, p. 399.

[7] Koliševski, *I Kongres na KPM*. The following is summarized from pp. 43-47.

[9] Ulam, *Titoism*, p. 22. Insofar as this statement is applied to Macedonia it should be somewhat qualified.

[10] *Četvrti Kongres SKOJ-a (12-14 Oktobra, 1948)*, p. 136. In 1935 SKOJ had between 2,000 and 3,000 members.

[11] Tito, *V Kongres*, p. 52.

[12] *Ibid.*, p. 54.

[13] *Ibid.*, p. 56.

[14] Koliševski, *I Kongres na KPM*, pp. 47-48.

[15] Aleksandar Ranković, *V Kongres*, p. 172.

[16] Koliševski, *I Kongres na KPM*, p. 49.

[17] Milovan Djilas, *V Kongres*, p. 262.

[18] Andrejev, born in Skopje, joined the CPY in 1923. At the time of the Fifth Conference he was the oldest party official from Macedonia, according to a former party member. Satorov, a Bulgarian reputed to have had a consistently anti-Serb attitude (Barker, *Macedonia*, p. 84), was elected to the Provincial Committee in 1937. He went into a short eclipse after a reorganization in 1939 because of his "factionalist" position on the nationality question. However, by October 1940 he was the Provincial Organizational Secretary.

[19] *Solunci* (also *Solunaši*) were World War I soldiers, mostly Serbs from Austro-Hungary, in the Yugoslav Volunteer Corps. They fought on the Salonika Front and many were given land confiscated in the reforms of the 1920's.

[20] Koliševski, *I Kongres na KPM*, pp. 49-53. See also *I.A.*, II, p. 384.

[21] Vlahov served as District Governor at Priština, a largely Albanian town north of the present Macedonian boundary line. Swire, *Bulgarian Conspiracy*, p. 137.

CHAPTER 4

[1] Hugh Seton-Watson, *The East European Revolution* (New York, 1951) p. 66.

[2] C. O. Ostović, *The Truth About Yugoslavia* (New York, 1952) pp. 163, 164, quoted from *Dokumenti o Jugoslaviji, Istina o 25 i 27 Martu* (Paris, 1951).

[3] Stephen Clissold, *Whirlwind* (London, 1949) p. 27; Shoup, *Communism*, p 49ff.

[4] According to the MPO, Mihailov was in Warsaw when the Germans attacked Poland. After he had been interned by the Germans for some time, friends in Hungary obtained permission for him to leave. Bulgaria would accept him only on its own terms, i.e., his ceasing to work for an independent Macedonia, and nobody else would have him except Ante Pavelić. Mihailov believed the wishes of the Macedonians would be respected after the war and, therefore, did not order his agents in Macedonia to fight against the Bulgarian or Serbian nationalists or the Communists. In 1942 and 1943 the Germans unsuccessfully tried to persuade him to go to Skopje to set up a Pavelić-type government. He finally went there on a brief survey mission in September 1944. See below pp. 112-113.

[5] Barker, *Macedonia*, p. 79.

[6] Seton-Watson, *East European Revolution*, p. 123.

[7] H.R. Wilkinson, *Maps and Politics: A Review of the Ethnographic Cartography of Macedonia* (Liverpool, 1951), p. 298. The larger figure would include almost all post-World War I Serb settlers.

[8] See S.R. Ladas, *The Exchange of Minorities: Bulgaria, Greece, and Turkey* (New York, 1932) for data on the large-scale population transfers in the 1920's.

[9] Lazar Mojsov, *Bulgarskata Rabotnička Partija (Komunisti) i makedonskoto nacionalno prašanje* (Skopje, 1948), pp. 74, 78. Mojsov's assertion that in the spring of 1941 the CPY took a stand against Yugoslavia's dismemberment conflicts with Clissold's view.

[10] Kološevski, *I Kongres na KPM*, p. 57-58.

[11] Mojsov, *Bulgarska Radnička Partija*, p. 81.

[12] *Istorijski Arhiv*, Vol. VII, *Makedonija u Narodnoslobodilačkom Ratu i Narodnoj Revoluciji 1941-1944*, Jovan Marjanović, ed., (Belgrade, 1951) hereinafter cited as *I.A.* VII, pp. 50-51.

[13] *I.A.* VII, p. 389. The decision of the Executive Committee of the Comintern is reproduced, together with a letter from the CC CPB acknowledging that decision.

[14] It is possible that the Bulgarian Party received different instructions or that the CPY records exaggerate the degree of Comintern acceptance of Tito's Macedonian claim. It is of interest that although footnotes in the *Arhiv* claim that the originals of almost all the documents reproduced therein are in the archives of the CC CPY, in the case of these two communications the archives have only copies.

[15] *I.A.* VII. One of Pavlović's reports is reproduced on pp. 42-44. The critical comments appear on p. 386 of the "Explanations and Commentaries" section. On p. 391 it is noted that Pavlović was recalled from Macedonia and sent into action in Bosnia. He was killed in January 1942.

[16] *Ibid.*, p. 391. Barker states that after Kološevski's arrest, "Balgaranov immediately came forward and took over the relics of the Regional [Provincial] Committee," *Macedonia*, p. 90. It should be stressed that the detailed CPY version of developments in Macedonia was not available to Barker. In any case, her conclusion that the Committee reverted to the Šatorov line is entirely correct, and Balgaranov's role was likely pre-eminent in this period.

[17] A description of Andrejev's "mistakes" is given in *I.A.* VII, pp. 391, 392, 395-398.

[18] Tito, *V Kongres*, p. 129-130.

[19] Ranković, *V Kongres*, p. 200.

[20] *I.A.* VII, p. 61, 62.

[21] According to Barker, "It was not until the beginning of 1943 that Tito again tried to retrieve the position in Macedonia." *Macedonia*, p. 91. Radosavljević arrived in Macedonia on August 25, 1942. *I.A.* VII, p. 401.

[22] *I.A.* VII, pp. 398-399.

[23] *Ibid.*, the Proclamation is reproduced on pp. 135-140. Most of the remaining historical data in this chapter was culled from the same volume of the *Arkiv*.

[24] Also of interest is comment in the *Arhiv* about reference in the Proclamation to the counter-*četa* military detachments. According to this source, these bands were formed of old IMRO hands in 1941 by the Bulgarian occupation authorities. It is admitted that "a great number of people suffered" at the hands of the counter-*četas* and that it was not until 1943 that the units were, "in general", liquidated. *I.A.* VII, p. 401.

CHAPTER 5

[1] Seton-Watson, *East European Revolution*, p. 125.

[2] *I.A.* VII. The letter is reproduced on pp. 187-194.

[3] Barker, *Macedonia*, p. 91.

[4] *I.A.*, VII, pp. 204-211.

[5] *I.A.* VII, pp. 210-211.

[6] *Ibid.*, VII, p. 214. The unattributed quotations which follow in this chapter are also from Volume VII.

[7] *I Kongres na KPM*, p. 70.

[8] *I.A.* VII, p. 403. Of the CC's eight members of 1943, Koliševski, Uzunovski, Gigov, Temelkovski, and Aceva were full members of the CC CPY at the time of the Fifth Congress in 1948. Naceva and Andrejev were only candidate members. The average age of the CC CPM members of 1943 was 29, another indication of the defection or demise of the old hands of the CPY's Macedonian organization.

[9] Although Andrejev ostensibly sided with Tito on the Cominform Resolution issue, he was arrested in 1950, and charged with being a Cominformist.

[10] Koliševski, *I Kongres na KPM*, p. 69. It is not clear when Balgaranov left Macedonia. Šatorov had been in Bulgaria since October 1941, according to *I.A.* VII, p. 388. Later both were commissioned as officers in the Bulgarian Army of the Fatherland Front Government. Mojsov, *Bulgarska Radnička Partija*, p. 131.

[11] *I.A.* VII, p. 247.

[12] *Ibid.*, pp. 222-227.

[13] There was considerable variation in the size of Partisan "regular" units at this time. When a unit acquired 150 men it was usually given brigade status. Later in the war the brigades had between 400 and 700 men. Each brigade was divided into four battalions; each battalion into four *četas*. Every unit from a *četa* on up had a political commissar at least equal in rank to the military commander.

[14] Emphasis supplied.

[15] *I.A.*, VII, pp. 229-245.

[16] Among these were probably some of the pro-Tito Macedonians for whose arrests the CPY blamed the Bulgarian Communists.

[17] In this letter Tempo made several other references to the fact that Italian-held territory in Macedonia was more fruitful for the CPY than was that occupied by the Bulgarians.

[18] See p. 78-79 above.

[19] Koliševski, *I Kongres na KPM*, p. 73-74.

[20] At this time Bulgaria occupied additional territory in the Lake Ohrid-Prespa area over which she had a dispute with Italy in August, 1941. John A. Lukacs, *The Great Powers in Eastern Europe* (New York, 1953), p. 456.

[21] *I.A.* VII, pp. 257-261.

[22] The Partisans at least tacitly played this game themselves on occasion. In 1942, Communists in Slavonia were instructed not to interfere with Ustaša destruction of Orthodox churches. It has not been proved that the CP instigated this vandalism, but it was stupid from the Ustaša and occupiers' point of view, for it electrified Serbian resistance. Partisan recruitment of the minority Serbs soared.

[23] The last named four men were treated separately from Mihailov in CPM proclamations because they were in Macedonia. According to the MPO, any guerrilla action they took was on their personal initiative. Many IMRO members fought on the side of the Partisans, assuming the IMRO would take over after the war. Kitinčev was the occupation mayor of Skopje. Džuzelov and Dimitri Čkatrov were heroes of the 1927 IMRO trial, after which the latter was imprisoned for twelve years; both were executed by the Communists after the war.

[24] In the Manifesto's appeals to various ethnic groups, the Vlahs were included for the first time.

[25] See p. 80.

[26] The extremely poor state of communications between the CPM and the CC CPY in this period is sometimes forgotten.

[27] *I.A.* VII, pp. 262-265.

[28] *I.A.*, VII, pp. 265-269.

[29] Much of the data from which the following observations are drawn were made available by a former Partisan and member of an Agitprop team.

[30] The real Communist enemies in Macedonia were the Četniks, the Bulgarophiles, the IMRO and the unorganized out-and-out Autonomists. As we have seen, these groups were not declared as enemies simultaneously. Some were manipulated to help decrease the potentialities of the others. In the end, however, all were declared enemies.

[31] Djilas, *V Kongres,* pp. 281-283.

[32] Vladimir Dedijer, *Tito* (New York, 1953), pp. 180-183, 189, 209, 210.

CHAPTER 6

[1] Vladimir Dedijer, *Jugoslovensko-Albanski Odnosi 1939-1948,* (Belgrade, 1949), p. 10.

[2] *Ibid.,* p. 11.

[3] *Ibid.,* pp. 27.

[4] Clissold, *Whirlwind,* p. 143.

[5] Dedijer, *Jugoslovensko-Albanski Odnosi,* p. 89.

[6] *I.A.* VII, pp. 237-242.

[7] Dedijer, *Jugoslovensko-Albanski Odnosi,* p. 127.

[8] William Hardy McNeill, *The Greek Dilemma* (Philadelphia, 1947) p. 264.

[9] Greek anti-Communists made capital out of agreements allegedly made by representatives of ELAS and EAM (National Liberation Front) with the Bulgarian occupation authorities. It was purported that the terms provided that the administration of Greek Macedonia would be given over to EAM and SNOF when the Bulgarians and Germans withdrew and that the Greek Communist Party would work for Macedonian autonomy within a Slav Federation. C.M. Woodhouse, *Apple of Discord* (London, 1948), pp. 296-297.

[10] *I.A.,* VII, pp. 240, 241.

[11] Svetozar Vukmanović-Tempo, *How and Why the People's Liberation Struggle of Greece Met with Defeat* (London, 1950) p. 52.

[12] Vranje is about fifty miles north-northeast of Skopje and is outside the boundaries of Macedonia.

[13] *I.A.* VII, p. 239.

[14] *Ibid.,* pp. 244-245.

[15] Vladimir Dedijer, *Dnevnik,* Vol. II (Belgrade, 1946) p. 472. In an extensive footnote (pp. 472-490) Dedijer reviewed the Partisans' military undertakings in Macedonia, as related to him by Tempo. In the account of Tempo's conversations with the representatives of the other Balkan CP's, there are a number of references to his having spoken "in the name of the Supreme [Yugoslav] Staff."

[16] Harry N. Howard, in Kerner, *Yugoslavia* (Berkeley, 1949), pp. 345-346.

[17] Fitzroy MacLean, *Escape to Adventure* (Boston, 1951), p. 251.

[18] Dedijer, *Tito,* pp. 204-205.

[19] *Zbornik na dokumenti od ASNOM,* pp. 48-49.

[20] *The Slavonic Nations in the Fight Against Fascism* (Moscow, 1941), p. 20. At the same Congress (August 10, 11, 1941) Alexei Tolstoy stated, "The whole world has already heard about the heroism of the Polish, Montenegrin, Serbian and Macedonian partisans." At that time, the inclusion of the latter was of course thoroughly imaginative. Macedonia was not included in the Congress' "Manifesto to the Oppressed Slavonic Nations," while Serbs, Croats, Slovenes, Bulgarians, Carpathian-Ukrainians, etc., were.

[21] Barker, *Macedonia,* pp. 95, 101.

[22] Dedijer, *Tito*, p. 209. At the Tehran Conference, held the same time as Jajce, the Partisans were recognized as an "Allied Army" but no suggestion of legal governmental authority was ascribed to them.

[23] *Ibid.*, p. 210.

[24] According to some sources, the USSR felt so strongly about this that it ordered Tito to cooperate with Axis forces in opposing an Allied invasion. Tito's representative, General Vladimir Velebit, reportedly made such an offer to the German General Edmund von Glaise-Horstenau, but the proposal was rejected by Hitler. See Stefan T. Possony, *A Century of Conflict*, p. 267. Possony gives as his sources Walter Hagen, *Die Geheime Front* (Zurich, 1950) and Derek Kartun, *Tito's Plot Against Europe* (New York, 1950).

[25] *I.A.* VII, pp. 265-269.

[26] *Ibid.*, pp. 286-287.

[27] Barker, *Macedonia*, p. 97.

[28] *I.A.*, VII, p. 409.

[29] *Ibid.*, pp. 271-274.

[30] *Opštepropaganda* is the Agitprop term for approved but "unofficial" propagation of the Party line on an issue. The rule was that "responsible" agitators, i.e., those who spoke officially for the Party or for one of its sub-groups, could not usually employ the *Opštepropaganda* line, for it often differed from the official line. Agitprop agents not formally attached to a Party unit were instructed to utilize the *Opštepropaganda* adaptations of the official line according to specified local or temporal needs.

[31] *I.A.*, VII, pp. 289-293.

[32] *Ibid.*, p. 287. About a month before, the "Hristo Botev" Batallion, largely composed of deserters from the Bulgarian forces, had been formed by the CPY in eastern Macedonia.

[33] *I.A.*, VII, p. 410. The CPB was accused of continuing to inform on leaders loyal to the CPY. In the 1948 trial of the occupation police chief, Asen Bogdanov, it was claimed that one of his agents was Anka Balgaranova, wife of none other than Bojan Balgaranov.

[34] *Ibid.*, p. 315.

[35] Koliševski, *I Kongres na KPM*, pp. 83-85.

[36] The official military history of the Macedonian Partisans, written by their Chief of Staff, covers the period from June to November 1944. Mihajlo Apostolski, *Završnite Operacii na N.O.V. za Oslovoduvanjeto na Makedonija* (Skopje, 1953).

[37] Koliševski, *I Kongres na KPM*, p. 85.

[38] There is pointed omission here and elsewhere to Bulgarian contributions. The emphasis on Macedonian *action* was an appeal and a threat as well as a commendation, for the last Axis campaign in Macedonia was in full swing at the time.

39 Awaiting the full liberation of Yugoslavia and desiring to be near enough to return as quickly as possible, King Petar and many members of the Yugoslav government-in-exile were in Cairo.

40 These excerpts of Pijade's article are from *I.A.*, pp. 316-322. Emphasis supplied. This is a literal translation including Pijade's technical errors, such as calling the Englishman Brailsford a Norwegian.

41 Barker attributes significance to the use of the word *Sobranje*, or "assembly" which is "identical with the Bulgarian word, instead of the word *Veće* or 'council' used in the other Yugoslav lands." *(Macedonia*, p. 97.) This was a concession to clarity rather than to Bulgarophilism, for *sobranje* was and is the word used by Macedonians for assembly or council.

42 The decisions of ASNOM are reproduced on pp. 340-345 of *I.A.* VII.

43 *Ibid.*, pp. 346-347.

44 *Ibid.*, p. 413.

45 *Ibid.*, pp. 348-353.

46 Woodhouse, *Apple of Discord*, pp. 192-199.

47 The Communists had obtained the services of the Chief Secretary in the office of Pavelić.

CHAPTER 7

1 *I.A.*, VII, pp. 328-330.

2 *Ibid.*, pp. 330-331.

3 *Ibid.*

4 Barker, *Macedonia*, pp. 110-111, quoting from Gaston Coblentz in the *New York Herald Tribune* (European Edition), August 20, 1949.

5 McNeill, *Greek Dilemma,* pp. 265-266.

6 After Sofia sued for peace with the Allies, the USSR declared war on Bulgaria in order to occupy the country and have a voice in the peace treaty at the conclusion of the war. Bulgaria, though an ally of Germany, never declared war on the Soviet Union. The Soviet Union declared war on Bulgaria September 5, 1944. Three days later the Bulgarian government asked for an armistice.

7 *I.A.*, VII, pp. 413-414.

8 Speech of Madolev to the Fifth Congress of the CPB, *Rabotnichesko Delo*, December 23, 1948.

9 Letter of Vukmanović-Tempo and Koliševski. *I.A.*, VII, pp. 359-361.

10 Madolev speech, *Rabotnichesko Delo*, December 23, 1948.

11 Letter dated November 8, 1944, *I.A.*, VII, pp. 369-375.

[12] The Yugoslavs have remained sensitive on this question. In 1968 when a series of bitter polemics on the Macedonian question broke out, one of the issues raised by Sofia was the role of the Bulgarian Army in liberating areas of Macedonia and Serbia. For the Yugoslav response at that time, see *Borba*, October 2, 1968. and the speech of Tito in Leskovac, *Borba*, October 22, 1968.

[13] *I.A.*, VII, p. 415.

[14] *Ibid.*, pp. 366-367. Emphasis in original.

[15] *I.A.*, VII, pp. 367-369.

[16] Aleksandar Ranković, *II Kongres Komunističke partije Srbije*, p. 226; Vladimir Dedijer, *Tito*, p. 304.

[17] According to the MPO, 800 families were moved out of the Nevrokop District alone.

[18] Dimitar Mitrev, *Pirinska Makedonija vo borba za nacionalno osloboduvanje*, p. 281.

[19] The results of the 1946 Bulgarian census for the Pirin district have never been published. However, both Yugoslavs and Bulgarians have frequently stated that the census showed seventy percent of the population to be Macedonian, but specific numerical figures are never cited. For example, see Crvenkovski's speech reported in *Borba*, February 3, 1968.

[20] Mitrev, *Pirinska Makedonija*, pp. 288-290.

[21] Mojsov, *Bulgarska Radnička partija*, pp. 223-224. Emphasis supplied.

[22] Mitrev, *Pirinska Makedonija*, pp. 302-308. See Shoup's discussion of this resolution in *Communism and the Yugoslav National Question*, pp. 151-152.

[23] *Documents on International Affairs*, 1947-1948(London, 1952), pp. 290-292.

[24] *Ibid.*, p. 292.

[25] *Ibid.*, pp. 293-294; Georgi Dimitrov, *Political Report: V Congress of the Bulgarian Communist Party*, p. 65.

[26] Dimitrov, *Political Report*, p. 64.

[27] See R.V. Burks, *The Dynamics of Communism in Eastern Europe*, pp. 99-101; and Philip Mosley, *The Kremlin and World Politics*, pp. 230-232.

[28] Evangelos Kofos, *Nationalism and Communism in Macedonia*, pp. 164-166.

[29] Mitrev, *Pirinska Makedonija*, pp. 326-335; Dimitrov, *Political Report*, p. 67.

[30] Mojsov, *Bulgarska Radnička Partija*, p. 274.

[31] *Pravda*, January 29, 1948.

[32] Dedijer, *Tito*, p. 321; Milovan Djilas, *Conversations with Stalin*, pp. 175-178.

[33] *Documents on International Affairs*, 1947-1948, pp. 293-294. The Slavic inhabitants of the Pirin District considered themselves Bulgarians. Compulsory instruction in the Macedonian language, compulsory subscriptions to Macedonian newspapers, and a

party decision that the inhabitants of the Pirin region should be enumerated in the 1946 census as Macedonians were necessary to encourage these people to consider themselves Macedonians.

34 Dimitrov, *Political Report*, p. 70.

35 See *The Trial of Traicho Kostov and His Group*.

36 MPO officials maintained that Ljupčo Arsov and Vera Aceva had Cominformist inclinations and that Cvetko Uzunovski was dropped from the CC CPM because of Bulgarophile Cominformism. This thesis is also held by Anton Ciliga, who pointed to a new influx of Serbs into Macedonia after 1948 as a counter to Cominform exploitation of Bulgarophilism. See his *La Yougoslavie sous la Ménace*, pp. 67-70.

37 *Nova Makedonija*, May 10, 1949.

38 *Borba*, July 3, 1952.

39 The ratio of expulsions to party membership was one to thirty-one in the MPR, one to twenty-three in Bosnia-Hercegovina, one to twenty in Croatia and one to six in Montenegro. Figures were not released by the Serbian and Slovenian parties. [Paul S. Shoup, *Communism and the National Question in Yugoslavia* (Columbia University: Unpublished Ph. D. Thesis, 1961), pp. 163-164.] The meaning of these figures is not distorted by any divergence in the ratio of party members to total republic population. Although this ratio in 1949 was higher in Montenegro (4.3% of the republic population were party members), party membership in the other republics averaged between 2.1 percent (Bosnia-Hercegovina) and 2.7 percent (Slovenia).

40 *Borba*, June 19, 1945.

41 Josip Broz Tito, *Isgradnja nova jugoslavije*, I, p. 158.

42 *Borba*, August 26, 1946.

43 Barker, *Macedonia*, p. 118.

44 Kofos, *Nationalism and Communism in Macedonia*, pp. 166-167, 170-173.

45 *Ibid.*, pp. 175-177.

46 Pijade, quoted in *KPJ i makedonskoto prašanje*, p. 98.

47 Hamilton Fish Armstrong, *Tito and Goliath*, p. 192; Kofos, *Nationalism and Communism in Macedonia*, pp. 179-183.

48 *Nova Makedonija*, August 3, 1949.

49 Vukmanović Tempo, *How and Why the People's Liberation Struggle in Greece Met with Defeat*, p. 77.

CHAPTER 8

1 *Osnivački kongres KP Bosne i Hercegovine*, pp. 11-12.

2 Report of the CC to the Second Congress of the LCM, *Nova Makedonija*, May 26,

1952. At the Sixth Congress of the CPY (Zagreb, 1952) the name of the party was changed to the League of Communists of Yugoslavia. The republic parties also became Leagues.

[3] *Borba,* May 22, 1945.

[4] *Ustav, FNRJ* (Belgrade, 1950), Article I.

[5] This practice in the Security service continued at least until the purge of Aleksandar Ranković in July, 1966.

[6] For an excellent summary of the nationality composition of the Federal Yugoslav governments and the central party organs from 1945 to 1963, see Shoup, *Communism and the Yugoslav National Question,* pp. 274-275.

[7] *Borba,* January 31, 1954 .

[8] *Borba,* April 20, 1958. Gligov returned to Skopje to become a member of the LCM Executive Committee and Secretary of the Skopje party committee.

[9] *Borba,* July 1, 1963. They included Risto Džunov, Kiro Gligorov, Nikola Minčev, Borko Temelkovski, Trajče Grojovski, plus the Chairman of the MSR Executive Council.

[10] *Ibid.* These were Arsov, Crvenkovski, Gigov, Aleksandar Grličkov, Koliševski, Smilevski and Blagoje Taleski.

[11] *Borba,* May 19, 1967. Arsov, Gigov, Koliševski, and Smilevski remained on the new council and five new Macedonian members were elected: Mihajlo Apostolski, Mito Hadživasilev, Slavko Janevski, Elisije Popovski. and Borko Temelkovski. Azem Zulfčari, also from the Macedonian Republic, was also elected to the Council. However, Zulfičari is of Albanian nationality.

[12] *Borba,* May 18, 1969.

[13] Shoup lists only 5 Macedonians on the CC [p. 275]. The apparent reason is that there is no biography on Cvetko Uzinovski in *Ko je Ko u Jugoslaviji,* the source used by Shoup to determine nationality of government and party officials. There is no doubt of Uzinovski's Macedonian nationality, however. The records of the Fifth Party Congress indicate that he was born in Macedonia and was a member of the Macedonian party leadership [*V Kongres KPJ: Stenografske Bilješke,* p. 799.] His name is unmistakably Macedonian. Before the communist take-over the Slavic-Macedonians used the Bulgarian patronymic "-ov" in their surnames. After the Macedonians were recognized by the CPY to be a distinct nationality and the process of de-Bulgarization got underway, the patronymic "-ski" was added to Macedonian names. In order to avoid the charge of following the old Yugoslav policy of Serbianizing the Macedonians, the Communists used the Polish or Russian patronymic "-ski" rather than the Serbian patronymic "-ić," Macedonian names thus have both patronymic endings— "-ov" plus "-ski." For example, Uzin*ov-ski,* Smil*ev-ski,* Crven*kov-ski,* Koliš*ev-ski.*

[14] *V Kongres KPJ: Stenografske Bilješke,* pp. 796-804.

[15] *VI Kongres SKJ,* pp. 286-288. In addition to the six who had been chosen in 1948, Ljupčo Arsov, Crvenkovski, Minčev and Naumovski were elected to full membership.

The Central Revision Commission included Burzevski and Dimitar Vlahov.

[16] *VII Kongres SKJ*, pp. 421-424. All of the Macedonian members of the CC chosen in 1953 except Uzinovski were re-elected. New members of the Committee were Risto Džunov, Mito Hadživasilev, Krste Markovski, Lazar Mojsov, and Blagoje Talevski.

[17] *VIII Kongres SKJ*, pp. 279-282. Vera Aceva, who had been a member of the Central Committee since 1948, was dropped from the 1964 CC but became a member of the Control Commission. Arsov, Naumovski, Mito Hadživasilev, Markovski, and Talevski were also dropped from CC membership. New Members of the committee for the first time were Kiro Gligorov, Aleksandar Grličkov, Kiro Hadživasilev, Boško Stankovski, Jani Bocevski, Slavko Miloslavlevski, Dane Petkovski, and Pavel Davkov. (The last three do not have biographies in *Ko je Ko*, but Mitoslavlevski and Petkovski have obviously Macedonian names and Davkov became a member of the Executive Committee of the LCM in 1965.) Shoup gives figures for the CC and Executive Committee for 1963 at a time when the membership of both organs had been altered since the Seventh Congress. The figures and individuals listed here, however, are based on the elections which took place at the Eighth Congress, December 7-13, 1964.

[18] Macedonian members of the Executive Bureau are Krste Crvenkovski and Kiro Gligorov. The seven Macedonian representatives chosen at the Fifth LCM Congress in November 1968 were Crvenkovski, Angel Cemerski, Koliševski, Dimce Belovski, Gligorov, Slavko Milosavlevski, and Azem Zulfičari (of Albanian nationality).

[19] *Ustav, SFRJ* (Belgrade, 1963), Article 226, p. 80.

[20] See speech of Georgov in Titov Veles, *Nova Makedonija*, November 2, 1958.

[21] *Borba*, December 23, 1952.

[22] *Borba*, November 24, 1953. For a discussion of the 1953 elections, see Thomas T. Hammond, "Yugoslav Elections: Democracy in Small Doses," *Political Science Quarterly*, 70:1 (March, 1955), pp. 57-74.

[23] *III Kongres SKM*, p. 30.

[24] For the text of the 1953 constitutional law and a discussion of the changes from the 1946 constitution, see *Constitution of the Federal People's Republic of Jugoslavia* (Belgrade: Union of Jurists Associations of Yugoslavia, 1960). See also Fred Warner Neal, *Titoism in Action: The Reforms in Yugoslavia after 1948*, pp. 89-117.

[25] Text in *Ustav Socialističke Federativne Republike jugoslavije sa ustavima socialističkih republika i statutim autonomnih pokrajina* (1963).

[26] *Politika*, December 27, 1968.

[27] *VIII Kongres SKJ*, p. 244. Party Statute VII:28.

[28] Report by Lazar Koliševski, *VIII Kongres SKJ*, p. 221.

[29] For details on these reorganizations see *Borba*, September 18, 1966; *Borba*, October 5, 1966.

[30] Opening address to the 5th Plenum of the CC LCY by Mijalko Todorović, *Borba*, October 5, 1966.

[31] One of the best attempts to quantify the differences in economic and political development between northern and southern Yugoslavia is Jack Fisher, *Yugoslavia—a Multinational State: Regional Difference and Administrative Response.*

[32] *V Kongres KPJ*, p. 454.

[33] *Five Year Plan for the Development of the National Economy of the Federative People's Republic of Yugoslavia in the Period from 1947 to 1951*, Article 5 , p. 75; Article 8, p. 81.

[34] Koliševski report, *I Kongres na KPM*, p. 98.

[35] Speech of Vidoe Smilevski to the Sixth Congress of the CPY, *Borba*, November 6, 1952.

[36] From 1947-1952 36.6 percent of industrial investment in Macedonia was concentrated on electric power development—more than twice the percentage spent in any other sector. M. Murgasanski, "Razvitok na industrijata vo NR Makedonija (1945-1952) godina," in *Industrijata vo N.R. Makedonija*, p. 217.

[37] Some 15.3 percent of industrial investment between 1946 and 1952 was made in this sector. *Ibid.*

[38] *Borba*, March 1, 1952.

[39] Wilkinson, "Jugoslav Macedonia in Transition," *The Geographic Journal*, 118 (December, 1952), p. 396.

[40] *Borba*, November 3, 1951. These figures were said to be high by most observers. One estimate put the percentage of collectivized arable land in Macedonia at only 25 percent in mid-1951.

[41] *Borba*, November 3, 1951.

[42] *Borba*, March 23, 1954. Only Montenegro experienced a greater decline in the number of cooperatives (9.9 percent) from the 1952 figures. The other republics had smaller declines—in Slovenia the number dropped to 44 percent, Serbia to 37 percent, Croatia to 22 percent, and Bosnia-Hercegovina to 16 percent.

[43] See Anton Ciliga's discussion of this point in his *La Yougoslavie sous la ménace intérieure et extérieure*, p. 120.

[44] For 1951, 1952, and 1953 per capita income in Macedonia relative to the Yugoslav average per-capita income went below its 1950 level, while it increased slightly in Montenegro and significantly in Bosnia-Hercegovina. *Indeks, Mesečni pregled privredne statistike FNRJ*, 1:9 (December, 1952), pp. 36; 3:8 (August, 1954), p. 44; 3:10 (October, 1954), p. 44. The rate of economic growth in Macedonia between 1947 and 1955 was the lowest of the underdeveloped republics.

[45] Edvard Kardelj, speech to the Conference of Cities in Split, *Oslobodjenje*, May 8, 1954.

234   YUGOSLAV COMMUNISM — MACEDONIAN QUESTION

[46] See *Industrijata NRM*, pp. 243-244; *Društveni plan privrednog razvoja Jugoslavije, 1957-1961*, p. 53; *Jugoslovenski pregled*, 9:2-3 (February-March, 1965), p. 46.

[47] For a discussion of some of the problems involved see, F.E. Ian Hamilton, *Yugoslavia: Patterns of Economic Activity*, pp. 131-153; and Shoup, *Communism and the Yugoslav National Question*, pp. 240-248.

[48] *Treći plenum CK SKJ: Aktuelni problemi borbe saveza komunista jugoslavije za spovodjenje reforme*, pp. 219-220.

[49] Nešo Markovski, "Pred sednicu Centralnog komiteta SK Makedonije: Efikasnost se ne postiže uopštenim zaključcima," *Komunist*, April 21, 1966.

[50] *Politika*, April 26, 1966; *Komunist*, April 28, 1966.

[51] Carl Gustaf Ströhm, "Staatsman im Banus-Palais: Ein Besuch bei Vladimir Bakarić," *Christ und Welt*, July 7, 1967.

[52] Antun Vratuša, "Multinationality in the Light of Yugoslav Socialist Development," *Socialist Thought and Practice*, 5 (January, 1962), p. 28.

[53] From 1947 to 1965 the agricultural population of Macedonia declined from 71.5 percent to 43.3 percent, while the non-agricultural population has increased from 28.5 percent to 52.7 percent. *Komunist*, October 10, 1968.

[54] *Indeks*, 12:3 (March, 1963), pp. 44, 48. Figures on the number of unemployed by republic were not published in *Indeks* after March 1963. See also *Rad*, September 22, 1967. In Bitolj there was one unemployed for every three employed. Of the unemployed in Macedonia, 76.3 percent were unskilled workers.

[55] Speech of Kiro Gligorov, *Borba*, November 20, 1968.

[56] *Borba*, November 19, 1968.

CHAPTER 9

[1] Horace G. Lunt, "A Survey of Macedonian Literature," *Harvard Slavic Studies*, I (1953), pp. 364-366. See also his *Grammar of the Macedonian Literary Language*.

[2] Lunt, a leading American scholar who has written on the Macedonian language, concentrates on the elements of difference between the central Macedonian dialect and the Bulgarian *literary* language which is based on the Eastern Bulgarian dialect. Although linguists may find enough differences to declare their dialect a separate language, the Slavic inhabitants of Macedonia considered themselves to be Bulgarians. The fact that the language spoken by the Saxons of northwest Germany differed significantly from *Hochdeutsch* (which is based on Central and south German dialects) does not mean that the Saxons did not consider themselves to be German.

[3] The *Serbian* Cyrillic alphabet with minor modification was adopted for the Macedonian language. See R.G.A. deBray, *Guide to the Slavonic Languages*, p. 247.

[4] Krum Tošev, "Die Mazedonische Schriftsprache," *Südost Forschung,* XV (1956), pp. 499-500.

[5] "Macedonicus" [Ivan Mihailov], *Stalin and the Macedonian Question,* p. 34.

[6] Krume Kepeski, *Makedonska gramatika* (Skopje, 1946), p. 8.

[7] Blaže Koneski, *Gramatika na makedonskiot literaturen jazik* (Skopje, 1966), p. 37.

[8] Kiro Miljovski, *Za nekoi prašanja od rabotata nad našata nacionalna istorija,* p. 18. The position which Miljovski condemns pretty well represents the truth of the matter.

[9] Blaže Koneski, a leading Macedonian linguist, author, and first president of the recently established Macedonian Academy of Sciences has played a key role in the development of the language. He has done a great deal of work in this area. See, for example, his *Za makedonskata literatura,* Izbrani, IV, and his *Kon makedonskata prerodba: makedonskite učebnici od 19 vek.*

[10] Lunt, "A Survey of Macedonian Literature," p. 382. Actually, the "Macedonian for intimate friends" which Lunt writes about was very different from today's official language. While it may be true that "many Macedonians *un*consciously slip into Serbian," it should be added that many others *con*sciously "slip into Serbian," carefully avoiding unconscious slips into their native dialects which are close to Bulgarian.

[11] At a literary exposition in Skopje after the Cominform break, books in almost every language, including Chinese, were displayed. However, there were no books in Bulgarian. Ciliga, *La Yougoslavie sous la ménace,* p. 69.

[12] Horace G. Lunt's, "A Survey of Macedonian Literature" is probably the best discussion of Macedonian literature up to 1952. However, his work is dated by much that has been written since then. Blaže Koneski, ed., *Makedonska kniževnost,* Srpska kniževna zadruga 368, pp. 161-200, deals with postwar Macedonian literature, but the coverage is superficial. Miodrag Drugovac, *Biographia Litteraria: 55 kritički impressii,* critically reviews some of the most recent Macedonian works.

[13] Wilkinson, "Jugoslav Macedonia in Transition," p. 396.

[14] H.N. Brailsford, "The New Yugoslavia—Macedonian Renaissance," *The New Statesman and Nation,* 41 (January 13, 1951), p. 31. In his *Macedonia* (1906) Brailsford was a protagonist of the view that the Macedonian Slavs were Bulgarians.

[15] Speech in Titov Veles, November 2, 1958. Reprinted in *Aspekti na makedonskoto prašanje,* p. 371.

[16] Kiril Nikolov, *Za makedonskata nacija,* p. 9.

[17] *I Kongres na KPM,* p. 253.

[18] Vidoe Smilevski, "Osvrt na razvoj makedonskog nacionalnog pitanja," *Komunist,* January, 1950, pp. 81-118.

[19] Kiro Miljovski, *Za nekon prašanje od rabota nad našata nacionalna istorija,* p. 8. The article first appeared in *Socialistička zora,* No. 3 (1949).

[20] Nikolov, *Za makedonskata nacija*, p. 9.

[21] *Spomeni na Gorče Petrov*, p. 2.

[22] Nikolov, *Za makedonskata nacija*, p. 25.

[23] *Nova Makedonija*, February 10, 1952.

[24] Dančo Zografski, *Makedonija do balkanskata vojna*, pp. 282-283.

[25] "Content Analysis of Three Yugoslav Newspapers," unpublished results of research project by the Bureau of Media Research, Department of Journalism, Indiana University, 1954. The newspapers audited were *Borba* (Belgrade), *Nova Makedonija* (Skopje), and *Oslobodjenje* (Sarajevo), with coverage of Tuesday, Friday and Sunday issues for the last six months of 1952.

[26] See for example the Institute's series, "Materijali za makedonskata nacional revolucionerna istorija," which included six volumes by 1955; the five volume *Turski dokumenti za makedonskata istorija* (1951-1958) by Panta Dzambazovski; and Ljuben Lape, *Izveštia od 1903 godina* (1954). Some of the early non-documentary works include Dančo Zografski's *Za rabotničkoto dviženje vo makedonija do balkanskata vojna* (1950) and Zografski, Abadziev, Mitrev, and Kermidčiev, *Egejska makedonija vo našata nacionalna istorija* (1951).

[27] Koliševski's speech was reprinted in his *Aspekti na makedonskoto prašanje*, pp. 343-388.

[28] While no attempt is made here to produce a bibliography of recent Macedonian historical works, some of the works along the lines indicated above are: Hristo Andonovski, *Meglenskata oblast vo narodno-osloboditelnoto dviženje na egejska makedonija* (Skopje: Kultura, 1960); Kiril Jiljovski, *Makedonskoto prašanje vo nacionalnata program na KPJ (1919-1937)*, (Skopje: Kultura, 1962); Aleksandar T. Hristov, *KPJ vo rešavanjeto na makedonskoto prašanje (1937-1944)*, (Skopje: Kultura, 1962); Ivan Katardziev, *KPJ vo makedonija do obznanata* (Skopje: Kultura, 1961); Kliment Dzambazovski, *Kulturno-opštestvenite vrski na makedoncite co srbija vo tekot na xix vek* (Skopje: Institut za nacionalna istorija, 1960); Manol Pandevski, *Političkite partii i organizacii vo makedonija (1908-1912)*, (Skopje: Kultura, 1965); Dančo Zografski, *Jugoslovenskite sociajalisti za makedonskoto prašanje* (Skopje: Kultura, 1962); Zografski, *Razvitokot na kapitalističkite elementi vo makedonija za vreme na turskoto vladeenje* (Skopje: Kultura, 1967). The most comprehensive attempt thus far to treat Macedonian history is the recently published three volume work sponsored by the Institute of National History-Skopje, *Istorija na Makedonskiot Narod* (Skopje: Nova Makedonija, 1969).

[29] *VIII Kongres SKJ*, pp. 35-36.

[30] *IV Kongres na SKM*, pp. 56-57.

[31] See George G. Arnakis, "The Role of Religion on the Development of Balkan Nationalism," in Charles and Barbara Jelavich, eds., *The Balkans in Transition*. The classic examples are the Serbs and Croats. Although both groups speak essentially the same language, Serbs are Orthodox and Croats are Roman Catholic. The Muslim Serbo-Croatian

speaking population of Bosnia and Hercegovina has been claimed by both nationalities. But in Yugoslav nationality censuses since 1945, these Muslims have preferred to call themselves "Muslims" or Yugoslavs of "Unspecified Nationality." The Albanians are one of the few exceptions to this generalization. Although a single nationality, they are religiously split—seventy percent Muslim, twenty percent Orthodox and ten percent Roman Catholic.

[32] A number of observers prematurely announced the establishment of a Macedonian church. One example was an article in the *New York Times* of August 30, 1945, quoted by Mathew Spinka in Robert J. Kerner, ed., *Yugoslavia*, p. 255.

[33] *Nova Makedonija*, September 15, 1951.

[34] *Politika*, May 15, 1952.

[35] *Politika*, June 6, 1952.

[36] *Borba*, February 26, 1955.

[37] *Politika*, February 24, 1955.

[38] *Borba*, April 19, 1957.

[39] *Borba*. May 24, 1957.

[40] *Nova Makedonija*, October 5, 1958.

[41] *Ustav na Makedonskata provoslavna crkva*, Article I, p. 5. For accounts of the conference see *Nova Makedonija*, October 5, 1958; October 6, 1958; October 7, 1958; *Borba*, October 7, 1958.

[42] *Borba*, October 11, 1958. The account of Tito's interview with German was perfunctory—nothing was said about their conversation or how "cordial" it was. In contrast, the account of the Koliševski-Dositej meeting stated: "After congratulating them [Dositej and the church officials with him], Lazar Koliševski expressed his satisfaction that the question of the Orthodox Church in Macedonia was settled. He stayed with them for a rather long conversation."

[43] After the Cominform resolution of 1948, Bulgaria and the Soviet Union continued to recognize the existence of a separate Macedonian nationality, although they called for the creation of an Autonomous Macedonia in a federation with Bulgaria and other Balkan states. It was not until 1958 that Bulgaria publicly denied the existence of Macedonians.

[44] These grievances are enumerated in an editorial in *Nova Makedonija*, September 30, 1967.

[45] By becoming autocephalous, the Macedonian church would chose its own Patriarch and would have absolute and complete autonomy in church affairs—appointment and removal of bishops, etc.

[46] *Pravoslavlje* [Organ of the Belgrade Patriarchate], August 31, 1967.

[47] *Pravoslavlje*, August 31, 1967.

[48] For accounts of the conference see *Nova Makedonija,* July 16, 1967; July 18, 1967; July 19, 1967; July 20, 1967; July 21, 1967.

[49] *Politika,* October 29, 1967.

[50] The question of Macedonian church autonomy aroused intense interest among the Macedonian population. An all-Yugoslav public opinion survey found very little interest on the average in the Serbian-Macedonian church controversy—only 26 percent of those interviewed answered a question dealing with the controversy. However, 41 percent of Macedonians, but only 17 percent of Serbs responded to the question. *Svet,* December 7, 1968.

[51] Ironically, this was on the very same day that Nikola Minčev, President of the Macedonian Executive Council, presented Dositej his Order of the Yugoslav Banner with Sash. Dositej had just returned from a three week visit to Macedonian emigrants in Canada and the United States. A bishopric of the Macedonian church was created for the Macedonian faithful in Canada, the United States and Australia. Both Crvenkovski and Dositej were pleased with the "enthusiastic" acceptance of the church's independence by emigrants.

[52] *Glasnik,* September 15, 1967.

[53] *Pravoslavlje,* September 15, 1967.

[54] *Nova Makedonija,* October 26, 1967.

CHAPTER 10

[1] In Yugoslavia there are five "Yugoslav nationalities"—Serbs, Croats, Sloven, Macedonians, and Montenegrins. All other nationalities are "national minorities." Each of the privileged "Yugoslav nationalities" is entitled to its own national republic. Although Albanians and Hungarians constitute a large portion of the population the Serbian autonomous provinces of Kosmet and the Vojvodina respectively, they are not one of the "Yugoslav nationalities," and they have not been given republic status.

[2] The boundary between the Republic of Macedonia and the Republic of Serbia (including Kosmet) closely parallels that advocated by the Macedonian Dimitar Jaranov in 1930 and that of IMRO maps after 1934. Wilkinson, *Maps and Politics,* pp. 232-310.

[3] Krste Crvenkovski, "Treba se upornije i sistematskije boriti za sprovodjenje pisma CK SKJ u delo," *Komunist,* September, 1953, p. 653.

[4] *Borba,* March 28, 1954.

[5] The Albanians in Tirana claimed that by 1957 some 30,000 Albanians from Yugoslavia "were forced to abandon their Albanian hearth, the land of their forefathers . . . and betake themselves to the swampy regions of Turkey." *Zëri i popullit,* March 24, 1957. By 1966 it was claimed that figure was a staggering (and unrealistic) 250,000! *Zëri i popullit,* August 31, 1966.

[6] The Serbs, who numbered 42,728 in 1961, have their own schools which are taught in Serbian. The Vlahs, probably the third largest minority, have been largely assimilated by the Macedonian Slavs.

[7] *Narodnostite vo samoupravnoto opštestvo, xiv sednica na centralniot komitet na CK na makedonija* [March, 1968], p. 62.

[8] *III Kongres na SKM*, p. 60.

[9] *Nova Makedonija*, November 6, 1968.

[10] *III Kongres na SKM*, p. 57.

[11] *Borba*, October 19, 1952.

[12] Shoup, *Communism and the Yugoslav National Question*, pp. 278-279.

[13] *III Kongres na SKM*, p. 119.

[14] *Narodnostite vo samoupravnoto opštestvo*, p. 35.

[15] *Borba*, March 29, 1968.

[16] Hoxha is a common Albanian name. Envir Hoxha and Fadil Hoxha are not related.

[17] *Politika*, December 30, 1968. Zufličari had earlier advocated closer links between Albanians in Macedonia and the Kosmet. In an interview with *Rilindija* (the Albanian language newspaper in Priština) of November 22, 1967, he spelled out a number of specific suggestions to strengthen ties between Yugoslav Albanians. Crvenkovski opposed this point of view at the Central Committee session on minorities and Zulfičari changed his mind. For accounts of the events, statements, and speeches on the uprising, see *Nova Makedonija*, December 24, 1968, through early January 1969. *Borba* and *Politika* also carried frequent articles on events during this same time.

18 *Borba*, December 29, 1968.

CHAPTER 11

1 Speech to the 5th LCM Congress, *Borba*, November 19, 1968.

2 *Nova Makedonija*, May 27, 1962.

3 *Ibid.*

4 "Nationalist Criticism," *Izvestia na instituta po istoria na BKP*, No. 3-4 (Sofia: B'lgarskata Komunisticheska partia, 1958), p. 509. Koliševski quotes this article in his Titov Veles speech of November 2, 1958.

5 *Kathimerini*, Athens, September 14, 1962.

6 *Komunist*, November 21, 1968.

7 *III Kongres na SKM*, p. 80. Emphasis supplied.

[8] *Vjesnik u srijedu,* January 10, 1968.

[9] "Resolution Adopted on 12 July 1948 by the Sixteenth Plenum of the Central Committee of the Bulgarian Worker's Party . . . ," *Documents on International Affairs, 1947-1948,* pp. 293-294.

[10] Dino G. K'osev, *Borbite na Makedonskiia narod na osvobozhdenie* (Sofia: Narodna prosveta, 1950), pp. 165-167.

[11] According to a semi-official document published by the Historical Institute of the Bulgarian Academy of Sciences in November 1968, it was at the April plenum of the CC of the CPB in 1956 that the party changed its position on the existence of the Macedonian nationality. See "The Macedonian Problem: Historical-Political Aspects," translated by Radio Free Europe, *Bulgarian Press Survey, No.* 694 (February 17, 1969), p. 28.

[12] There were 187,789 Macedonians in Bulgaria—the third largest national group following Bulgarians and Turks. Of this number 178,862 lived in the Blagoevgrad Okrug (Pirin Macedonia). *Prebroyalvane na naselenieto v narodna republika B'lgaria na 1 XII 1956 godina* (Sofia: Tsentralno statichesko upravlenie pri ministerskiia s'vet, 1960), Vol. II, p. 106.

[13] For the reasons behind this decision and details of Soviet-Yugoslav relations, see Richard Lowenthal, "Tito's Gamble," *Encounter* (October, 1958), pp. 56-65; Vaclav L. Beneš and others, eds., *The Second Soviet-Yugoslav Dispute: Full Text of Main Documents,* Slavic and East European Series, Vol. 14 (Bloomington: Indiana University Publications, 1959); Robert Bass and Elizabeth Marbury, eds., *The Soviet-Yugoslav Controversy, 1948-1958: A Documentary Record* (New York: Prospect Books, 1959); and Donald S. Zagoria, *The Sino-Soviet Conflict, 1956-1961*(Princeton: Princeton University Press, 1961), pp. 176-187.

[14] For an analysis of the reasons for the change in Soviet policy, see William E. Griffith, *The Sino-Soviet Rift* (Cambridge, Mass.: MIT press, 1964), pp. 43-52.

[15] Speech of Krste Crvenkovski to the Macedonian Central Committee, *Borba,* February 3, 1968.

[16] *Delo* Ljubljana, February 12, 1968.

[17] Speech at Pirot, *Borba,* September 29, 1965.

[18] *Borba,* February 3, 1968.

[19] The April 1965 attempted *coup d'état* which was led by former western Bulgarian partisans was one indication of disaffection with the undeviatingly pro-Moscow line followed by Zhivkov.

[20] In 1948 Yugoslavia was prosecuting territorial claims against all three of its non-communist neighbor states—against Greece for Aegean Macedonia, against Italy for Trieste and the Free Territory, and against Austria for parts of Carinthia and Styria.

[21] *Nova Makedonija,* August 1, 1952.

[22] Lazar Mojsov, *Okolu prosanjeto na makedonskoto nacionalno maitsinstvo vo grcija,* p. 329.

[23] Reuters, London, July 19, 1954.

[24] *Komunist,* January 11, 1962 .

[25] *Nova Makedonija,* April 8, 1962.

[26] Vassos Vassilou, dispatch from Belgrade in *Acropolis,* Athens, April 22, 1962.

[27] *New York Times,* February 4, 1965.

[28] *Borba,* August 10, 1968. See also *Nova Makedonija,* August 9, 1968.

CONCLUSION

[1] Although there has been an extensive debate carried on among various intellectuals in the Soviet Union [See Grey Hodnett, "What's in a Nation?" *Problems of Communism,* 16:5 (September-October, 1967), pp. 2-15], Stalin's writings remain the basis of the communist position on the national question. In his report to the Sixteenth Party Congress, Stalin declared:

> . . . We, who are in favor of the fusion of national cultures in the future into one common culture (both in form and in content) with a single, common language, are at the same time in favor of the blossoming of national cultures at the present time, in the period of the dictatorship of the proletariat. But there is nothing strange in this. The national cultures must be permitted to develop and expand and to reveal all their potential qualities, in order to create the conditions necessary for the fusion into a single, common culture with a single common language. [Josef Stalin, *Marxism and the National Question,* pp. 208-209.]

Stalin specified that the fusion of nationalities would not occur until the "victory of socialism on a worldwide scale," but there was no question about the future merging of nations.

As recently as the Twenty-Second Party Congress in 1961, the Soviet Party reaffirmed this aspect of the national question:

> Full-scale communist construction constitutes a new stage in the development of national relations in the U.S.S.R. in which the nations will draw closer together until complete unity is achieved. . . . However, the obliteration of national distinctions, and especially of language distinctions is a considerably longer process than the obliteration of class distinctions. [Jan F. Triska, ed., *Soviet Communism Programs and Rules* (San Francisco: Chandler, 1962), p. 107.]

[2] *III Kongres na SKM,* p. 54.

[3] *Vjesnik,* December 2, 1967.

INDEX